English in Thermal Energy and Power Engineering

热能与动力工程专业英语

（第3版）

主　编　李瑞扬　吕　薇
副主编　夏新林　赵玉晓
主　审　朱群益

哈尔滨工业大学出版社

内容提要

本书涵盖了热能与动力工程专业的主要分支学科,以培养热能与动力工程专业学生的专业英语阅读能力为主要目标。全书共分八个部分,主要内容为:流体力学与流体机械,热力学与传热,燃料及燃烧,制冷与空调,锅炉设备,涡轮机,环保、腐蚀,部分参考译文等,书后附录中还给出了常用缩写词和常用计量单位换算。本书有较强的实用性和知识性,高等院校热能与动力工程专业的本科生和研究生可根据其选修方向有针对性地学习相关单元。

本书既可作为高等学校热能与动力工程专业学生的专业英语教材,也可供从事有关热能与动力工程专业的工程技术人员学习、参考之用。

图书在版编目(CIP)数据

热能与动力工程专业英语/李瑞扬,吕薇主编.—3版.

哈尔滨:哈尔滨工业大学出版社,2008.12(2017.1 重印)

ISBN 978-7-5603-1451-8

Ⅰ.热… Ⅱ.①李… ②吕… Ⅲ.①热能-英语-高等学校-教材②动力工程-英语-高等学校-教材 Ⅳ.H31

中国版本图书馆 CIP 数据核字(2008)第 186907 号

责任编辑	徐 雁
封面设计	卞秉利
出版发行	哈尔滨工业大学出版社
社　　址	哈尔滨市南岗区复华四道街 10 号　邮编 150006
传　　真	0451-86414749
网　　址	http://hitpress.hit.edu.cn
印　　刷	哈尔滨工业大学印刷厂
开　　本	880mm×1230mm　1/32　印张 12.75　字数 329 千字
版　　次	2008 年 12 月第 3 版　2017 年 1 月第 11 次印刷
书　　号	ISBN 978-7-5603-1451-8
定　　价	28.00 元

(如因印装质量问题影响阅读,我社负责调换)

第3版前言

热能与动力工程专业英语一书自2000年1月出版以来,受到了广大高校师生和英语爱好者的欢迎,目前国内已有多所高等院校将此书作为教材,并在教学中收到良好效果。还有许多热工人员将此书作为科研工作中翻译英文资料的重要参考书。本书出版以来已修订2次,重印6次,读者反馈意见较好,为了进一步满足教学要求和读者需要,增强本书的科学性和实用性,综合各校使用的情况,结合我们多年来的教学经验和体会,在保证本书基本体系和主要内容不变的前提下,在第2版基础上作了如下补充和修改。

(1)为更方便读者阅读和查阅单词,在每课课文后补充了单词表,而全书后词汇索引表(按字母顺序排列)仍保留。

(2)为突出内容的完整性,在内容编排上进行了适当增减和调整,充实了能突出反映本学科相关的内容。

(3)对各课生词及译文进行了核准。

由于参与修订本书的人员及分工有变,书的各章节的负责人员、主编、主审等发生变化。全书由英文、译文和附录组成,英文部分共分七部分,其中第一部分、第六部分由赵玉晓编写,第三部分、第四部分由吕薇编写,第二部分由夏新林编写,第五部分、第七部分及附录等由李瑞扬编写。全书由李瑞扬、吕薇主编,由朱群益主审。

由于编者水平有限,对书中的不足之处,请广大读者批评指正。

编 者
2008年11月

CONTENTS

1 Fluid Mechanics and Fluid Machines
- 1.1 Definition of a Fluid and Classification of Fluid Flow .... (1)
- 1.2 Historical Development of Fluid Mechanics .... (6)
- 1.3 The Characteristics of Fluids .... (11)
- 1.4 Scope Significance and Trend of Fluid Mechanics .... (14)
- 1.5 The Principles of Fluid Machines .... (20)
- 1.6 Turbulent Flow .... (23)

2 Thermodynamics and Heat Transfer
- 2.1 Basic Concepts of Thermodynamics .... (27)
- 2.2 Thermodynamic Systems .... (31)
- 2.3 General Characteristics of Heat Transfer .... (33)
- 2.4 Conduction .... (36)
- 2.5 Natural Convection .... (40)
- 2.6 Radiation .... (43)

3 Fuels and Combustion
- 3.1 Heat of Combustion .... (47)
- 3.2 Combustion Equipment .... (51)
- 3.3 Fuel-ash .... (54)
- 3.4 The Mechanisms of Gaseous Fuels Combustion .... (58)
- 3.5 The Combustion of Liquid Fuels and Solid Fuels .... (62)
- 3.6 Nuclear Fuels .... (68)
- 3.7 Liquid By-product Fuels .... (72)

4 Refrigeration and Airconditioning
- 4.1 The Ideal Basic Vapor Compression Refrigeration Cycle .... (75)
- 4.2 Refrigerant Evaporators .... (79)

ii English in Thermal Energy and Power Engineering

    4.3   Refrigeration ··· (82)
    4.4   Absorption Heat Pumps ······································· (85)
    4.5   Comfort and Discomfort ······································ (89)
    4.6   Compressor Failure ··· (93)
    4.7   Operation and Maintenance of the Airconditioning Plant ············ (97)
    4.8   Air-conditioning cycle equipment ····························· (101)

5 Boiler
    5.1   Boiler and Its Development ··································· (105)
    5.2   Stokers ··· (108)
    5.3   Boiler Circulation ·· (113)
    5.4   Fossil-fuel Boilers for Electric Utilities ······················· (119)
    5.5   Spreader Stoker ·· (123)
    5.6   Economizers and Air Heaters ································· (128)
    5.7   Selection of Coal-burning Equipment ························· (133)
    5.8   Oil and Gas Burning Equipment ······························ (140)
    5.9   Furnace ·· (145)
    5.10 Gas and Fuel Oil – fired Furnaces ··························· (148)
    5.11 Boiler Design ·· (152)
    5.12 Superheaters and Reheaters ·································· (162)

6 Turbine
    6.1   Steam Turbine ··· (171)
    6.2   Gas Turbine ··· (177)
    6.3   Compressor ·· (184)
    6.4   Gas Turbine Plants ··· (187)
    6.5   Classification of Steam Turbines ······························ (191)
    6.6   Current Practice and Trends of Turbine ······················ (195)
    6.7   The Modern Steam Power Plant ······························ (198)
    6.8   Wind Turbines ··· (206)
    6.9   The Principle of Steam Turbine ······························ (212)

7 Environmental Protection, Corrosion and Others
    7.1   Ash Removal and Disposal ··································· (219)

7.2 Oil-ash Corrosion ……………………………………… (224)
7.3 Control of Pollutant Gases …………………………… (230)
7.4 Fans ……………………………………………………… (236)
7.5 Stokers …………………………………………………… (240)
7.6 Flue Gas Desulfunzation ……………………………… (245)
7.7 Steam Separation ……………………………………… (250)
7.8 Pulverizers ……………………………………………… (255)
7.9 Prevention of Scaling in Boilers ……………………… (260)
7.10 Air Pollution …………………………………………… (265)
7.11 Pressure Measurement ………………………………… (267)
7.12 Clean Coal Teachnologies …………………………… (275)

参考译文

流体的定义和流体流动的分类(1.1) ……………………… (280)
流体力学发展史(1.2) ……………………………………… (282)
热力系统的基本概念(2.1) ………………………………… (284)
导热(2.4) …………………………………………………… (286)
液体燃料的燃烧(3.5) ……………………………………… (288)
核燃料(3.6) ………………………………………………… (290)
液态副产品燃料(3.7) ……………………………………… (292)
理想的基本蒸气压缩制冷循环(4.1) ……………………… (293)
吸收式热泵(4.4) …………………………………………… (295)
压缩机故障(4.6) …………………………………………… (297)
锅炉水循环(5.3) …………………………………………… (299)
电力公用事业电站燃用矿物燃料的锅炉(5.4) …………… (303)
燃油燃气锅炉炉膛设计(5.10) …………………………… (305)
过热器和再热器(5.12) …………………………………… (307)
汽轮机(6.1) ………………………………………………… (312)
燃气轮机(6.2) ……………………………………………… (315)
除灰及灰的处理(7.1) ……………………………………… (319)
油灰腐蚀(7.2) ……………………………………………… (321)
压力测量(7.11) …………………………………………… (325)

洁净煤技术(7.12) ………………………………… (327)
Words and Expressions …………………………………… (330)
附录Ⅰ　常用缩写词 ………………………………… (364)
附录Ⅱ　常用计量单位换算 ………………………… (393)

1

Fluid Mechanics and Fluid Machines

1.1 Definition of a Fluid and Classification of Fluid Flow

A fluid is a substance that deforms continuously when subjected to a shear stress, no matter how small that shear stress may be. A shear force is the force component tangent to a surface, and this force divided by the area of the surface is the average shear stress over the area. Shear stress at a point is the limiting value of shear force to area as the area is reduced to the point.

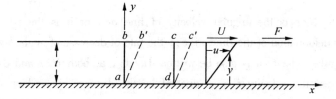

Fig. 1.1 Deformation resulting from application of constant shear force.

In Fig. 1.1 a substance is placed between two closely spaced parallel plates, so large that conditions at their edges may be neglected.

The lower plate is fixed, and a force F is applied to the upper plate, which exerts a shear F/A on any substance between the plates. A is the area of the upper plate. When the force F causes the upper plate to move with a steady (nonzero) velocity, no matter how small the magnitude of F, one may conclude that the substance between the two plates is a fluid.

The fluid in immediate contact with a solid boundary has the same velocity as the boundary, i.e., there is no slip at the boundary. This is an experimental fact which has been verified in countless tests with various kinds of fluids and boundary materials. The fluid in the area $abcd$ flows to the new position $ab'c'd$, each fluid particle moving parallel to the plate and velocity u varying uniformly from zero at the stationary plate to U at the upper plate. Experiments show that, other quantities being held constant, F is directly proportional to A and to U and is inversely proportional to thickness t. In equation form

$$F = \mu \frac{AU}{t}$$

in which μ is the proportionality factor and includes the effect of the particular fluid. If $\tau = F/A$ for the shear stress,

$$\tau = \mu \frac{U}{t}$$

The ratio U/t is the angular velocity of line ab, or it is the rate of angular deformation of the fluid, i.e., the rate of decrease of angle bad. The angular velocity may also be written du/dy, as both U/t and du/dy express the velocity change divided by the distance over which the change occurs. However, du/dy is more general, as it holds for situations in which the angular velocity and shear stress change with y. The velocity gradient du/dy may also be visualized as the rate at which one layer moves relative to an adjacent layer. In differential form,

$$\tau = \mu \frac{du}{dy} \tag{1.1}$$

is the relation between shear stress and rate of angular deformation for one-dimensional flow of a fluid. The proportionality factor μ is called the viscosity of the fluid, and Eq. (1.1) is Newton's law of viscosity.

Materials other than fluids cannot satisfy the definition of a fluid. A plastic substance will deform a certain amount proportional to the force, but not continuously when the stress applied is below its yield shear stress. Acomplete vacuum between the plates would cause deformation at an ever-increasing rate. If sand were placed between the two plates, Coulomb friction would require a finite force to cause a continuous motion. Hence, plastics and solids are excluded from the classification of fluids.

Fluids may be classified as Newtonian or non-Newtonian. In Newtonian fluid there is a linear relation between the magnitude of applied shear stress and the resulting rate of angular deformation (μ constant in Eq. 1.1). In non-Newtonian fluid there is a nonlinear relation between the magnitude of applied shear stress and the rate of angular deformation.

An ideal plastic has a definite yield stress and a constant linear relation of τ to du/dy. A thixotropic substance, such as printer's ink, has a viscosity that is dependent upon the immediately prior angular deformation of the substance and has a tendency to take a set when at rest. Gases and thin liquids tend to be Newtonian fluids, while thick long-chained hydrocarbons may be non-Newtonian.

For purposes of analysis, the assumption is frequently made that a fluid is nonviscous. With zero viscosity the shear stress is always zero, regardless of the motion of the fluid. If the fluid is considered to be nonviscous, it is then called an ideal fluid.

Fluid flow may be classified in many ways, such as steady or nonsteady, rotational or irrotational, compressible or incompressible, and viscous or nonviscous.

Fluid flow can be steady or nonsteady. When the fluid velocity at any given point is constant in time, the fluid motion is said to be steady. That is, at any given point in a steady flow the velocity of each passing fluid particle is always the same. At some other point a particle may travel with a different velocity, but every other particle which passes this second point behaves there just as this particle did when it passed this point. These conditions can be achieved at low flow speeds, a gently flowing stream is an example. In nonsteady flow, as in a tidal bore, the velocities are a function of the time. In the case of turbulent flow, such as rapids or a waterfall, the velocities vary erratically from point to point as well as from time to time.

Fluid flow can be rotational or irrotational. If the element of fluid at each point has no net angular velocity about that point, the fluid flow is irrotational. We can imagine a small paddle wheel immersed in the moving fluid. If the wheel moves without rotating, the motion is irrotational; otherwise it is rotational. Rotational flow includes vortex motion, such as whirlpools.

Fluid flow can be compressible or incompressible, Liquids can usually be considered as flowing incompressible. But even a highly compressible gas may sometimes undergo unimportant changes in density. Its flow is then practically incompressible. In flight at speeds much lower than the speed of sound in air (described by subsonic aerodynamics), the motion of the air relative to the wings is one of nearly incompressible flow.

Fluid flow can be viscous or nonviscous. Viscosity in fluid motion is the analogy of friction in the motion of solids. In many cases, such as in lubrication problems, it is extremely important. Sometimes, however, it is negligible. Viscosity introduces tangential forces between layers of fluid in relative motion and results in dissipation of mechanical energy.

Words and Expressions

component [kəm'pəunənt] n. (组成)部分,成分
tangent ['tændʒənt] a. 正切的,相切的
space [speis] v. 把……分隔开,留间隔
magnitude ['mægnitjud] n. 大小,量值
slip [slip] n. 滑动,滑动量
stationary ['steiʃənəri] a. 固定的,稳定的
inversely [in'və:sli] ad. 相反地
angular ['æŋgjulə] a. 角形的,用角度量的
adjacent [ə'dʒeisənt] a. 接近的,邻近的
yield [ji:ld] n. 屈服(点),极限
vacuum ['vækjuəm] n. 真空
Newtonian [nju'təuniən] a. 牛顿的
linear ['liniə] a. 线性的,直线的
thixotropic [ˌθiksə'trɔpik] a. 触变性的
hydrocarbon ['haidrəu'ka:bən] n. 碳氢化合物
nonviscous ['nɔn'viskəs] a. 非黏性的
plot [plɔt] v. 作图(表示)
ordinate ['ɔ:dinit] n. 纵坐标
irrotational [ˌirəu'teiʃənl] a. 不旋转的
incompressibly [ˌinkəm'presəbli] ad. 不可压缩地
waterfall ['wɔtəfɔ:l] n. 瀑布
tidal ['taidl] a. 潮汐的
bore [bɔ:] n. 激浪
rapid ['ræpid] n. 急流
erratically [i'rætikəli] ad. 不稳定地,无规律地
vortex ['vɔ:teks] n. 涡流,漩涡
whirlpool ['hwə:lpu:l] n. 漩涡

dissipation [ˌdisiˈpeiʃən] n. 消耗,消散
shear stress 剪切力,切应力
parallel to 与……平行
proportionality factor 比例系数
relative to 相对于,关于
Coulomb friction 库伦系数
take a set 凝固,硬化

1.2 Historical Development of Fluid Mechanics

The science of fluid mechanics began with the need to control water for irrigation and navigation purposes in ancient China, Egypt, Mesopotamia, and India. Although these civilizations understood the nature of channel flow, there is no evidence that any quantitative relationships had been developed to guide them in their work. It was not until 250 B. C. that Archimedes discovered and recorded the principles of hydrostatics and buoyancy. In spite of the fact that the empirical understanding of hydrodynamics continued to improve with the development of fluid machinery, better sailing vessels, and more intricate canal systems, the fundamental principles of classical hydrodynamics were not founded until the seventeenth and eighteenth centuries. Newton, Daniel Bernoulli, and Leonard Euler made the greatest contributions to the founding of these principles.

In the nineteenth century, two schools of thought arose in the treatment of fluid mechanics, one dealing with the theoretical and the other with practical aspects of fluid flow. Classical hydrodynamics, though a fascinating subject that appealed to mathematicians, was not applicable to many practical problems because the theory was based on inviscid fluids. The practicing engineers at that time needed design procedures that involved the flow of viscous fluids; consequently, they developed empirical equations that were usable but narrow in scope. Thus, on the one hand, the mathematicians and physicists developed theories that in many cases could not be used by the engineers, and on the other hand, engineers used empirical equations that could not be used outside the limited range of application from which they were derived. In a sense, these two schools of thought have persisted to the present day, resulting in the mathematical field of hydrodynamics and the practical science of hydraulics.

Near the beginning of the twentieth century, however, it was necessary to merge the general approach of the physicists and mathematicians with the experimental approach of the engineer to bring about significant advances in the understanding of flow processes. Osborne Reynolds' paper in 1883 on turbulence and later papers on the basic equations of liquid motion contributed immeasurably to the development of fluid mechanics. After the turn of the century, in 1904, Ludwing Prandtl proposed the concept of the boundary layer. In his short, convincing paper Prandtl, at a stroke, provided an essential link between ideal and real fluid motion for fluids with a small viscosity and provided the basis for much of modern fluid mechanics.

The development of fluid mechanics in the twentieth century may be divided into four periods.

Low speed aerodynamics, 1900 ~ 1935

The first development of fluid mechanics was closely associated with aeronautical science. Because of the stringent requirement on weight, one needs reliable theoretical prediction to practical problems. As a result, one has to combine the essential features of old hydrodynamics and hydraulics into one rational science of fluid mechanics. Some of the important developments in these periods are: (a) Prandtl's boundary layer theory; (b) Kutta-Joukowski's wing theory to explain the phenomenon of air lift; (c) the theory of turbulent flow by von Kármán and others. In this period, the velocity of the fluid flow is low and the temperature difference in the flow is small. Consequently, we may neglect the compressibility effect of the fluid. Both the gas and the liquid may be treated by the same method of analysis. There is practically no difference in principle for hydrodynamics and aerodynamics.

Aerothermodynamics, 1935 ~ 1950

The speed of the gas flow was gradually increased from subsonic to supersonic speed. The compressibility effect of the gas is no longer negligible. We have to treat gas and liquid separately. For gasdynamics, we have to consider the mechanics of the flow simultaneously with the thermodynamics of the gas. Hence the term of aerothermodynamics was suggested for this new branch of fluid mechanics. In this field the most important parameter is the Mach number. However, the temperature range of the gas or air was still below 2 000K and the air may be considered as an ideal gas with constant specific heat. The molecular structure has very little influence on the gas flow and we may use the same formula to deal with monatomic gas and polyatomic gas. Many new phenomena, such as shock wave, supersonic flow, etc., were analyzed in this period.

Physics of fluid, 1950 ~ 1960

This is the start of the space age. The speed of the flow and the temperature of the fluid are high enough so that we have to consider the interaction of mechanics of fluid with other branches of physics and that the molecular structure of the gas has a large influence on the fluid flow. We have to consider the influence on dissociation, ionization, and thermal radiation. New subjects such as aerothermochemistry, magnetogasdynamics, and plasma dynamics, and radiation gasdynamics have been extensively studied. We have to deal with the whole physics of fluids.

New era of fluid mechanics, 1960 and on

In the above three periods, our main interests are still the flow of fluids which consists of liquid, gas, or plasma only. During the recent years, the interest of many technical developments is so broad that we have to deal with flow problems beyond those of fluid alone. For instance, we have to deal with the mixture of solid and fluid, the so-called two-phase flow. In many rheological problems, the fluids behave partly as ordinary fluid and partly as solid. In the above three periods, we treat the fluid flow problems mainly according to the principles of classical physics. In many new problems of fluid flow, we have to consider the principles beyond those of classical physics such as superfluid for which the quantum effects are important even for macroscopic properties (quantum fluid mechanics); relativistic fluid mechanics in which the relativistic mechanics should be used because the velocity of the flow is no longer negligible in comparison with the speed of light. We are also interested in bio-fluid mechanics in which we study the interaction between the physical science of fluid flow and biological science. Modern developments in fluid mechanics, as in all fields, involve the use of high-speed computers in the solution of problems. Remarkable progress has been made in this area, and there is an increasing use of the computer in fluid dynamic design.

It should be noted that even though we divide the development of modern fluid mechanics into the above four periods, there are overlaps in time for these periods as far as the study of various subjects are concerned. For instance, the study of turbulent flow of low speed fluid flow which was one of the major subjects in the first period is still a very active research subject at the present time and many basic problems are far from being solved yet.

Words and Expressions

hydrostatics ['haidrəu'stætiks] n. 流体静力学
buoyancy ['bɔiənsi] n. 浮力
empirical [em'pirikl] a. 经验的,实验的
hydrodynamics ['haidrəudai'næmiks] n. 流体动力学
inviscid [in'visid] a. 无黏性的
turbulence ['tə:bjuləns] n. 紊流,湍流
convincing [kən'vinsiŋ] a. 有说服力的
viscosity [vis'kɔsiti] n. 黏性,黏度
aerodynamics ['ɛərəudai'næmiks] n. 空气动力学
aeronautical [,ɛərəu'nɔ:tikl] a. 航空(学)的
stringent ['strindʒənt] a. 严格的
compressibility [kem,presi'biliti] n. 压缩性,压缩系数
aerothermodynamics n. 空气热力学
subsonic ['sʌb'sʌnik] a. 亚音速的
monatomic [,mɔnə'tɔmik] a. 单原子的
polyatomic [,pɔliə'tɔmik] a. 多原子的
dissociation [dis,səusi'eiʃən] n. 离解作用,分离
ionization [,aiənai'zeiʃən] n. 电离
magnetogasdynamics n. 磁性气体动力学
plasma ['plæzmə] n. 等离子体
rheological [,riə'lɔdʒikl] a. 流变的
quantum ['kwɔntəm] n. 量子
relativistic [,relətiv'vistik] a. 相对论性的
bio-fluid ['baiə'flui:d] n. 生物流体
overlap ['əuvəlæp] n. 重叠(部分)

at a stroke　一下子，一次
shock wave　冲击波
two-phase flow　两相流

1.3　The Characteristics of Fluids

A fluid is a substance which may flow; that is, its constituent particles may continuously change their positions relative to one another. Moreover, it offers no lasting resistance to the displacement, however great, of one layer over another. This means that, if the fluid is at rest, no shear force (that is a force tangential to the surface on which it acts) can exist in it. A solid, on the other hand, can resist a shear force while at rest; the shear force may cause some displacement of one layer over another, but the material does not continue to move indefinitely. In a fluid, however, shear forces are possible only while relative movement between layers is actually taking place. A fluid is further distinguished from a solid in that a given amount of it owes its shape at any particular time to that of a vessel containing it, or to forces which in some way restrain its movement.

The distinction between solids and fluids is usually clear, but there are some substances not easily classified. Some fluids, for example, do not flow easily: thick tar or pitch may at times appear to behave like a solid. A block of such a substance may be placed on the ground, but, although its flow would take place very slowly, yet over a period of time—perhaps several days—it would spread over the ground by the action of gravity, that is, its constituent particles would change their relative positions. On the other hand, certain solids may be made to "flow" when a sufficiently large force is applied; these are known as *plastic solids*.

Even so, the essential difference between solids and fluids remains. Any fluid, no matter how "thick" or viscous it is, begins to flow, even if imperceptibly, under the action of the slightest net shear force. Moreover, a fluid continues to flow as long as such a force is applied. A solid, however, no matter how plastic it is, does not flow unless the net shear force on it exceeds a certain value. For forces less than this value the layers of the solid move over one another only by a certain amount. The more the layers are displaced from their original relative positions, however, the greater are the forces resisting the displacement. Thus, if a steady force is applied, a state will be reached in which the forces resisting the movement of one layer over another balance the force applied and so no further movement of this kind can occur. If the applied force is then removed, the resisting forces will tend to restore the solid body to its original shape.

In a fluid, however, the forces opposing te movement of one layer over another exist only while the movement is taking place, and so static equilibrium between applied force and resistance to shear never occurs. Deformation of the fluid takes place continuously so long as a shear force is applied. But if this applied force is removed the shearing movement subsides and, as there are then no forces tending to return the particles of fluid to their original relative positions, the fluid keeps its *new* shape.

Fluids may b sub-divided into liquids and gases. A fixed amount of a liquid has a definite volume which varies only slightly with temperature an pressure. If the capacity of the containing vessel is greater than this definite volume, the liquid occupies only part of the container, and it forms an interface separating it from its own vapour, the atmosphere or any other gas present.

On the other hand, a fixed amount of a gas, by itself in a container, will always expand until its volume equals that of the container. Only then can it be in equilibrium. In the analysis of the behaviour of fluids the most important difference between liquids and gases is that, whereas under ordinary conditions liquids are so difficult to compress that they may for most purposes be regarded as incompressible, gases may be compressed much more readily. Where conditions are such that an amount of gas undergoes a negligible change of volume, its behaviour is similar to that of a liquid and it may then be regarded as incompressible. If, however, the change in volume is not negligible, the compressibility of the gas must be taken into account in examining its behaviour.

In considering the action of forces on fluids, one can either account for the behavior of each and every molecule of fluid in a given field of flow or simplify the problem by considering the average effects of the molecules in a given volume. In most problems in fluid dynamics the latter approach is possible, which means that the fluid can be regarded as a *continuum*— that is, a hypothetically continuous substance.

The justification for treating a fluid as a continuum depends on the physical dimensions of the body immersed in the fluid and on the number of molecules in a given volume. Let us say that we are studying the flow of air past a sphere with a diameter of 1 cm. A continuum is said to prevail if the number of molecules in a volume much smaller than the sphere's is sufficiently great so that the average effects (pressure, density, and so on) within the volume either are constant or change smoothly with time. The number of molecules in a cubic meter of air at room temperature and sea-level pressure is about 10^{25}. Thus the number of molecules in a volume of 10^{-19} m^3 (about the size of a dust particle, which is very much smaller than the sphere) would be 10^6. This number of molecules is so large that the average effects within the microvolume are indeed virtually constant. On the other hand, if the 1 cm sphere were at an altitude of 305 km, there would be only one chance in 10^8 of finding a molecule in the microvolume, and the concept of an average condition would be meaningless. In this case, the continuum assumption would not be valid. It may thus be concluded that the assumption of a continuum is valid for fluid flow except in the rarest conditions, such as those encountered in outer space.

Words and Expressions

constituent [kən'stitjuənt] a. 组成的
tangential [tæn'dʒenʃəl] a. 切向的
restrain [ris'trein] v. 限制,约束
equilibrium [ˌi:kwi'libriəm] n. 平衡(状态),均衡
interface ['intə(:)feis] n. 相互关系,分界面
molecule ['mɔlikju:l] n. 微小颗粒,分子
continuum [kən'tinjuəm] n. 连续体

1.4 Scope Significance and Trend of Fluid Mechanics

Fluid mechanics, as the name indicates, is that branch of applied mechanics which is concerned with the statics and dynamics of liquids and gases. Dynamics, the study of motion of matter, may be divided into two parts - dynamics of rigid bodies and dynamics of non-rigid bodies. The latter is usually further divided into two general classifications—elasticity (solid elastic body) and fluid mechanics.

The subject of fluid mechanics can be subdivided into two broad categories: hydrodynamics and gas dynamics. Hydrodynamics deals primarily with the flow of fluids for which there is virtually no density change, such as liquid flow or the flow of gas at low speeds. Hydraulics, for example, the study of liquid flows in pipes or oper channels, falls within this category. The study of fluid forces on bodies immersed in flowing liquids or in low-speed gas flows can also be classified as hydrodynamics.

Gas dynamics, on the other hand, deals with fluids that undergo significant density changes. High-speed gas flowing through a nozzle or over a body, the flow of chemically reacting gases, or the movement of a body through the low density air of the upper atmosphere falls within the general category of gas dynamics.

An area of fluid mechanics not classified as either hydrodynamics or gas dynamics is aerodynamics, which deals with the flow of air past aircraft or rockets, whether it be low-speed incompressible flow or high-speed compressible flow.

There are, however, two major aspects of fluid mechanics which differ from solid-body mechanics. The first is the nature and properties of the fluid itself, which are very different from those of a solid. The second is that, instead of dealing with individual bodies or elements of known mass, we are frequently concerned with the behavior of a continuous stream of fluid, without beginning or end.

Knowledge and understanding of the basic principles and concepts of fluid nechanics are essential in the analysis and design of any system in which a fluid is the working medium. Mary applications of fluid mechanics make it one of the most vital and fundamental of all engineering and applied scientific studies. The flow of fluids in pipe and channels makes fluid mechanics of importance to civil engineers. The study of fluid machinery such as pumps, fans, blowers, compressors, turbines, heat exchangers, jet and rocket engines, and the like, makes fluid mechanics of importance to mechanical engineers. Lubrication is an area of considerable importance in fluid mechanics. The flow of air over objects, aerodynamics, is of fundamental interest to aeronautical and space engineers in the design of aircraft, missiles and rockets. In meteorology, hydrology and oceanography the study of fluids is basic since the atmosphere and the ocean are fluids. And today in modern engineering many new disciplines combine fluid mechanics with classical disciplines. For example, fluid mechanics and electromagnetic theory are studied together as magnetogas-dynamics. In new types of energy conversion devices and in the study of stellar and ionospheric phenomena, magnetogasdynamics is vital.

On the contrary, the collapse of the Tacoma Narrows Bridge in U.S.A. is evidence of the possible consequences of neglecting the basic principles of fluid mechanics. On a memorable day in November 1940, Nature decided to teach us all a lesson. The wind could not even be considered strong on that day, but it happened to disturb the great Tacoma Narrows suspension bridge cyclically with a frequency close to the bridge's natural frequency of vibration. The entire bridge started to dance. Traffic was stopped; and an astonished public watched the bridge itself to pieces.

We see that a good familiarity with fluid mechanics is essential to the modern engineer and scientist, and it is probably obvious that fluid mechanics and its applications is a broad subject with far-flung fields of specialization. What we should do is to master the basic concepts and principles of fluid mechanics. Once these fundamentals are mastered more advanced books and research literature may be studied to increase one's understanding of more specialized aspects of fluid mechanics.

The significance of fluid mechanics becomes apparent when we consider the vital role it plays in our everyday lives. When we turn on our kitchen faucets, we activate flow in a complex hydraulic network of pipes, valves, and pumps. When we flick on a light switce, we are drawing energy either from a hydroelectric source that operates by the flow of water through turbines or from a thermal power source derived from the flow of steam past turbine blades. When we drive our cars, pneumatic tires provide suspension, hydraulic shock absorbers reduce road shocks, gasoline is pumped through tubes and later atomized, and air resistance creates a drag on the auto as a whole; and when we stop, we are confident in the operation of the hydraulic brakes. Very complex fluid processes are also involved in the manufacture of the paper on which this book is printed, And our very lives depend on a very important fluid mechanic process—the flow of blood through our veins and arteries.

Some of the most significant environmental problems facing society today involve fluid mechanics. For example, coastal cities often discharge their wastewater (usually treated) into the sea, near the sea bed, far enough from shore so that the wastes become sufficiently diluted with the ambient sea water to render the resulting mixture harmless. The process involves mixing the wastewater with the ambient liquid, a complex turbulence phenomenon. The degree of mixing is a function of the characteristics of the wastewater and the ambient liquid (such as density) as well as the discharge velocity of the wastewater. Also involved in this process are the velocity and pattern of coastal currents. In addition to the fluid mechanics of such a problem, the contaminants in the mixture may change both chemically and biologically in the process. Thus sophisticated models linking the basic flow model with other aspects of the problem are required to design a satisfactory waste disposal system. Such models are generally developed and used by multidisciplinary teams that may include engineers, mathematicians, chemists, and bioscientists. There is an increasing need for engineers who have the ability and mathematical skills to assist in the generation of, and to use, sophisticated computational models of this type. Other problems, sinilar in nature, that involve fluid mechanics include air pollution and underground hazardous waste problems.

Modern developments in fluid mechanics, as in all fields, involve the use of high-speed computers in the solution of problems. Remarkable progress is being made in this area, and the use of the computer in fluid dynamic design is increasing. In the design of aircraft, computers are used to predict the flow over engine nacelles and appendages in order to select configurations that minimize aerodynamic drag. The NASA publication on wind tunnels (1) explains the role of computers in aircraft design. Computational solutions for wind forces on buildings and structures are used to complement measurements on wind tunnel models to insure the safety and structural integrity of the full-scale structures.

The ever-increasing speed and memory capacity of modern computers are leading to even more exciting applications of computers in fluid mechanics. Computer solutions for the motion of terrestrial winds and weather fronts are leading to more accurate forecasting of local weather conditions. The coupling of fluid mechanics with heat transfer and chemical kinetics in computational solutions will lead to improved designs for industrial power and propulsion systems. As space stations and space travel become more feasible, computers will play a vital role in the design of flow systems in microgravity environments that are difficult to examine through terrestrial experimentation. The application of computers to the analysis of flows in biological systems is only beginning, but it will continue to grow as the mechanics of flows in these systems becomes better understood.

The science of fluid mechanics is developing at a rapid rate. Armed with more detailed measurements and numerical models, fluid mechanicians have developed higher levels of understanding that have led to sophisticated designs and applications of fluid systems. Still, there are many areas in which only rudimentary information and physical models are available. Turbulence is a prime example. Even though we presently have high-speed computers at our disposal, the solutions are only as valid as the equations we use to describe the basic flow phenomena. And there is currently no general analytic model that completely describes the nature of turbulence. We have good data on turbulence in straight pipes, so reliable empirical formulas have been developed to describe the turbulence in such a simple case. But turbulence in high-shear flows, buoyant flows, and compressible flows is still the subject of extensive study. Analyses of the flow of multiphase mixtures such as solids in a liquid (slurries) and bubbles in a liquid still rely heavily on empiricism. In oil recovery operations, the the engineer is confronted with the problem of the flow of immiscible liquids, such as oil in water, which is not well understood. These are areas which represent exciting challenges to current and future practitioners of fluid mechanics.

Words and Expressions

classification [ˌklæsifiˈkeiʃən] n. 分类,分类法
elastic [iˈlæstik] a. 弹性的
subdivide [ˈsʌbdiˈvaid] v. 把……再分
nozzle [ˈnɔzl] n. 喷嘴
compressible [kəmˈpresəbl] a. 可压缩的
blower [ˈbləuə] n. 鼓风机
lubrication [ˌljuːbriˈkeiʃən] n. 润滑(作用)
meteorology [ˌmiːtjəˈrɔlədʒi] n. 气象学
hydrology [haiˈdrɔlədʒi] n. 水文学
oceanography [ˌəuʃjəˈnɔgrəfi] n. 海洋学
discipline [ˈdisiplin] n. 学科
stellar [ˈstelə] a. 星球的,恒星的
ionospheric [ˌaiənəˈsferik] a. 电离层的
narrows [ˈnærəuz] n. 海峡
suspension [səsˈpenʃən] n. 熟悉,通晓
far-flung [ˈfaːˈflʌŋ] a. 辽阔的,漫长的
specialization [ˌspeʃəlaiˈzeiʃən] n. 专门化,学科
faucet [ˈfɔːsit] n. 龙头,旋塞
pneumatic [njuːˈmætik] a. 空气的,气体的,气动的

ambient ['æmbiənt] a. 周围的,大气的
contaminant [kən'tæmineit] n. 污染物,毒害
nacelle [næ'sel] n. 机舱
appendage [ə'pendidʒ] n. 附属物
configuration [kən‚figju'reiʃən] n. 结构,形状,外形
integrity [in'tegriti] n. 完整,完全,完善
terrestrial [ti'restriəl] a. 地球(上)的,陆地的
propulsion [prə'pʌlʃən] n. 推进(装置),推动
rudimentary [‚ru:di'mentəri] a. 基本的,初步的
buoyant ['bɔiənt] a. 浮升的
immiscible [i'misəbl] a. 不溶混的
and the like   等等,诸如此类
civil engineer   土木工程师
fall within   属于……(之列)

1.5 The Principles of Fluid Machines

A fluid machine is a device either for converting the energy held by a fluid into mechanical energy or vice versa. The mechanical energy is usually transmitted by a rotating shaft: a machine in which energy from the fluid is converted directly to the mechanical energy of a rotating member is known as a *turbine* (from the Latin *turbo*, a circular motion); if, however, the initial mechanical movement is a reciprocating one the term *engine* or *motor* is used. A machine in which the converse process—the transfer of energy from moving parts to the fluid—takes place is given the general title of *pump*. When the fluid concerned is a gas other terms may be used. If the primary object is to increase the pressure of the gas, the machine is termed a compressor. On the other hand, a machine primarily used for causing the movement of a gas is known as a *fan* of *blower*. In this case the change in static pressure is quite small—usually sufficient only to overcome the resistance to the motion—and so the variation of density is negligible and the fluid may be regarded as incompressible.

No attempt will be made here to describe constructional details or the practical operation of any of these machines. Our concern is simply with the basic principles of mechanics of fluids which are brought into play.

Although a great variety of fluid machines is to be found, any machine may be placed in one of two categories: the *positive-displacement* group or the *rotodynamic* group. The functioning of a positive-displacement machine derives essentially from changes of the volume occupied by the fluid within the machine. This type is most commonly exemplified by those machines, such as reciprocating pumps and engines, in which a piston moves to and from in a cylinder (a suitable arrangement of valves ensures that the fluid always moves in the direction appropriate to either a pump or an engine). Also in this category are diaphragm pumps, in which the change of volume is brought about by the deformation of flexible boundary surfaces (an animal heart is an example of this form of pump), and gear pumps in which two rotors similar to gear wheels mesh together within a close-fitting housing. Although hydrodynamic effects may be associated with a positive-displacement machine, the operation of the machine itself depends only on mechanical and hydrostatic principles. This is not to say that such a machine is easy to design, but since few principles of the mechanics of fluids are involved our consideration of positive-displacement machines in there will be very brief.

Rotodynamic machines, on the other hand, do present hydrodynamic problems. All these machines have a rotor, that is, a rotating element through which the fluid passes. In a turbine this rotor is called the *runner*; for a pump the term *impeller* is more often used. The fluid has a component of velocity and therefore of momentum in a direction tangential to the rotor, and the rate at which this tangential momentum is changed corresponds to a tangential force on the rotor. In a turbine there is a reduction of the tangential momentum of the fluid in the direction of movement of the rotor; thus energy is transferred from the fluid to the rotor and hence to the output shaft. In a pump, energy from the rotor is used to increase the tangential momentum of the fluid; subsequent deceleration of the fluid produces a rise in pressure.

Rotodynamic machines have a number of advantages over the positive-displacement type. The flow from most positive-displacement machines is unsteady whereas, for normal conditions of operation, that from a rotodynamic machine is essentially steady. Most positive-displacement machines require small clearances between moving and stationary parts, and so are unsuited to handing fluids which may contain solid pariticles; in general, rotodynamic machines are not restricted in this way. If discharge from a positive-displacement pump is prevented—for example, by the closing of a valve—the pressure within the pump rises and so either the pump stops or some part of the casing bursts; if the discharge valve of a rotodynamic pump is closed, however, the rotating impeller merely churns the fluid round, and the energy consumed is converted to heat. Moreover, for dealing with a given overall rate of flow a rotodynamic machine is usually less bulky than one of positive-displacement type.

Words and Expressions

vice versa　反过来(也是这样)
reciprocate　[ri′siprəkeit]　v. 互换(位置),往复移动
compressor　[kəm′presə]　n. 压缩机
blower　[′bləuə]　n. 鼓风机,风扇
piston　[′pistən]　n. 活塞,柱塞
cylinder　[′silində]　n. 气缸,圆筒

rotor ['rəutə] n. 转子,旋转部
hydro-static a. 流体静力(学)的
decelerate [di:'seləreit] v. (使)减速
clearance ['kliərəns] n. 余隙
churn [tʃə:n] v. 搅拌

1.6 Turbulent Flow

The majority of flows that are of engineering interest are turbulent. They are, unfortunately, the most difficult to analyze. In principle, and largely in fact, we can solve most laminar flow problems with the computing power that is available today. The same statement cannot be made of turbulent flows; the opposite is true and there seems to be little hope of achieving that goal in the near future.

Professor D. Allan Bromley (1986) in a review of the state of physics asserts:

One of the most intractable problems in all of physics has been that of turbulence; anyone who has watched the flow of water around an obstacle or watched the smoke rise from a lighted cigarette has observed the transition from ordered laminar flow into ever more complex eddies and finally into completely chaotic motion. Such motion, at the interface between ordered and chaotic, has defied numerical analysis and yet has enormous importance; it is responsible for the drag on ships and planes moving through fluids, it is responsible for most of the noise from jet aircraft, and it is responsible for the ultimate damage to human heart valves, buffeted over periods of years in turbulnt blood flow.

Despite the negative tone of Bromley's assessment, a world without turbulence is unimaginable. The phenomenon is fundamental to life itself. Since it increases diffusion by a couple of orders of magnitude, it would be impossible for air-breathing animals to obtain sufficient oxygen without turbulence. All other natural processes would change so drastically that the face of the earth would be unrecognizable by humans. Perhaps life could evolve in a nonturbulent environment, but even that supposition is far from obvious.

Air and water are the two most common fluids, The natural flows of the atmosphere (wind) and earth take place at highly turbulent Reynolds numbers. The approximation of potential flow can often yield some solutions. Laminar flow is rate in the above-ground environment and its study contributes mainly to a general understanding of the principles of fluid mechanics, many of which translate into the analysis of turbulent flows.

Exactly what is meant by the word "turbulence" must remain somewhat intuitive. Even after a study of the phenomenon, a concise definition is difficult to formulate. Hinze (1959) writes, "Turbulent fluid motion is an irregular condition of flow in which the various quantities show a random variation with time and space coordinates, so that statistically distinct average values can be discerned." The random feature is one of the primary items that makes the study of turbulence difficult. The other feature, not mentioned in the above definition, is that turbulence is strongly three-dimensional. When combined with the fact that the motion takes place over a large range of scales (say, 0.1 mm to several kilometers in the case of geophysical motions), these characteristics create almost insurmountable difficulty.

Turbulence is a phenomenon whose physics are known at a molecular of microscopic level but not at the "macroscopic" level necessary for computation. Despite huge resources and a large amount of research activity spanning more than 30 years, the numerical weather forecasting problem remains largely unsolved even though early optimism predicted that long-term numerical forecasts were just over the horizon. Current models for weather forecasting use about an eighty-kilometer grid spacing. If all the turbulent processes were to be included in the model, the grid spacing would have to be about 1 mm. Since al parts of the earth interact, the grid would have to cover the globe, requiring some 10^{18} grid points. Such a calculation is far beyond the capacity of present-day computers or any foreseeable computer. Research efforts are underway to invent models that can be accurate at much larger grid scales. Current models can compute accurately at large grid scales for a short time but eventually (sqy about two weeks in real time), the interaction of the large scale phenomena with the small scale phenomena renders the calculation worthless. (There are, of course, other obstacles besides raw computing power that stand in the way of long-range forecasts. Obtaining data for initial or corrective conditions on a small scale may be an even more insurmountable problem.)

The "butterfly effect" is a tongue-in-cheek description of the process of atmospheric disturbance. The story is that a butterfly decides to fly from the limb of a tree to a nearby flower in, say, Beijing, thereby creating an atmospheric disturbance. The disturbance is magnified by nonlinear atmospheric processes, eventually causing thunderstorms and tornados in some distant location like St. Louis.

The potential economic benefits of a long-range weather forecast are tremendous. Perhaps agriculture would benefit most. Farmers could decide when to plant, when to fertilize, and when to harvest. They could choose what crops to plant and use a variety that is resistant to either drought or to wet conditions. Crop failure, wasted energy, and associated economic resources would become rare. A host of other fields would benefit: transportation; construction; control of damage due to floods, hurricanes, and tornados; water supply and waste disposal are obvious examples. Of course such forecasts would be important to Jane while she is deciding whether to hold her wedding in the church or in the garden.

One of the misconceptions regarding turbulence is that some fluids are turbulent. It is true that any fluids, especially air and water, have low viscosities so that when they move, the movement tends to be turbulent. It is, however, the *flow* that is turbulent. This apparently self-evident statement is important in that the properties or parameters of turbulence are sometimes attributed to the fluid, whereas the fluid has no such property.

Words and Expressions

intractable [in'træktəbl] *a.* 难处理的
eddy ['edi] *n.* 涡流,漩涡
chaotic [kei'ɔtik] *a.* 浑沌的,混乱的
buffet ['bʌfit] *v.* 打击,与……搏斗
diffusion [di'fju:ʒən] *n.* 漫射,(气流的)滞止
intuitive [in'tjuitiv] *a.* 直觉的,直观的
discern [di'sə:n] *v.* 辨别,分清,看出
insurmountable [ˌinsə:'mauntəbl] *a.* 不可克服的,难以超越的
molecular [mou'lekjulə] *a.* 分子的
optimism ['ɔptimizəm] *n.* 乐观(主义)
grid [grid] *n.* 格子,格栅
underway 在进行中
render ['rendə] *v.* 反映,执行
butterfly ['bʌtəflai] *n.* 蝴蝶
non-linear *a.* 非线性的
tornado [tɔ:'neidəu] *n.* 龙卷风,旋风
tremendous [tri'mendəs] *a.* 巨大的,惊人的
hurricane ['hʌrikən] *n.* 台风
viscosity ['vis'kɔsiti] *n.* 黏性,黏滞度
parameter [pə'ræmitə] *n.* 参数

2

Thermodynamics and Heat Transfer

2.1 Basic Concepts of Thermodynamics

Most applications of thermodynamics require that the system and its surroundings be defined. A thermodynamic system is defined as a region in space or a quantity of matter bounded by a closed surface. The surroundings include everything external to the system, and the system is separated from the surroundings by the system boundaries. These boundaries can be either movable or fixed; either real or imaginary.

Two master concepts operate in any thermodynamic system, energy and entropy. Entropy (s) measures the molecular disorder of a given system. The more shuffled a system is, the greater its entropy; conversely, an orderly or unmixed configuration is one of low entropy.

Energy is the capacity for producing an effect, and can be categorized into either stored or transient forms. Stored forms of energy include:

thermal (internal) energy, u—the energy (possessed by a system) caused by the motion of the molecules and/or intermolecular forces;

potential energy, $P.E.$ —the energy possessed by a system caused by the attractive forces existing between molecules, or the elevation of the system:
$$P.E. = mgz \qquad (2.1)$$
where m = mass
g = local acceleration of gravity
z = elevation above a horizontal reference plane

kinetic energy, $K.E.$ —the energy possessed by a system caused by the velocity of the molecules:
$$K.E. = mv^2/2 \qquad (2.2)$$
where m = mass
v = velocity of the fluid streams crossing system boundaries

chemical energy, E_c—energy possessed by the system caused by the arrangement of atoms composing the molecules.

nuclear (atomic) energy, E_a—energy possessed by the system from the cohesive forces holding protons and neutrons together as the atom's nucleus.

Transient energy forms include:

heat, Q—the mechanism (that transfers energy across the boundary of systems with differing temperatures), always in the direction of the lower temperature.

work—the mechanism that transfers energy across the boundary of systems with differing pressures (or force of any kind), always in the direction of the lower pressure; if the total effect produced in the system can be reduced to the raising of a weight, then nothing but work has crossed the boundary. Mechanical or shaft work, W, is the energy delivered or absorbed by a mechanism, such as a turbine, air compressor or internal combustion engine.

Flow work is energy carried into or transmitted across the system boundary because a pumping process occurs somewhere outside the system, causing fluid to enter the system. It can be more easily understood as the work done by the fluid just outside the system on the adjacent fluid entering the system to force or push it into the system. Flow work also occurs as fluid leaves the system.

$$\text{Flow Work (per unit mass)} = pV \qquad (2.3)$$

where p is the pressure and V is the specific volume, or the volume displaced per unit mass.

A property of a system is any observable characteristic of the system. The state of a system is defined by listing its properties. The most common thermodynamic properties are: temperature (T), pressure (p) and specific volume (V) or density (ρ). Additional thermodynamic properties include entropy, stored forms of energy and enthalpy.

Frequently, thermodynamic properties combine to form new properties. Enthalpy (h), a result of combining properties, is defined as:

$$h = u + pV \qquad (2.4)$$

where u = internal energy

p = pressure

V = specific volume

Each property in a given state has only one definite value, and any property always has the same value for a given state, regardless of how the substance arrived at that state.

A process is a change in state that can be defined as any change in the properties of a system. A process is described by specifying the initial and final equilibrium states, the path (if identifiable) and the interactions that take place across system boundaries during the process. A cycle is a process, or more frequently, a series of processes wherein the initial and final states of the system are identical. Therefore, at the conclusion of a cycle all the properties have the same value they had at the beginning.

A pure substance has a homogeneous and invariable chemical composition. It can exist in more than one phase, but the chemical composition is the same in all phases.

If a substance exists as vapor at the saturation temperature, it is called saturated vapor. (Sometimes the term dry saturated vapor is used to emphasize that the quality is 100%.) When the vapor is at a temperature greater than the saturation temperature, it is superheated vapor. The pressure and temperature of superheated vapor are independent properties, since the temperature can increase while the pressure remains constant. Gases are highly superheated vapors.

Words and Expression

thermodynamics　[ˈθəməudaiˈnæmiks]　n. 热力学
entropy　[ˈentrəpi]　n. 熵(热力学函数)
shuffle　[ˈʃʌfl]　vt. 搅乱,弄混
configuration　[kənˈfigjuˈreiʃən]　n. 构造,结构
categorize　[ˈkætigəraiz]　v. 把……分类
transient　[ˈtrænziənt]　a. (物)瞬变的
thermal　[θəːməl]　a. 热的
elevation　[ˌeliˈveiʃən]　n. 高度
acceleration　[ækˌseləˈreiʃən]　n. (物)加速,加速度
kinetic　[kaiˈnetik]　a. 动力(学)的,动力的
cohesive　[kəuˈhiːsiv]　a. 内聚的
proton　[ˈprəutən]　n. 质子
neutron　[ˈnjuːtrɔn]　n. 中子
mechanism　[ˈmekənizəm]　n. 机械装置,机械结构
shaft　[ʃaːft]　n. 轴
compressor　[kəːmˈpresə]　n. 压缩机,压气机
combustion　[kəmˈbʌstʃən]　n. 燃烧

adjacent [ə'dʒeisənt] a. 邻近的,因此相连的
specific volume 比容
displace [dis'pleis] vt. 排(水)
enthalpy [en'θælpi] n. 焓
equilibrium [iːkwi'libriəm] n. 平衡,均衡
homogeneous [hɔ'mɔdʒinəs] a. 均匀的
saturation [ˌsætʃə'reiʃən] n. 饱和(状态)
saturated ['sætʃəreitid] a. 饱和的

2.2 Thermodynamic Systems

In the engineering world, objects normally are not isolated from one another. In most engineering problems many objects enter into a given problem. Some of these objects, all of these objects, or even additional ones may enter into a second problem. The nature of a problem and its solution are dependent on which objects are under consideration. Thus, it is necessary to specify which objects are under consideration in a particular situation. In thermodynamics this is done either by placing an imaginary envelope around the objects under consideration or by using an actual envelope if such exists. The term system refers to everything lying inside the envelope. The envelope, real or imaginary, is referred to as the boundaries of the system. It is essential that the boundaries of the system be specified very carefully. For example, when one is dealing with a gas in a cylinder where the boundaries are located on the outside of the cylinder, the system includes both the cylinder and its contained gas. On the other hand, when the boundaries are placed at the inner face of the cylinder, the system consists solely of the gas itself.

When the boundaries of a system are such that it cannot exchange matter with the surroundings, the system is said to be a closed system (see Fig.2.1(a)). The system, however, may exchange energy in the form of heat or work with the surroundings. The boundaries of a closed system may be rigid or may expand or contract, but the mass of a closed system cannot change. Hence, the term control mass sometimes is used for this type of system. When the energy crossing the boundaries of a closed system is zero or substantially so, the system may be treated as an isolated system (Fig.2.1(b)).

In most engineering problems, matter, generally a fluid, crosses the boundaries of a system in one or more places. Such a system is known as an open system (see Fig.2.1(c)). The boundaries of an open system are so placed that their location does not change with time. Thus, the boundaries enclose a fixed volume, commonly known as the control volume.

Sometimes a system may be a closed system at one moment and an open one the next. For example, consider the cylinder of an internal combustion engine with the boundaries at the inner walls. With the valves closed, the system is a closed one. However, with either or both of the valves open, the system becomes an open system.

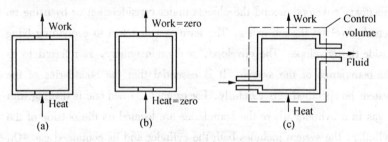

Fig. 2.1 Types of systems
(a) Closed system (b) Isolated system (c) Open system

Frequently the total system to be considered may be large and complicated. The system may be broken down into component parts and an analysis of the component parts made. Then the performance of the entire system can be determined by the summation of the performance of the individual component systems. For example, consider the liquid-vapor part of a steam power plant as an entire system. This system, which is closed, contains the steam generator, the steam turbine, the steam condenser, the feed-water pumps, and the feed-water heaters. Any or all of these units may be considered separately by throwing a boundary around them. Since a fluid enters and leaves each of these smaller systems, each one is an open system and must be analyzed as such.

Words and Expression

isolate ['aisəleit] v. 使隔离,使独立
additional [ə'diʃənəl] a. 额外的,附加的,补充的
imaginary [i'mædʒinəri] a. 虚构的,想像的
envelope ['enviləup] n. 壳层,外壳,包裹物
cylinder ['silində] n. 圆筒,圆柱体,汽缸
boundary ['baundəri] n. 界线,分界,边界
location [ləu'keiʃən] n. 地点,位置,场地
individual [ˌindi'vidjuəl] a. 个别的,单独的,一个人的

2.3 General Characteristics of Heat Transfer

Heat or thermal energy is transferred from one region to another by three modes: conduction, convection and radiation. Each is important in the design or application of heating, air-conditioning or refrigeration equipment. Heat transfer is among the transport phenomena that include mass transfer, momentum transfer or fluid friction and electrical conduction. Transport phenomena have similar rate equations and flux is proportional to a potential difference. In heat transfer by conduction and convection, the potential difference is the temperature difference. Heat, mass and momentum transfer, because of their similarities and interrelationship in many common physical processes, receive unified treatment in some textbooks.

Thermal conduction is the mechanism of heat transfer whereby energy is transported between parts of a continuum from the transfer of kinetic energy between particles or groups of particles at the atomic level. In gases, conduction is a result of elastic collision of molecules; in liquids and electrically nonconducting solids, it is believed to be caused by longitudinal oscillations of the lattice structure. Thermal conduction in metals occurs like electrical conduction, through motions of free electrons. The second Law of Thermodynamics states that thermal transfer occurs in the direction of decreasing temperature. In solid opaque bodies, the significant heat transfer mechanism is thermal conduction, since there is no net material flow in the process. With flowing fluids, thermal conduction dominates in the region very close to a solid boundary where the flow is laminar and parallel to the surface, and there is no eddy motion.

Thermal convection may involve energy transfer by eddy mixing and diffusion in addition to conduction. Consider heat transfer to a fluid flowing inside a pipe. If the Reynolds number is sufficiently great, three different flow regions will exist. Immediately adjacent to the wall is a laminar sublayer where heat transfer occurs by thermal conduction; outside the laminar sublayer is a transition region called the buffer layer, where both eddy mixing and conduction effects are significant; beyond the buffer layer and extending to the center of the pipe is the turbulent region, where the dominant mechanism of transfer is eddy mixing.

In most equipment, the main body of fluid is in turbulent flow, and the laminar layer exists at the solid walls only. In cases of low velocity flow in small tubes, or with viscous liquids such as oil (i.e., at low Reynolds numbers), the entire flow may be laminar with no transition or eddy region.

When fluid currents are produced by sources external to the heat transfer region, for example, a blower or pump, the solid-to-fluid heat transfer is termed forced convection. If the fluid flow is generated internally by nonhomogeneous densities caused by temperature variation, the heat transfer is termed free or natural convection.

In conduction and convection, heat transfer takes place through matter. For radiant heat transfer, there is a change in energy form; from internal energy at the source to electromagnetic energy for transmission, then back to internal energy at the receiver. Whereas conduction and convection are affected primarily by temperature difference and somewhat by temperature level, the heat transferred by radiation increases rapidly as the temperature increases.

Although some generalized heat transfer equations have been mathematically derived from fundamentals, usually they are obtained from correlations of experimental data. Normally, the correlations employ certain dimensionless numbers from analyses such as dimensional analysis or analogy.

Words and Expression

momentum [məu'mentəm] n. 动量,运动量
friction ['frikʃən] n. 摩擦(力),阻力
collision [kə'liʒən] n. 猛烈相撞,抵触(意见)冲突
lattice ['lætis] n. 格子,晶格
laminar ['læminə] a. 成薄层的,薄层状的
diffusion [di'fju:ʒən] n. 扩散,散布
nonhomogeneous ['nɔnhɔmə'dʒi:niəs] a. 非均匀的
correlation [ˌkɔri'leiʃən] n. 相互关联,交互作用,关联式
analogy [ə'nælədʒi] n. 类比,类推

2.4 Conduction

Heat transferred by conduction may be thought of as the heat transferred through a substance (or combination of substances) from a region of high temperature to a region of low temperature by the progressive exchange of energy between the molecules of the substance. In the process of transferring heat by conduction, no bodily displacement of the molecules occurs. In the case of metals, however, electron movement greatly assists in heat transfer by conduction.

The fundamental law of conduction is credited to Fourier. This law may be illustrated as follows. Consider steady-state, unidirectional heat flow through a solid, as is indicated in Fig.2.2. Take a slab of the solid having a cross-sectional area A normal to the path of heat flow. Let the thickness of the slab be dx, and let the temperature difference across the slab be dt. From his experimental work Fourier developed the following relationship:

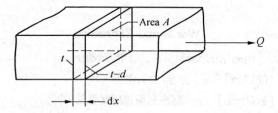

Fig.2.2 Fourier's law of heat conduction

$$Q = -kA \frac{dt}{dx} \qquad (2.5)$$

where Q = heat flow per unit of time

k = proportionality factor, called the thermal conductivity

dt/dx = rate of change in temperature with distance in the direction of heat flow.

In the SI system of units, thermal conductivity may be expressed as
$$W/m^2 \div K/m = W/mK$$

Extensive experimental investigations have established the values of thermal conductivities of many substances and the effect of temperature on these conductivities. Note that the thermal conductivity of any metal is very high in comparison with that of any gas. The reported values of thermal conductivities of metals are valid only for metals of a given degree of purity. Particularly for those metals with the highest values of thermal conductivity, the introduction of a slight amount of another metal will cause a significant change in the thermal conductivity.

The best heat-insulating solids owe their insulating properties to the air or to other gases contained in cells within the material. These cells cause the heat to flow through the solid material through a long tortuous passage. In addition, the available cross-sectional area of the solid material is much less than the projected area. Experimental evidence shows that many small unicellular pockets of gas are much more effective than a series of connected cells having the same total volume in giving insulating value to a substance. There may be considerable variation in the thermal conductivity of any given insulating material because the conductivity depends on its density, the size and number of its air cells, and its absorbed moisture.

There are several accepted methods of experimentally determining the thermal conductivity of solids. When proper care is used, fairly accurate values can be obtained for the thermal conductivity of a given solid of specified composition. It is much more difficult, however, to determine the thermal conductivity of a gas, a vapor, or a liquid, since it is almost impossible to eliminate the heat transferred by convection, which occurs simultaneously with that transferred by conduction, without introducing difficulties in the accurate measurement of other factors. For these reasons there are differences of perhaps 10 to 25 percent in reported values of the thermal conductivities of fluids.

Fig.2.3 shows the heat conduction in a simple wall. It is assumed that the width and height of the wall are so large in comparison with the thickness of the wall that the heat flow may be considered to be unidirectional. One face of the wall is maintained at a uniform temperature t_1, and the other face is kept at temperature t_2. The heat flow through the wall may be obtained by integration of Eq.2.5.

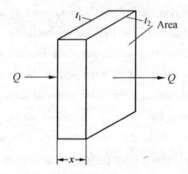

Fig.2.3   Conduction through a single wall

An examination of the thermal conductivities of the various materials shows that, for many materials, the thermal conductivity may be taken as constant over an appreciable range in temperature. Furthermore, for most materials, the thermal conductivity is a straight-line function of temperature within the range of temperature for which information is available. Thus, the arithmetic mean thermal conductivity k_m may be used as the true thermal conductivity. For the simple wall, Eq.2.5 may be integrated as follows:

$$Q = \frac{k_m A}{x}(T_1 - T_2) \qquad (2.6)$$

According to Eq.2.6, the rate of heat flow is proportional to the heat-flow area, the temperature difference causing heat flow, and the term

k_m/x. This term is known as the thermal conductance.

When the thermal conductivity does not vary linearly with temperature, the mean thermal conductivity k_m cannot be determined readily. In such a case it becomes desirable to express the thermal conductivity as a function of temperature in Eq.2.5 and then to perform the integration.

Words and Expression

progressive [prə'gresiv] a. 进行的
bodily ['bɔdili] a. 具体的,有形的
credit (to) v. 把……归于,认为……
Fourier's law 傅里叶定律
unidirectional ['juːnidi'rekʃənl] a. 单向的
slab [slæb] n. 厚片,平板
cross-sectional area 横截面积
proportionality [prə'pɔːʃə'næliti] n. 比例
conductivity [ˌkɔndʌk'tiviti] n. 导热系数
purity ['pjuəriti] n. 纯度
insulating ['insjuleitiŋ] a. 绝热的
tortuous ['tɔːtjuəs] a. 弯曲的
projected area 投影面积
unicellular ['juːni'seljulə] a. 单细胞的,单孔的
convection [kən'vekʃən] n. 对流
integration [ˌinti'greiʃən] n. 积分
appreciable [ə'priːʃiəbl] a. 相当大的
conductance [kən'dʌktəns] n. 导热率
linearly ['liniəli] ad. 线性地

2.5 Natural Convection

Heat transfer involving motion in a fluid caused by the difference in density and the action of gravity is called natural or free convection. Heat transfer coefficients for natural convection are generally much lower than for forced convection, and it is therefore important not to ignore radiation in calculating the total heat loss or gain. Radiant transfer may be of the same order of magnitude as natural convection, even at room temperatures, since wall temperatures in a room can affect human comfort.

Natural convection is important in a variety of heating and refrigeration equipment: (1) gravity coils used in high humidity cold storage rooms and in roof-mounted refrigerant condensers, (2) the evaporator and condenser of household refrigerators, (3) baseboard radiators and convectors for space heating and (4) cooling panels for air conditioning. Natural convection is also involved in heat loss or gain to equipment casings and interconnecting ducts and pipes.

Consider heat transfer by natural convection between a cold fluid and a hot surface. The fluid in immediate contact with the surface is heated by conduction, becomes lighter and rises because of the difference in density of the adjacent fluid. The motion is resisted by the viscosity of the fluid. The heat transfer is influenced by: (1) gravitational force due to thermal expansion, (2) viscous drag and (3) thermal diffusion. It may be expected to depend on the gravitational acceleration g, the coefficient of thermal expansion β, the kinematic viscosity $v\ (=\mu/\rho)$, and the thermal diffusivity $\alpha = (k/\rho c_p)$. These variables can be expressed in terms of dimensionless numbers: the Nusselt number, Nu, is a function of the product of the Prandtl number, Pr, and Grashof number, Gr, which, when combined, depend on the fluid properties, the temperature difference between the surface and the fluid, Δt, and the characteristic length of the surface, L. The constant c and exponent n depend on the physical configuration and nature of flow.

The entire process of natural convection cannot be represented by a single value of exponent n, but can be divided into three regions: (1) turbulent natural convection for which n equals 0.33, (2) laminar natural convection, for which n equals 0.25 and (3) a region that has ($Gr \cdot Pr$) less than for laminar natural convection, for which the exponent n gradually diminishes from 0.25 to lower values. Note that, for wires, the ($Gr \cdot Pr$) is likely to be very small, so that the exponent n is 0.1.

To calculate the natural convection heat transfer coefficient, determine ($Gr \cdot Pr$) to find whether the boundary layer is laminar or turbulent, then apply the appropriate equation. The correct characteristic length indicated must be used. Since the exponent n is 0.33 for a turbulent boundary layer, the characteristic length cancels out, and the heat transfer coefficient is independent of the characteristic length. Turbulence occurs when length or temperature difference is large. Since the length of a pipe is generally greater than its diameter, the heat transfer coefficient for vertical pipes is larger than for horizontal pipes.

Convection from horizontal plates facing downward when heated (or upward when cooled) is a special case. Since the hot air is above the colder air, there is no theoretical reason for convection. Some convection is caused, however, by secondary influences such as temperature differences on the edges of the plate. As an approximation, a coefficient of somewhat less than half of the coefficient for a heated horizontal plate facing upward can be used.

Since air is often the heat transport fluid, simplified equations for air are given. Other information on natural convection is available in the general heat transfer references.

Observed differences in the comparisons of recent experimental and numerical results with existing correlations for natural convective heat transfer coefficients indicate that caution should be taken when applying coefficients for (isolated) vertical plates recommended by ASHRAE for situations with vertical surfaces in enclosed spaces (buildings). Improved correlations for calculating natural convective heat transfer from vertical surfaces in rooms under certain temperature boundary conditions have been developed.

Natural convection can affect the heat transfer coefficient in the presence of weak forced convection. As the forced convection effect, i.e., the Reynolds number, increases, the "mixed convection" (superimposed forced-on-free convection) gives way to the pure forced convection regime. Since the heat transfer coefficient in the mixed convection region is often larger than that calculated based on the natural or forced convection calculation alone, attention is called to references on combined free and forced convection heat transfer. The reference given before summarizes natural, mixed, and forced convection regimes for vertical and horizontal tubes. Local conditions influence the values of the convection coefficient in a mixed convection regime, but the references permit locating the pertinent regime and approximating the convection coefficient.

Words and Expression

humidity [hju(:)'miditi] *n*. 湿度
roof-mounted 屋顶安装的
baseboard *n*. 踢脚板
casings ['keisiŋz] *n*. 壳
ducts [dʌkts] *n*. 风管,管道
viscous ['viskəs] *a*. 黏性的,黏滞的
diffusivity [ˌdifjuː'siviti] *n*. 扩散性,扩散系数

Nusselt number   努谢尔特数
Prandtl number   普朗特数
Grashof number   格拉晓夫数
diminish   [di′miniʃ]   vt. 减小,减少
turbulence   [′tə:bjuləns]   n. 紊流,扰动
correlation   [ˌkɔri′leiʃən]   n. 关系式
ASHRAE = American Society of Heating Refrigerating and Air-conditioning Engineers   美国供热制冷和空调工程师协会
superimpose   [′sju:pərim′pəuz]   vt. 加上,附加,叠加
forced-on-free convection   加上自然对流影响的受迫对流
regime   [rei′ʒi:m]   n. 区域,状态
pertinent   [′pə:tinənt]   a. 恰当的,相关的

2.6 Radiation

Every free surface emits energy in the form of electromagnetic waves; the amount of energy is a function of the surface temperature. This emitted energy is known as radiant thermal energy. The nature of this radiant energy is not completely understood, but laws have been formulated that describe its behavior. It is recognized that, as with other forms of radiant energy, radiant heat energy is transmitted in the form of electromagnetic waves. The complete formulation of the laws governing radiant heat energy must consider that this energy is quantized, that is, the energy is transferred in quanta. In contrast with other modes of heat transfer, no medium is required to transmit radiant energy. In fact some gases, for instance, carbon dioxide and water vapor, absorb some of the radiant energy passing through them.

For a fixed set of conditions, any free surface emits radiant energy of varying wavelengths. The frequency of vibration (ν) of radiant waves is dependent solely on the source of radiation and is independent of the medium through which they pass. The velocity of radiant waves (V) is a function solely of the medium through which they pass. Thus, the wavelength ($\lambda = V\nu$) is a function of both the source and the medium.

All free surfaces receive radiant energy from all other surfaces that they can "see," that is, surfaces in direct line of sight. Most problems in radiation deal with the net radiant energy exchanged between a given surface and those that surround it. In common parlance, the term "heat exchanged by radiation" is used. It must be emphasized, however, that radiation is not heat. Heat is conducted to a surface. By virtue of the temperature of a surface, electromagnetic waves transmit energy from the surface. When these strike another surface, part of the energy will be absorbed, tending to increase the temperature of the surface struck by them, and part will be reflected. When the object is transparent, or partially so, to radiant waves, some or all of the radiant energy received by the surface will pass into the object. The transparency of an object to radiant energy is a function of the wavelength of the radiant waves. These statements relating to the radiant energy received by a surface may be put in equation form as follows:

$$\alpha + \rho + \tau = 1 \tag{2.7}$$

where α = absorptivity, or the portion of the radiant energy that is absorbed;

ρ = reflectivity, or the portion of the radiant energy that is reflected;

τ = transmissivity, or the portion of the radiant energy that is transmitted.

A black surface has an absorptivity close to unity. For this reason the term blackbody has been used to designate an imaginary object whose surface has an absorptivity of unity. Since no known surface completely absorbs radiant energy, the term blackbody refers to an ideal surface.

kirchhoff conceived a method of completely absorbing radiant energy. Assume that a hollow sphere contains a very small opening, as is indicated in Fig.2.4 Radiation entering this opening will be received by the back wall of the sphere. Here it will be partially absorbed and partially reflected to other parts of the walls of the sphere. The reflected waves are, in turn, partially reflected, so that each reflected portion is a progressively smaller portion of the energy entering the sphere until ultimately all of it is absorbed. Strictly speaking, some of the reflected radiant energy will pass out through the hole. However, the surface area of the sphere is πD^2. Hence, when the diameter of the sphere is chosen to be 50 times that of the opening, the inside surface area is 10 000 times that of the opening, and it may be assumed that the hollow sphere absorbs all of the radiant energy.

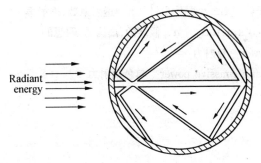

Fig.2.4 Radiant energy absorbed in a hollow sphere

The amount of radiant energy emitted by a surface is a function of the nature of the surface and its temperature. The term blackbody is also used to denote a surface that emits the maximum conceivable amount of radiant energy at any given temperature. There is no actual surface that is a perfect emitter, but the hollow-sphere concept may be used to establish a standard. The process of emission from the inner surface of the sphere is the reverse of that of absorption.

The total radiant energy emitted in a unit time by a unit area is known as the total emissive power and is designated by E. Since radiant energy is emitted over a range of wavelengths,

$$E = \int_{\lambda=0}^{\lambda=\infty} E_\lambda d\lambda \qquad (2.8)$$

where E_λ is the monochromatic emissive power. It is assumed that E_λ in Eq.2.8 is a continuous function of λ.

Words and Expression

emit [i'mit] v. 放射,发出
frequency ['fri:kwənsi] n. 频繁,频率
vibration [vai'breiʃən] n. 振动,动摇,共鸣,感应
transparency [træns'pɛərənsi] n. 透明,透明物,透明性,透明度
reflectivity [riflek'tiviti] n. 反射率
transmissivity [træzmi'siviti] n. 透射系数,透射率
assumed [ə'sju:md] a. 假装的,虚构的,假想的
emissive power 辐射力
monochromatic emissive power 单色辐射力

3

Fuels and Combustion

3.1 Heat of Combustion

In a boiler furnace (where no mechanical work is done) the heat energy evolved from the union of combustible elements with oxygen depends on the ultimate products of combustion and not on any intermediate combinations that may occur in reaching the final result.

A simple demonstration of this law is the union of 1 lb of carbon with oxygen to produce a specific amount of heat. The union may be in one step to form the gaseous product of combustion, CO_2, or under certain conditions the union may be in two steps, first to form CO, producing a much smaller amount of heat and, second the union of the CO so obtained to form CO_2, releasing 9 755 Btu. However, the sum of the heats released in the two steps equals the 14 100 Btu evolved when carbon is burned in one step to form CO_2 as the final product.

That carbon may enter into these two combinations with oxygen is of utmost importance in the design of combustion equipment. Firing methods must assure complete mixture of fuel and oxygen to be certain that all of the carbon burns to CO_2 and not to CO. Failure to meet this requirement will result in appreciable losses in combustion efficiency and in the amount of heat released by the fuel, since only about 28% of the available heat in the carbon is released if CO is formed instead of CO_2.

Measurement of heat of combustion

In boiler practice the heat of combustion of a fuel is the amount of heat, expressed in Btu, generated by the complete combustion, or oxidation, of a unit weight (1 lb in the United States) of fuel. Calorific value or "fuel Btu value" are terms also used.

The amount of heat generated by complete combustion is a constant for any given combination of combustible elements and compounds and is not affected by the manner in which the combustion takes place, provided it is complete.

The heat of combustion of a fuel is usually determined by direct measurement in a calorimeter of the heat evolved during combustion. Combustion products within a calorimeter are cooled to the initial temperature and the heat absorbed by the cooling medium is measured to determine the higher or gross heat of combustion.

For solid fuels and most liquid fuels, calorimeters of the "bomb" type, in which combustible substances are burned in a constant volume of oxygen, give the most satisfactory results. With bomb calorimeters properly operated, combustion is complete, all of the heat generated is absorbed and measured, and heat from external sources either can be excluded or proper corrections can be applied.

For gaseous fuels, calorimeters of the continuous or constant – Flow type are usually accepted as standard. The principle of operation is the same as for the bomb calorimeter except that the heat content is determined at constant pressure rather than at constant volume. For most fuels, the difference in the heating values from the constant-pressure and constant-volume determinations is small and is usually neglected.

For accurate heat values of solid and liquid fuels calorimeter determinations are required. However, approximate heat values may be determined for most coals if the ultimate chemical analysis is known. Dulong's formula gives reasonably accurate results (within 2 to 3%) for most coals and is often used as routine check of values determined by calorimeter:

$$\text{Btu/lb} = 14\ 544\ C + 62\ 028(H_2 - O_2/8) + 4\ 050\ S \qquad (3.1)$$

In this formula, the symbols represent the proportionate parts by weight of the constituents of the fuel—carbon, hydrogen, oxygen and sulfur—as determined by an ultimate analysis; the coefficients represent the approximate heating values of the constituents in Btu per lb. The term $O_2/8$ is a correction applied to the hydrogen in the fuel to account for the hydrogen already combined with the oxygen in the form of moisture. This formula is not generally suitable for calculating the Btu values of gaseous fuels.

High and low heat values

Water vapor is one of the products of combustion for all fuels which contain hydrogen. The heat content of a fuel depends on whether this water vapor is allowed to remain in the vapor state or is condensed to liquid. In the bomb calorimeter the products of combustion are cooled to the initial temperature and all of the water vapor formed during combustion is condensed to liquid. This gives the high, or gross, heat content of the fuel with the heat of vaporization included in the reported value. For the low, or net heat of combustion, it is assumed that all products of combustion remain in the gaseous state.

While the high, or gross, heat of combustion can be accurately determined by established (ASTM) procedures, direct determination of the low heat of combustion is difficult. Therefore, it is usually calculated using the following formula:

$$Q_L = Q_H - 1\ 040\ W \qquad (3.2)$$

where:

Q_L = low heat of combustion of fuel, Btu/lb

Q_H = high heat of combustion of fuel, Btu/lb

W = lb water formed per lb of fuel

1 040 = factor to reduce high heat of combustion at constant volume to low heat of combustion at constant pressure

In the United States the practice is to use the high heat of combustion in boiler combustion calculations. In Europe the low heat value is used.

Words and Expressions

boiler ['bɔilə] n. 锅炉,煮器
furnace ['fə:nis] n. 火炉,炉膛
oxygen ['ɔksidʒən] n. 氧,氧气
ultimate ['ʌltimit] a. 最后的,最终的
failure ['feiljə] n. 失败,忽略
carbon ['ka:bən] n. 碳
calorimeter [ˌkælə'rimitə] n. 热量计,量热器
gross [grəus] a. 总体的,总的
bomb [bɔm] n. 高压弹,炸弹
approximate [ə'prɔksimit] a. 近似的,大概的
routine [ru:'ti:n] a. 日常的,例行的
hydrogen ['haidrədʒən] n. 氢,氢气

3.2 Combustion Equipment

A steam generating system is large and complex. It consists of combustion equipment, furnace, and various heat transfer surfaces. In addition, the steam generating system has some auxiliary equipment needed for efficient operation. These auxiliaries include at least the boiler fans (forced-draft and induced-draft), stack, precipitatoer, and SO_2 removal system.

The selection of combustion equipment depends on the type of the fuel used. For solid fuels such as coal, three combustion systems (mechanical stoker, pulverizer burner and cyclone-furnace) are generally suitable. Mechanical stokers were first developed in the history of the boiler. Almost any coal can be burned on some type of stoker. Other advantages of stokers include low power requirements and large operating range. Because of the small capacity, they are seldom used for today's central electric power station.

The pulverizer-burner system was introduced in the third decade of last century. This system overcomes the size limitation of the mechanical stoker. Modern pulverizing systems are so well developed that they can burn almost any type of coal, particularly those in the higher grades and ranks. In addition, the system has improved response to the load change, higher combustion efficiency, and less manpower required in operation.

Fig. 3.1 shows a typical firing system for pulverized coal. The function of this system is to pulverize the coal, deliver the coal powder to the burners, and accomplish complete combustion in the furnace. The system must operate in continuous process and can adjust itself to the load demand in a reasonable time. There are two major equipment components, pulverizer and burner, in the system. The pulverizer receives coal from the coal bunker through the coal feeder, and produces the coal powder according to the fitness requirement. At the same time the pulverizer receives the hot air from the primary-air fan for drying and transporting the coal powder to the burners. Each pulverizer is usually connected with several burners. In operation, the coal feed is proportioned to the load demand, and the primary air supply is adjusted to the rate of coal feed. The air-coal ratio is so determined that the air-coal mixture leaving the pulverizer should have a proper temperature and moisture. Generally, the temperature and moisture are, respectfully, 65℃ and 1% to 2% for bituminous coals.

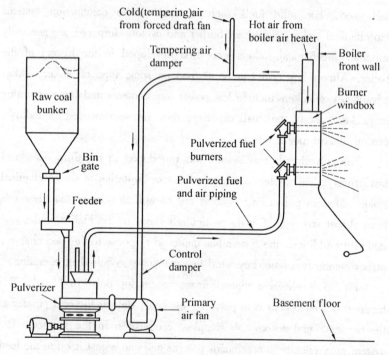

Fig. 3.1 Typical firing system for pulverized coal

In addition to delivering a sufficient amount of air, the primary air fan is designed to maintain a high velocity of the air-coal mixture in pulverizer discharge lines. The velocity must be such that there is no settling and drifting of coal in the piping. At the burner the air-coal mixture is combined with secondary air and both injected into furnace. As indicated in Fig. 3.1, both primary air and secondary air are from the boiler air preheater. When the moisture of coal is below the maximum level, or the boiler is in a low load condition, cold air is used to temper the primary air.

Combustion equipment for oil and natural gas is relatively simple. There is no need for a coal pulverizer, coal crusher, or other fuel preparation facilities. Because of the high viscosity of the fuel oil, some types of heaters are usually needed in the oil storage tank to warm the oil and to facilitate pumping. Oil pumps receive the oil from the strainers and discharge it to the burners through heaters. To maintain a good combustion, the temperature of the fuel oil entering the burners should be around 65℃. The recirculation lines are provided in the fuel oil system. The recirculation lines are used to prevent stagnant oil from collecting in the piping system and cooling to the point of solidification. The burners for the fuel oil are similar to those for the pulverized coal.

Words and Expressions

forced-draft　送风机
induced-draft　引风机
stoker　['stəukə]　n. 层燃炉
capacity　[kə'pæsiti]　n. 容量,生产力,功率
powder　['paudə]　n. 煤粉
bunker　['bʌŋkə]　n. 容器,仓
feeder　['fi:də]　n. 给煤机
fitness　['fitnis]　n. 适合,恰当
discharge　[dis'tʃa:dʒ]　vt. 排出,离开
settling　['setliŋ]　n. 沉淀,沉降

drifting   ['driftiŋ]   adj. 漂移,偏差
crusher   ['krʌʃə]   n. 破碎机
facilitate   [fə'siliteit]   vt. 使方便
strainer   ['streinə]   n. 过滤器,滤网
stagnant   ['stægnənt]   adj. 停滞的,不流动的
solidification   [ˌsɔlidifi'keiʃən]   n. 凝固,浓缩

3.3 Fuel-ash

Ash content of coal

The ash content of coals varies over a wide range. This variation occurs not only in coal from different parts of the world or from different seams in the same region but also in coal from different parts of the same mine. Some rock and earthy materials find their way into the mined product. Before marketing, some commercial coals are cleaned or washed to remove a portion of what would be reported as ash in laboratory determinations. In any case, the ash determinations of significance to the user are those made at the point of use, and the values noted below are on that basis.

The bulk of bituminous coal used for power generation in the U.S. has an ash content within the range of 6 to 20%. Low values of 3% or 4% are encountered infrequently, and such coals find other commercial uses, particularly in the metallurgical field. On the other hand, some coals may have an ash content as high as 30%. Many high-ash fuels are successfully burned in the Cyclone Furnace as well as in pulverized-coal-fired units. Their use is increasing in localities where the fuel costs indicate a favorable overall economy.

Nature of coal ash

The presence of ash is accounted for by minerals associated with initial vegetal growth or those which entered the coal seam from external sources during or after the period of coal formation. Appreciable quantities of inorganic material may be contributed to the commercial fuel by partial inclusion of adjacent rock strata in the process of mining.

Since quantitative evaluation of mineral forms is extremely difficult, the composition of the coal ash is customarily determined by chemical analysis of the residue produced by burning a sample of coal at a slow rate and at moderate temperature (1 350°F) under oxidizing conditions in a laboratory furnace. It is thus found to be composed chiefly of compounds of silicon, aluminum, iron, and calcium, with smaller amounts of magnesium, titanium, sodium and potassium.

The element sulfur is present in practically all coal, and its effect on equipment performance has been given much attention. Sulfur itself burns as a fuel with a relatively low heating value (3 980 Btu/lb when burned to SO_2), but its reputation, which is nearly all bad, results from the effect of its chemical combination with other elements. Under certain conditions some of these compounds corrode boiler components; others contribute to the fouling and slagging of gas passages and heating surfaces.

Some of the sulfur in coal is in combination with iron as FeS_2. Sulfur may also be present in the form of complex organic compounds and, in minor amounts, in combination with the alkaline earths (calcium and magnesium). When the fuel is burned, the sulfur compounds are normally converted to more or less stable mineral oxides and sulfur dioxide gas, SO_2. A very small part of the SO_2 thus formed is further oxidized to SO_3. These sulfur gases are carried along with the other combustion gases, and their presence, under certain conditions, can contribute to corrosion of boiler heating surfaces and to air pollution problems.

Coals may be classified into two groups based on the nature of their ash constituents. One is the bituminoustype ash and the other is the lignite-type ash. The term "lignite-type" ash is defined as an ash having more CaO plus MgO than Fe_2O_3. By contrast, the "bituminoustype" ash will have more Fe_2O_3 than CaO plus MgO.

Ash fusibility

The preferred procedure for the determination of ash fusion temperatures is outlined in ASTM Standard D-1857. Earlier procedure used only a reducing atmosphere for ash-fusibility determination whereas the standard adopted in 1968 offers the use of both reducing and oxidizing atmospheres. The previous method had loosely defined softening and fluid critical points; the new procedure uses improved definitions, as follows:

Initial deformation temperature, at which the first rounding of the apex of the cone occurs.

Softening temperature, at which the cone has fused down to a spherical lump in which the height is equal to the width at the base.

Hemispherical temperature, at which the cone has fused down to a hemispherical lump at which point the height is one half the width of the base.

Fluid temperature, at which the fused mass has spread out in a nearly flat layer with a maximum height of one sixteenth in.

The determination of ash fusion temperatures is strictly a laboratory procedure, developed in standardized form, which experience shows can be duplicated with some degree of accuracy. For example, the permissible differences of reproducibility between two furnace runs may range from 100 to 150°F. However, some bituminoustype ash, containing relatively large amounts of silica, may exhibit low ash-softening temperatures, yet exhibits high viscosity characteristics in its plastic range. Some lignite-type ash, containing large amounts of calcium and magnesium, may react with the refractory base (kaolin and alumina), or it may evolve gaseous products and swell, thereby causing changes in density of the ash cone. Methods for determining fusibility of coal ash used by countries outside the U.S. may also vary considerably. Thus, ash fusibility data should be used with care and its limitations recognized.

Ash melts when heated to a sufficiently high temperature. Following combustion, individual ash particles are generally in the form of tiny spheres (cenospheres) that appear hollow when viewed under a microscope. The form of the ash particles indicates that, during combustion of the coal, the particles were actually liquid and the spheres were formed as tiny bubbles by evolved gases trying to escape. What happens to these particles depends on their physical and chemical characteristics and on furnace conditions. If cooled promptly and sufficiently, the result is a dusty ash that may travel through the equipment, lodge on heating surfaces, drop out in soot hoppers and along flues, or collect at the base of the stack. Those particles that remain in suspension are carried out with the flue gases to the particulate-removal equipment and stack. The individual ash particles do not, however, always cool quickly to a solid state. If insufficiently cooled, they remain molten or sticky and tend to coalesce into large masses in the boiler furnace or other heat-absorption surfaces. This problem is dealt with by adequate design of burners and furnace arrangement for the fuels to be burned and by proper attention to boiler operation.

Words and Expressions

fuel-ash $n.$ 燃料灰
bulk   [bʌlk] $n.$ 大部分,堆
bituminous   [biˈtjuːminəs] $a.$ 烟煤的

cyclone ['saikləun] a. 旋风的
vegetal ['vedʒitl] a. 植物的,蔬菜的
slag [slæg] n. 熔渣,渣滓
sulfur ['sʌlfə] n. 硫磺,含硫磺的
fusibility [ˌfju:zə'biliti] n. (可)熔性,熔度
deformation [ˌdi:fɔ:'meiʃən] n. 变形
lump [lʌmp] n. 堆
hemispherical [ˌhemi'sferrikəl] a. 半球状的,半球体的

3.4 The Mechanisms of Gaseous Fuels Combustion

As has been found by experiment, the rates of combustion reactions substantially exceed the rates calculated using the law of mass action and Arrhenius' law by considering the number of active molecules of the initial substances entering a reaction. Actually, reactions do not occur immediately between the original molecules, but pass through a number of intermediate stages in which active molecular fragments (radicals and atoms of H, OH, O, etc.) participate along with molecules. As a result, each of these intermediate reactions has a low level of the activation energy E, since radicals and individual atoms possess a free valency, and can therefore form free-valency particles. Such reactions can proceed at a high rate. The start of a reaction between substances is preceded by a period during which active reaction centres in the form of charged particles accumulate in the medium, owing to the partial destruction of original molecules by other molecules which possess an energy higher than the energy of the atomic bonds in the original molecules. This is what is called the *induction period*.

The combustion of gaseous fuels. Combustion of gaseous fuels occurs by the laws of branched chain reactions which were discovered by Soviet Academician N.N. Semenov and C.N. Hinshelwood. The conversion of the original substances to the final products passes through a sequence of reaction links which are connected in succession with one another and develop in the volume of a combustible mixture like the branches of a tree develop from its trunk. This results in the formation of the final reaction products and of an even greater number of active centres which further ensure the development of the reaction in the confining volume.

Let us consider the mechanism of branched chain reactions, taking as an example the combustion of hydrogen in air. By the stoichiometric equation

$$2H_2 + O_2 = 2H_2O$$

the rate of the reaction between molecules of the combustible substance

$$w_{H_2O} = k_0 e^{-E/RT} C_{H_2}^2 C_{O_2} \qquad (3.3)$$

cannot be very large. Actually, however, combustion of hydrogen at temperatures above 500°C is an explosive chain reaction proceeding at a very high rate. Indeed, according to N.N. Semenov, the beginning of the active reaction is preceded by the formation of active centres:

$$H_2 + M^a \longrightarrow 2H + M$$

$$H_2 + O_2^a \longrightarrow 2OH$$

where M^a and O_2^a are active molecules which possess high energy levels in the volume.

Atoms and radicals formed by this mechanism actively enter the reactions with the surrounding molecules, i.e. chains of successive reactions develop which result in the formation of the final reaction products and ever greater number of active centres.

Fig. 3.2 schematically shows the first cycle of this reaction. As may be seen, each of the active hydrogen atoms H that has given rise to a chain reaction has produced three new active centres, owing to which the reaction progressively develops in the volume confining the gas mixture.

As the reaction products accumulate and the concentrations of the starting substances become lower, chains are disrupted more often in the volume and at the walls of the reactor:

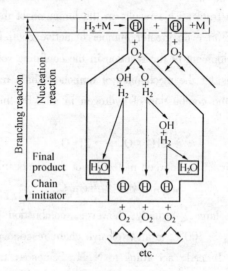

Fig. 3.2 Chain reaction cycle of hydrogen burning

○ — chain reaction exciter;

□ — final product

$$H + H \longrightarrow H_2$$

$$OH + H \longrightarrow H_2O$$

The actual reaction rate is described by the equation:

$$w_H = 10^{11} \sqrt{T} C_H C_{O_2} e^{-E'/RT} \qquad (3.4)$$

The decisive factors for the reaction rate are the concentrations of hydrogen atoms (reaction centres) and oxygen molecules, with the activation energy E' of the reaction between them being substantially lower than E in equation (3.3). Similar laws of chain reactions govern the combustion of carbon monoxide CO, methane CH_4 and other combustible gases.

It follows from the foregoing that a short time, the induction period, precedes the beginning of an active reaction, during which a sufficiently large quantity of active centres (atoms and radicals) accumulates in the reaction volume. During this period, the reaction is almost unnoticeable and its thermal effect is negligible. After this period, the reaction rate increases due to the development of a large number of parallel reaction chains over the whole volume, until an equilibrium between the appearance and disappearance of active centres is established. The reaction then attains its maximum rate and will proceed at this rate, provided that fresh portions of starting substances are regularly supplied to the combustion zone.

Combustion of a gaseous fuel in a mixture with air occurs at a very high rate (a ready methane-air mixture burns in a volume of 10 m^3 in 0.1 s). For this reason, the intensity of combustion of natural gas in steam boiler furnaces is limited by the speed at which it mixes with air in the burner, i.e. by physical factors. The difficulties which arise when high flows of gas and air should be mixed thoroughly in a very short time in a burner are linked with the fact that the volume flow rates of the gas and air differ substantially, as approximately 10 m^3 of air are needed for the combustion of 1 m^3 of gas. For thorough intermixing, gas must be introduced into the air flow in the form of numerous fine jets and at a high rate. For the same purpose, the air flow is thoroughly turbulized by special swirling arrangements.

Words and Expressions

mechanism ['mekənizəm] *n*. 机理,机构

intermediate [ˌintə'miːdjət] *a*. 中间的 *n*. 中间物

valency ['veilənsi] *n*. (化合)价,(原子)价

medium ['mi:diəm] n. 媒体
induction [in'dʌkʃən] n. 感应,诱导
sequence ['si:kwəns] n. 连续,次序
trunk [trʌŋk] n. 树干,主要部分
confine [kən'fain] v. 限制
concentration [ˌkɔnsen'treiʃən] n. 浓度,浓缩
thermal ['θə:məl] a. 热的
parallel ['pærəlel] a. 相似的,相同的 n. 相似处
approximately [ə'prɔksimətli] adv. 大概,近乎
swirl [swə:l] n. 旋涡,涡动

3.5 The Combustion of Liquid Fuels and Solid Fuels

The combustion of liquid fuels

In the combustion of liquid fuels (petroleum, fuel oil), both the ignition and combustion temperatures (especially the latter) turn out to be higher than the boiling temperature of the individual fuel fractions. For this reason, liquid fuel first evaporates from the surface under the effect of the supplied heat, then its vapours are mixed with air, preheated to the ignition temperature and start burning. A stable flame forms at a certain distance from the surface of liquid fuel (0.5 ~ 1 mm or more).

Fig. 3.3 schematically shows the combustion of a liquid fuel droplet in stagnant air. A vapour cloud forms around the droplet and diffuses into the environment, with the diffusion of oxygen of the air occurring in the opposite direction. As a result, the stoichiometric relationship between the combustible gases and oxygen is established at a certain distance r_{st} from the droplet, i.e. the burning fuel vapours form a spherical combustion front around it. The magnitude of r_{st} is equal to 4 ~ 10 droplet radii, i.e. $r_{st} = 4 \sim 10 r_d$, and depends heavily on the droplet size and the temperature in the combustion zone. In the zone where $r < r_{st}$, fuel vapours prevail, but their concentration decreases inversely with the distance from the liquid surface. The zone with $r > r_{st}$ contains primarily combustion products mixed with the oxygen that has diffused into the combustion zone. The highest temperature is established in the reaction zone. Although at both sides of this zone the temperature decreases gradually, its decrease is more intensive in the inside direction, i.e. on approaching the droplet, since some heat is spent there for heating fuel vapours.

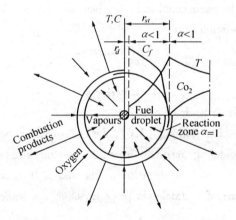

Fig.3.3 Mechanism and combustion characteristics of a liquid fuel droplet

Thus, the burning rate of a liquid fuel droplet is determined by the rate of evaporation from its surface, the rate of chemical reaction in the combustion zone, and the rate of oxygen diffusion to this zone. As stated earlier, the reaction rate in a gaseous medium is very high and cannot limit the total rate of combustion. The quantity of oxygen diffused through the spherical surface is proportional to the square of sphere diameter, and therefore, a slight removal of the combustion zone from the surface of the droplet (under oxygen deficiency) noticeably increases the mass flow rate of supplied oxygen. Thus, the rate of combustion of the droplet is mainly determined by evaporation from its surface. The combustion rate of liquid fuels is increased by atomizing the fuel just before burning, which substantially increases the total surface of evaporation. Besides all this, as the size of the droplets decreases, the intensity of evaporation per unit area of their surface increases. Fine liquid fuel droplets suspended in an air flow move at low Reynolds numbers, $Re \ll 4$. In such cases, the heat flow through a spherical surface is determined solely by the conductivity λ through the boundary layer, which is much thicker than the droplet diameter. Under such conditions, the heat-transfer coefficient α is given by Sokolsky's formula:

$$Nu = \alpha d / \lambda = 2 \qquad (3.5)$$

whence

$$\alpha = 2\lambda / d = \lambda / r \qquad (3.6)$$

where Nu is the Nusselt number.

As follows from formula (3.6), the heat exchange between a droplet and the surrounding medium increases as the size of the droplet decreases, i.e. with a decrease in its mass. It turns out that the evaporation time of a droplet is proportional to the square of its initial diameter.

The combustion of solid fuel

When combined with air in a furnace, pulverized coal first passes through the stage of thermal preparation (Fig. 3.4, I), which consists in the evaporation of residual moisture and separation of volatiles. Fuel particles are heated up to a temperature at which volatiles are evolved intensively (400 ~ 600℃) in a few tenths of a second. The volatiles are then ignited, so that the temperature around a coke particle increases rapidly and its heating is accelerated (III'). The intensive burning of the

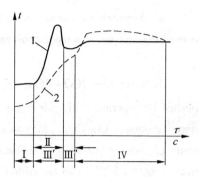

Fig.3.4 Temperature conditions of burning of an individual solid fuel particle
1—temperature of gaseous medium around the particle;
2—particle temperature;
I—thermal preparation zone;
II—zone of burning of volatiles;
III'—heating of coke particle due to burning of its volatiles;
III"—heating of coke particle from an external source;
IV—burning of coke particle

volatiles (II) takes up 0.2 ~ 0.5 s. A high yield of volatiles (brown coal, younger coals, oil shales, peat), produces enough heat through combustion to ignite coke particles. When the yield of volatiles is low, the coke particles must be heated additionally form an external source (III"). The final stage is the combustion of coke particles at a temperature above 800 ~ 1 000℃ (IV). This is a heterogeneous process whose rate is determined by the oxygen supply to the reacting surface. The burning of a coke particle proper takes up the greater portion (1/2 to 2/3) of the total time of combustion which may constitute 1 to 2.5 s, depending on the kind of fuel and the initial size of particles.

The reacting mechanism between carbon and oxygen seems to be as follows. Oxygen is adsorbed from the gas volume on the surface of particles and reacts chemically with carbon to form complex carbon-oxygen compounds of the type C_xO_y which then dissociate with the formation of CO_2 and CO. The resulting reaction at temperatures near 1 200℃ can be written as follows:

$$4C + 3O_2 = 2CO + 2CO_2 \qquad (3.7)$$

As has been established by experiment (L. Meyer, L. X. Khitrin), the ratio of the primary products, CO/CO_2, increases sharply with the increasing temperature of burning particles. For instance, the resulting equation at temperatures near 1 700℃ can be written in the form:

$$3C + 2O_2 = 2CO + CO_2 \qquad (3.8)$$

where the CO/CO_2 ratio is equal to two.

The primary reaction products are continuously removed from the surface of particles to the environment. In this process, carbon monoxide encounters the diffusing oxygen, which moves in the opposite direction, and reacts with it within the boundary gas film to be oxidized to CO_2, with the result that the concentration of supplied oxygen decreases sharply on approaching the surface of particles, while the concentration of CO_2 increases (Fig. 3.5(a)). At a high combustion temperature, carbon monoxide can consume all the oxygen supplied, which, consequently, will not reach the solid surface of particles (Fig. 3.5(b)). Under such conditions, the endothermic reduction reaction will occur on the surface of particles, i.e. CO_2 will be partially reduced to CO.

Thus, heterogeneous combustion of a carbon particle from its surface can be represented as a process embracing four subsequent reactions (according to A.S. Predvoditelev), two of which are the main ones:

$$C + O_2 = CO_2 + q_1$$
$$2C + O_2 = 2CO + 2q_2$$

the other two being secondary

$$2CO + O_2 = 2CO_2 - 2q_3$$

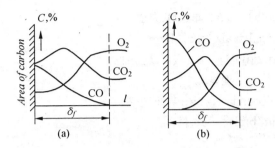

Fig. 3.5　Variations of concentration of gaseous substances at the surface of burning carbon
(a) burning at moderate temperatures;
(b) burning at high temperatures;
δ_f—thickness of boundary film

$$C + CO_2 = 2CO - q_4$$

where q is the thermal effect of a reaction, MJ/mol.

The thermal effect of the first reaction $q_1 = q_2 + q_3$, while $q_4 = 0.57 q_3$. The latter equation implies that even when the endothermic reaction takes place, the temperature of combustion is maintained at a rather high level due to a higher heat evolution in the volume.

As follows from an analysis of these reactions, the combustion of carbon from the surface takes place with partial gasification (formation of CO and its afterburning in the volume). This process accelerates the burning-off of coke particles.

Words and Expressions

evaporate　[i'væpəreit]　*v*. 使蒸发,使挥发
droplet　['drɔplit]　*n*. 小滴
diffuse　[di'fju:z]　*v*. 扩散,散开
spherical　['sferikəl]　*a*. 球的,球形的
deficiency　[di'fiʃənsi]　*n*. 缺乏,不够

solely ['səulli] adv. 单独地,完全
pulverize ['pʌlvəraiz] v. 将……粉碎
residual [ri'zidjuəl] a. 残留,剩余的
peat [pi:t] n. 泥煤块
boundary ['bəundəri] n. 界线,边界
embrace [im'breis] v. 包含

3.6 Nuclear Fuels

The principal source of heat energy, other than the sun, has traditionally been the combustion of fossil fuels such as wood, coal, oil and gas. A new source of energy, popularly called "atomic" energy was dramatically demonstrated during World War II when the Manhattan Project in the U.S. developed the atomic bomb. The subsequent naval propulsion and civilian power programs have successfully harnessed the fission of the atomic nucleus as a practical source of heat. This source, properly called "nuclear" energy, converts by fission some of the matter in the nucleus of the atom into energy, in accordance with Einstein's mass-energy equation:

$$E = mc^2 \tag{3.9}$$

where E is energy, m is mass and c is the velocity of light.

All practical applications of nuclear energy for the production of steam utilize the process of fission. The nucleus of a heavy atom splits into two principal fragments, each of which is the nucleus of a lighter atom. This is accompanied by the release of a very considerable amount of energy. In addition neutrons are released which can be used to fission additional atoms producing a "chain reaction," which is controlled to maintain a continuous production of heat.

Uranium

Uranium is the basic raw material of the nuclear power industry. It is a heavy, slightly radioactive chemical element of atomic number 92—the heaviest element that occurs in nature in more than trace quantities.

Chemically, uranium is a highly reactive metal with three principal valences, +3, +4 and +6. It has three crystalline phases and melts at 2 070°F. In the alpha phase, it is reasonably ductile and can be fabricated by standard metalworking techniques. Since small particles or chips of uranium are highly pyrophoric, machining operations and the storage of scrap require special precautions, such as use of coolant or an inert atmosphere.

Natural uranium is a mixture of three isotopes, uranium-234 (0.01%), uranium-235 (0.71%), and uranium-238 (99.28%). Uranium-234 is present in small amounts and is not significant. Uranium-235 is a fissionable isotope, and uranium-238 is generally known as a fertile isotope.

These three natural isotopes of uranium are radioactive and emit alpha particles. However, they have sufficiently long half lives so that only a minimum of precaution is required in handling natural uranium. Uranium is chemically toxic and must not be ingested. In areas where uranium is handled, the amount of uranium in the air must be kept below prescribed tolerances.

Uranium-235 is fissionable as a result of the absorption of a neutron by its nucleus. When one gram of uranium-235 is fissioned, the heat released is equivalent to approximately one megawatt-day (24 000 kwhr or 82 000 000 Btu). When one short ton of uranium-235 is fissioned, the heat released is equivalent to 22 billion kwhr or 75 thousand billion Btu, which is the quantity of heat contained in approximately three million tons of coal.

Uranium-235 can be fissioned by neutrons at various energy levels and a chain reaction can be maintained. It is a fissile material, which means that it can be fissioned by "slow" (low energy or thermal) neutrons.

Uranium-238 is not capable of sustaining a nuclear chain reaction but it is fissioned to some extent by high energy neutrons. When exposed to neutrons, as in a nuclear reactor, the uranium-238 nucleus, upon capture of a neutron, is ultimately transformed into plutonium-239, a fissile isotope of a new element. Plutonium-239 is capable of sustaining a chain reaction and, when fissioned, produces about the same amount of heat per gram as uranium-235. Because of this ability to be transmuted to a fissionable material, uranium-238 is known as a fertile material.

Uranium has become the basic raw material of the nuclear power industry because of its two principal isotopes, uranium-235 and uranium-238. The first is the only fissile material found in quantity in nature; the second is a fertile material from which fissile plutonium is produced. Since uranium-238 is 140 times as abundant as uranium-235, its ultimate potential as a source of power is very large.

Another fertile element, thorium, can be used for the production of power, but uranium is required for the conversion of thorium to a fissionable material.

Utilization of uranium

Unlike fossil fuels for steam generation which require a continuous feed of fuel for good combustion, nuclear fuel is utilized by a batch process. It is introduced into the nuclear furnace, or reactor, in the form of fabricated packages called "fuel assemblies."

These are assemblies of fuel rods, consisting of uranium oxide pellets contained in alloy cladding tubes. The term "cladding" does not imply deposition of one metal on another, but simply refers to the outer jacket of the nuclear fuel, which is used to prevent corrosion and the release of fission products to the coolant. For a large power reactor using fuel assemblies of this type, each assembly may be 14 ft or more in length and 8 in. square, or larger, in cross section. In pressurized water reactors, fuel rods must be designed to accommodate differential pressures of as much as 2 500 psi that occur early in life as a result of system pressure external to the cladding tubes. These tubes must also contain the internal pressure from gaseous fission products that accumulate during the life of the fuel.

The following requirements are basic to the utilization of fuel for the production of steam, whether the fuel is nuclear or fossil:

1. Control of heat release rate in the reactor or furnace.
2. Transfer of heat developed by the fuel into water for the production of steam.
3. Protection of the operators and control of the byproducts of the reaction.
4. A design which results in good fuel economics.

Words and Expressions

atomic [ə'tɔmik] *a*. 原子的,核子的,核能的
dramatically [drə'mætikəli] *adv*. 明显地,显著地
split [split] *v*. 劈开,分裂
uranium [ju'reiniəm] *n*. 铀
radioactive [ˌreidiəu'æktiv] *a*. 放射性的,放射引起的
isotope ['aisəutəup] *n*. 同位素,核素
toxic ['tɔksik] *a*. 有毒的,有害的
tolerance ['tɔlərəns] *n*. 容忍,抗拒药物的能力
plutonium [pluːˈtəuniəm] *n*. 钚

thorium ['θɔːriəm] n. [化]钍
pellet ['pelit] n. 小球,弹丸,锭片
coolant ['kuːlənt] n. 冷却剂,载热剂,冷却油

3.7 Liquid By-product Fuels

Pitch and tar

The liquid and semiliquid residues from the distillation of petroleum and coal are known as pitch and tar. Most of these residues are suitable for use as boiler fuels. Some handle as easily and burn as readily as does kerosine, whereas others give considerable trouble. To determine whether a particular pitch or tar might be a suitable fuel for a given installation, the following items are important:

Moisture. If the fuel contains moisture, it must be well emulsified to avoid reaching the burner in slugs. If there is a brief break in the continuous flow of fuel to the burners, the fires will be extinguished. Upon reestablishing the fuel flow, a furnace explosion might occur if there is any delay in reigniting the burners. Consequently, a slug of water in the fuel supply can be disastrous if it extinguishes the flame briefly. Tars and pitches containing as much as 35% moisture may be burned in properly designed units.

Flash and fire points. Flash point is defined as the lowest temperature at which, under specified conditions, a liquid fuel will vaporize sufficiently to flash into momentary flame when ignited. Fire point is the lowest temperature at which, under given conditions, a liquid fuel will vaporize to an extent to burn continuously when ignited. Many liquid fuels are blends of two or more different liquids. One of these might have low flash and fire points, whereas the other might have high flash and fire points. Such a fuel usually burns with a bright flame at the burner, where the low-flash-point constituents are burning off; but beyond, where the components whith the higher flash and fire points are burning, the flame is a dark yellow. Actually, if there is too little turbulence at the burner or if the burning products are quenched by passing too quickly from the active combustion zone, combustion is incomplete, and high unburned combustible olss results. Consequently, while the flash temperature is useful for determining the possible hazard involved in storing the fuel, the fire point determines its suitability for firing in a boiler. Fuels with fire points as high as 600 °F can be burned in properly designed equipment.

Viscosity. Practically all tars and pitches are burned in the same manner as fuel oil. They are reduced to a foglike dispersion in an atomizer located in a burner and then vaporized and burned. To produce the fine particles, the viscosity of the fuel must be correct – not over 180 Saybolt Universal Seconds (SUS) for most atomizers, although if favored by the burnerfurnace arrangement, viscosities as high as 1 000 SUS may be used.

Suspended matter. Many of these fuels contain suspended matter. If they are delivered to the burners in this condition, there will be:

1. Abnormal fouling of the atomizers, requiring frequent cleaning.

2. Excessive rate of wear of burner parts.

3. Deposition of unburned carbon throughout the unit or objectionable stack emission.

Such fuels should therefore be passed through strainers before they are fed to the burners.

Compatibility. When some of these fuels come into contact with ordinary fuel oil, they combine to form liver-like substances. If this happens in tanks or piping, trouble results. The mixture cannot be pumped from the tanks, and plugging of the piping often requires complete dismantling for cleaning. Burner operation, too, is erratic and spasmodic. Therefore, before mixing large quantities of tar or pitch with fuel oil, laboratory tests should be made at both storage and pumping temperatures to determine the compatibility of the fuels.

Words and Expressions

petroleum ['pi'trəuliəm] n. 石油
moisture ['mɔistʃə] n. 水分,湿气
emulsify [i'mʌlsifai] vt. 使乳化
extinguish [iks'tiŋgwiʃ] vt. 使熄灭,扑灭,使……不复存在
reestablish ['ri:is'tæbliʃ] vt. 重建,恢复,另行安装,使复原
viscosity [vis'kɔsəti] n. 黏稠,黏性
compatibility [kəmˌpæti'biliti] n. 兼容性

4

Refrigeration and Airconditioning

4.1 The Ideal Basic Vapor Compression Refrigeration Cycle

The equipment diagram for the basic vapor compression cycle is illustrated in Fig. 4.1. Minimum components of this cycle include compressor, condenser, expansion valve and evaporator. The ideal cycle considers heat transfer in the condenser and evaporator without pressure losses, a reversible adiabatic (isentropic) compressor, and an adiabatic expansion valve, connected by piping that has neither pressure loss nor heat transfer with the surroundings. The refrigerant leaves the evaporator at point 1 as a low pressure, low temperature, saturated vapor and enters the compressor, where it is compressed reversibly and adiabatically (isentropic). At point 2, it leaves the compressor as a high temperature, high pressure, superheated vapor and enters the condenser, where it is first desuperheated and then condensed at constant pressure. At point 3, the refrigerant leaves the condenser as a high pressure, medium

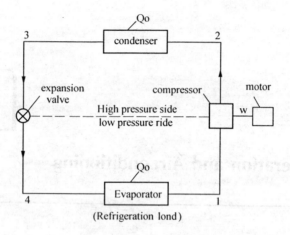

Fig.4.1 Equipment diagram for
basic vapor compression cycle

temperature, saturated liquid and enters the expansion valve where it expands irreversibly and adiabatically (constant enthalpy). At point 4, it leaves the expansion valve as a low pressure, low temperature, low quality vapor and enters the evaporator, where it is evaporated reversibly at constant pressure to the saturated state at point 1. Heat transfer to the evaporator and from the condenser occurs without a finite temperature difference between the fluid emitting the heat and the fluid that absorbs the heat, except during the desuperheating process in the condenser.

An energy balance and certain performance parameters can be derived from the first law of thermodynamics. Applying the steady flow equation for the first law to each of the components of the basic vapor compression cycle, the following relationships are derived:

1—2 Compression $_1\dot{W}_2 = -(h_2 - h_1)\dot{m}$ (4.1)

2—3 Condensing $_2\dot{Q}_3 = -(h_2 - h_3)\dot{m}$ (4.2)

3—4 Expansion Valve $h_3 = h_4$

4—1 Evaporator $_4\dot{Q}_1 = (h_1 - h_4)\dot{m}$ (4.3)

In applying the steady flow equation, kinetic energy and potential energy terms were omitted; because flow velocities are low to avoid fluid friction and undesirable pressure losses, and height variation within a given refrigeration system is usually small, these terms are numerically insignificant. Since the system is cyclic, the heat rejected in the condenser must be equal to the sum of the heat absorbed in the evaporator and the work of compression.

Coefficient of Performance (COP) is used to evaluate the performance of a refrigeration system. COP = refrigeration effect/net work input.

For the basic vapor compression cycle, from Eq. (4.1) and (4.3), the COP is

$$COP = (h_1 - h_4)/(h_2 - h_1)$$

In evaluating contributions of the compressor to thermodynamic systems, it is necessary to consider properties of the refrigerants at the inlet and outlet of the compressor, with the change in state between these points being (1) reversible and adiabatic (isentropic) for the ideal compressor; or (2) adiabatic and irreversible (with an increase in entropy in the fluid passing through the compressor) with the variation from the ideal compressor described by the adiabatic compressor efficiency.

An important thermodynamic consideration for the positive displacement compressor is the effect of the clearance volume, i. e., the volume the refrigerant occupies within the compressor that is not displaced by the moving member. For the piston compressor consider the clearance volume between piston and cylinder head when the piston is in a top, center position. After the cylinder discharges the compressed gas, the clearance gas reexpands to a larger volume as the pressure falls to the inlet pressure. Consequently, the compressor discharges a refrigerant mass less than the mass that would occupy the volume swept by the piston, measured at the inlet pressure and temperature. This effect is quantitatively expressed by the volumetric efficiency, η_v:

$$\eta_v = m_a / m_t \tag{4.4}$$

where

m_a = actual mass of new gas entering the compressor per stroke

m_t = theoretical mass of gas represented by the displacement volume and determined at the pressure and temperature at the compressor inlet

Volumetric efficiency measures the effectiveness of the compressor's piston displacement (size) in moving the refrigerant vapor through the cycle. Since refrigerants differ greatly in their specific volumes v_1, choice of refrigerant can affect the mass flow delivered by compressor displacement.

One of the design parameters of a multistage compressor is selection of the interstage pressure at which the refrigerant temperature is reduced by an intercooler. At optimum interstage pressure, total work is minimum. For two-stage compression of an ideal gas ($Pv = RT$), this occurs at the geometric mean of the suction and discharge pressures and results in equal work for the stages. The application of multistage compressors to refrigeration systems, however differs from gas compressors since cooling at the interstage pressure is usually accomplished by refrigerant diverted from some other part of the cycle.

Words and Expressions

compression [kəm'preʃən] n. 压缩
refrigeration [ri,fridʒə'reiʃən] n. 制冷
condenser [kən'densə] n. 冷凝器
valve [vælv] n. 阀门
evaporator [i'væpəreitə] n. 蒸发器

reversible [ri'və:səbl] *a*. 可逆的
reversibly [ri'və:səbli] *ad*. 可逆(倒)地
irreversibly [ˌiri'və:səbli] *ad*. 不可逆(转)地
isentropic [aisen'trɔpik] *a*. 等(定)熵的
refrigerant [ri'fridʒərənt] *n*. 制冷剂,冷冻剂,冷煤
adiabatically [ˌædiəbətikli] *ad*. 绝热地
superheated [sju:pəhi:tid] *a*. 过热的
desuperheated [di:'sju:pə'hi:tid] *a*. 降温,降低蒸气过热度
undesirable ['ʌndi'zaiərəbl] *a*. 令人不快的,讨厌的,不需要的
numerically [nju(:)'merikəli] *ad*. 在数字上,数值上的
insignificant [insig'nifikənt] *a*. 小的,微不足道的,不重要的
cyclic ['saiklik] *a*. 循环的
helical [helikəl] *a*. 螺旋的,螺旋形的
centrifugal [sen'trifjugəl] *a*. 离心的   *n*. 离心,离心机
clearance volume   余隙,容积
cylinder ['silində] *n*. 气缸,圆筒
reexpand ['ri:iks'pænd] *v*. 再膨胀
quantitatively ['kwɔntitətivli] *ad*. 定量地
volumetric [ˌvɔlju'metrik] *a*. 容积的
interstage [intə(:)'steidʒ] *a*. 级间的,中间的

4.2 Refrigerant Evaporators

Several types of evaporators can be used in multistage systems. A tubular, direct expansion evaporator oil easily and requires the smallest refrigerant charge. Where direct expansion is impractical, a flooded system or a recirculated system may be used, but these methods compound oil return problems.

Some problems that can become more acute in low-temperature systems than in high-temperature systems include oil transport properties, loss off capacity caused by static head from the depth of the pool of liquid refrigerant in the evaporator, deterioration of refrigerant boiling heat transfer coefficients, and higher specific volumes for the vapor.

The effect of pressure losses in the evaporator and suction piping is more acute in lowtemperature systems because of the large change in saturation temperatures and specific volume in relation to pressure changes at these conditions. Systems that operate near zero absolute pressure are particularly affected by pressure loss. For example, with R-12 and R-22 at 140 kPa suction and 27℃ liquid feed temperature, a 7 kPa loss increases the volume flow rate by about 5%. At 35 kPa suction and -7℃ liquid feed temperature, a 7 kPa loss increases the volume flow rate by about 25%.

The depth of the pool of boiling refrigerant in a flooded evaporator causes a liquid head or static pressure that is exerted on the lower part of the heat transfer surface. Therefore, the saturation temperature at this surface is higher than the pressure in the suction line, which is not affected by the static head. Although tubular dry expanded evaporators do not have appreciable static liquid head, gas pressure drops from the inlet to the outlet of the evaporator create a velocity head that causes a similar condition.

The liquid depth penalty for the evaporator can be eliminated if the pool of liquid is below the heat transfer surface and a refrigerant pump sprays the liquid over the surface. Of course, the pump energy is an additional heat load to the system, and more refrigerant must be used to provide the Net Positive Suction Head (NPSH) required by the pump. The pump is also an additional item to be maintained.

Another type of low-temperature evaporator is the flash cooler in which liquid refrigerant is cooled by boiling off some vapor. The remaining cold liquid can then be pumped from the flash cooler to the evaporator. There it is either top or bottom fed at a rate greater than the evaporation rate to ensure wetting of the entire evaporator surface for maximum heat transfer without an appreciable static head penalty. This liquid overfeed system is frequently used in large refrigerated warehouses with many evaporators.

Another less frequently used system pumps the liquid refrigerant as a secondary coolant from the flash cooler at low temperature. As the coolant passes through a secondary cooler, or coil, heat transfers to it from the material being cooled. The liquid temperature rises to develop a temperature range, but because pressure is maintained sufficiently above saturation by the liquid pump, the coolant does not evaporate until it returns via a restriction to the flash cooler. Sufficient refrigerant must be circulated to accommodate the temperature range. The flash cooler in this system is an accumulator receiver similar to that used in a liquid overfeed system, except that no excess refrigerant is fed to the remote heat transfer surface.

In both types of liquid recirculation systems, the cold liquid can be moved by mechanical pumps or by pressure from the compressor discharge.

Wods and Expressions

multistage ['mʌltisteidʒ] a. 多级(的),分阶段进行的
tubular ['tju:bjulə] a. 管的,管状的,由管构成的
deterioration [di,tiəriə'reiʃən] n. 恶化,磨损,损坏
penalty ['penlti] n. 惩罚,罚款,困难,障碍
spray [sprei] n. 喷雾,喷嘴,喷射
flash [flæʃ] n. 闪光,一瞬间 a. 瞬时的,迅速的
warehouse ['wɛəhəus] n. 仓库,货栈 vt. 把……入库
refrigerated warehouse 冷藏库
discharge [dis'tʃa:dʒ] n. 发射,卸货,偿还

suction ['sʌkʃən] n. 吸入,抽吸
suction piping 吸液管路

4.3 Refrigeration

Refrigeration was used by ancient civilizations when it was naturally available. The Roman rulers had slaves transport ice and snow from the high mountains to be used to preserve foods and to provide cool beverages in hot weather. Such natural sources of refrigeration were, of course, extremely limited in terms of location, temperatures, and scope. Means of producing refrigeration with machinery, called mechanical refrigeration, began to be developed in the 1 850s. Today the refrigeration industry is a vast and essential part of any technological society, with yearly sales of equipment amounting to billions of dollars in the United States alone.

Uses of Refrigeration

It is convenient to classify the applications of refrigeration into the following categories: domestic, commercial, industrial, and air conditioning. Sometimes transportation is listed as a separate category. Domestic refrigeration is used for food preparation and preservation, ice making, and cooling beverages in the household. Commercial refrigeration is used in retail stores, restaurants, and institutions, for purposes the same as those in the household. Industrial refrigeration in the food industry is needed in processing, preparation, and large-scale preservation. This includes use in food chilling and freezing plants, cold storage warehouses, breweries, and dairies, to name a few. Hundreds of other industries use refrigeration; among them are ice making plants, oil refineries, pharmaceuticals. Of course ice skating rinks need refrigeration.

Refrigeration is also widely used in both comfort air conditioning for people and in industrial air conditioning. Industrial air conditioning is used to create the air temperatures, humidity, and cleanliness required for manufacturing processes. Computers require a controlled environment.

Methods of Refrigeration

Refrigeration, commonly spoken of as a cooling process is more correctly defined as the removal of heat from a substance to bring it to or keep it at a desirable low temperature, below the temperature of the surroundings. The most widespread method of producing mechanical refrigeration is called the vapor compression system. In this system a volatile liquid refrigerant is evaporated in an evaporator; this process results in a removal of heat (cooling) from the substance to be cooled. A compressor and condenser are required to maintain the evaporation process and to recover the refrigerant for reuse.

Another widely used method is called the absorption refrigeration system. In this process a refrigerant is evaporated (as with the vapor compression system), but the evaporation is maintained by absorbing the refrigerant in another fluid.

Other refrigeration methods are thermoelectric, steam jet, and air cycle refrigeration. These systems are used only in special applications and their functioning will not be explained here. Thermoelectric refrigeration is still quite expensive; some small tabletop domestic refrigerators are cooled by this method. Steam jet refrigeration is inefficient. Often used on ships in the past, it has been largely replaced by the vapor compression system The air cycle is sometimes used in air conditioning of aircraft cabins. Refrigeration at extremely low temperatures, below about $-200°F$ ($-130°C$), is called cryogenics. Special systems are used to achieve these conditions. One use of refrigeration at ultralow temperatures is to separate oxygen and nitrogen from air and to liquefy them.

Refrigeration Equipment

The main equipment components of the vapor compression refrigeration system are the familiar evaporator, compressor, and condenser. The equipment may be separate or of the unitary (also called self-contained) type. Unitary equipment is assembled in the factory. The household refrigerator is a common example of unitary equipment. Obvious advantages of unitary equipment are that it is more compact and less expensive to manufacture if made in large quantities.

There is a variety of commercial refrigeration equipment; each has a specific function. Reach-in cabinets, walk-in coolers, and display cases are widely used in the food service business. Automatic ice makers, drinking water coolers, and refrigerated vending machines are also commonly encountered equipment.

Air conditioning includes the heating, cooling, humidifying, dehumidifying, and cleaning (filtering) of air in internal environments. Occasionally it will be necessary to mention some aspects of air conditioning when we deal with the interface between the two subjects. A study of the fundamentals and equipment involved in air conditioning is nevertheless of great value even for those primarily interested in refrigeration.

Words and Expressions

dairy ['dɛəri] n. 牛奶房,制酪场,制酪业
chill ['tʃil] n. & vt. 冷冻,使变冷,寒冷
brewery ['bruəri] n. 酿酒厂
pharmaceutical [ˌfaːməˈsjuːtikl] n. 制药厂
volatile ['vɔlətail] a. 挥发性的
thermoelectric [ˌθəːməuiˈlektrik] a. 热电的

cryogenics [kraiə'dʒeniks] n. 低温学,低温技术
ultralow ['ʌltrələu] a. 超低的
liquify ['likwifai] vt. 使液化
dehumidify [di:'hju:midifai] vt. 除湿
beverage ['bevəridʒ] n. 饮料
category ['kætigfəri] n. 种类,部类
humidity [hju:'miditi] n. 湿度
refrigerant [ri'fridʒərənt] n. 冷冻剂
absorption [əb'sɔ:pʃən] n. 吸收(过程)
unitary ['ju:nitəri] a. 具有单一特征的,整体式的,一体的
retail ['ri:teil] n. 零售,零卖
rink [riŋk] n. (室内)滑冰场,冰球场
fundamental [ˌfʌndə'mentl] a. 基础的
be replaced by 被代替
in large quantities 大量
a variety of 种种

4.4 Absorption Heat Pumps

Functions of Absorption Heat Pump

  An absorption heat pump extracts heat from a low-temperature heat source, such as waste heat or surface water, and delivers its heat output at a higher temperature for winter heating or other applications at a coefficient of performance greater than 1.

  In Japan and Sweden, absorption heat pumps have been installed in industrial and district heating plants using industrial waste heat to provide hot water, typically at 165°F, for winter heating or other purposes at a COP between 1.4 and 1.7.

  Absorption heat pumps can be used either for winter heating or for cooling in summer and heating in winter.

The coefficient of performance for cooling COPc for an absorption heat pump can be calculated. The coefficient of performance for heating for a two-stage absorption heat pump COP_{hp} can be calculated as

$$COP_{hp} = \frac{Q_{ab} + Q_{con}}{Q_{lg}} \qquad (4.5)$$

where Q_{ab} = heat removed from the absorber, Btu/h

Q_{con} = heat removed from the condenser, Btu/h

Q_{lg} = heat input to first-stage generator, Btu/h

Several absorbants, or working fluids, other than aqueous LiBr solution are being developed, such as $LiBr/ZnCl_2$ and $LiBr/ZnBr_2/CH_3OH$. $LiBr/H_2O$ is still the most widely used solution in absorption heat pumps.

Comparison Between Absorption and Vapor Compression Heat Pumps

Although the coefficient of performance for heating COP_{hp} for a centrifugal heat pump has a value between 4 and 4.5 and for an absorption heat pump it is only 1.3 to 1.7, electric energy used by a centrifugal machine is far more expensive than heat energy used by an absorption machine.

A life-cycle cost analysis should be performed during selection. When the ratio of cost per unit of electricity to natural gas is considered especially when demand charge, and higher electricity rates during peak hours are taken into account, absorption heat pumps may be more cost-effective in many locations.

Series-Connected Absorption Heat Pump

The series-connected absorption heat pump consists of two single-stage absorption heat pumps, each with an evaporator, absorber, generator, condenser, heat exchanger, and solution pump.

Liquid water refrigerant evaporates in the evaporator. Water vapor is extracted by the concentrated solution in the absorber. The heat of absorption transferred to the hot water in the absorber is then used for district heating. The diluted solution is pumped from the absorber to the generator through the heat exchanger. In the generator, steam from the plant boils off the water vapor from the diluted solution. The boiled-off water vapor is extracted to the condenser and condensed into liquid form. Latent heat of condensation is again transferred to the district heating hot water.

Concentrated solution from the generator flows to the absorber through the heat exchanger. Condensed liquid water enters the evaporator via a throttling orifice and is sprayed over the tube bundle in which flue gas cooling water flows from the plant. After absorbing the latent heat of vaporization from the flue gas cooling water, liquid water evaporates into water vapor in the evaporator.

In the series-connected absorption heat pump, the first-stage absorption heat pump is operated at higher temperatures and the second-stage heat pump is operated at lower temperatures.

During operation, the return hot water from district heating is heated from 144°F to 152°F in the absorber and condenser of the second-stage absorption heat pump, and from 152°F to 160.5°F in the absorber and condenser of the first-stage absorption heat pump. In the evaporator, heat is extracted from the lowtemperature heat source, the flue gas cooling water which enters the absorption heat pump at a temperature of 97.7°F and leaves at a temperature of 75.2°F. The high-temperature heat source, steam, is supplied at 320°F at a flow rate of 66 000 lb/h from the incineration plant. The average COP_{hp} for the seriesconnected absorption heat pump is about 1.6.

Operating Characteristics

The absorption heat transformer operates at two pressure levels: high pressure, including the evaporator and absorber, and low pressure, including the generator and condenser.

There are three temperature levels of input and output fluid streams:

(1) The fluid stream carrying the heat output from the absorber is at the highest temperature level.

(2) The heat source (the waste heat input to the evaporator and generator) is at the intermediate temperature level.

(3) The condenser cooling water in the condenser is at the lowest temperature level.

The purpose of an absorption heat transformer is to boost the temperature of the input waste heat fluid stream, and the function of an absorption heat pump is to attain a higher COP from the lower temperature heat source.

Words and Expressions

extract [iks'trækt] vt. 提取
coefficient [kəui'fiʃənt] n. 系数
absorbant [əb'sɔːbənt] n. 吸收剂
aqueous ['eikwiəs] a. 水的,水状的
solution [sə'ljuːʃən] n. 溶液,溶体
life-cyclen 整个使用周期
cost-effective a. 划算的,经济的
series-connected a. 串联的
concentrated [kən'sentreitid] a. 浓缩的
diluted [dai'ljuːtid] a. 稀释的
boil off 汽化

latent ['leitənt] *a*. 潜在的
latent heat 潜热
via [vai] *prep*. 经过,通过
throttle ['θrɔtl] *vt*. 节流
orifice ['ɔrifis] *n*. (管子等的)孔
spray [sprei] *v*. 喷射
tube bundle 管束
flue [flu:] *a*. 烟道
flue gas *a*. 烟气,废气
boost [bu:st] *vt*. 升高,增加
incineration [insinə'reiʃən] *n*. 焚烧,煅烧

4.5 Comfort and Discomfort

One of the goals of the environmental engineer and architect is to ensure comfortable conditions in a building. Thermal pleasure can only be achieved locally over part of the body or temporarily in the context of a situation which is in itself uncomfortable. Continuous thermal pleasure extending over a period of hours is not possible. We are left simply with the idea of comfort as a lack of discomfort; this may seem an uninspiring definition, but nevertheless it presents a real practical challenge.

General thermal discomfort will be felt if a person is either too hot or too cold. In addition there are several potential sources of local discomfort, such as cold feet or draughts.

Any guide to comfort must relate these forms of discomfort to the physical variables of the environment, so that a permissible range of the variables may be recommended. It is conventional to treat overall thermal discomfort in terms of, thermal sensation.

For other forms of discomfort it is not possible to base the definition of discomfort simply on a scale of overall thermal sensation. It is possible to be thermally neutral and so want the temperature neither raised nor lowered, yet still be uncomfortable because of some non-uniformity in the environment, such as a draught or radiant asymmetry. The most direct way of finding if someone is uncomfortable is simply to ask him. Usually the subject is asked to make a decision as to whether he is comfortable or uncomfortable, or whether he finds the thermal conditions acceptable or uncomfortable. Different people may be expected to become uncomfortable at different levels of external stress, so if the proportion of people voting uncomfortable at different levels of external stress, so if the proportion of people voting uncomfortable is plotted against the level of stimulus, we should expect to get a curve of the shape. This is an ideal presentation, since the end user of the information is now able to trade off the proportion of people made uncomfortable against the cost of controlling the uncomfortable stimulus.

How well can we achieve such a presentation in practice? In laboratory studies the control and measurement of the potentially comfortable stimulus can be done to any required degree of accuracy. The stimulus might be, for instance, radiant asymmetry. A subject is then exposed to several levels of radiant asymmetry, with the other environmental variables held constant; the subject is asked to say if he is uncomfortable or not. After sufficient subjects have been exposed to various levels of radiant energy, a curve of the form may be plotted.

This experimental paradigm has formed the basis for much of the work on comfort, but has some weaknesses. The subject is asked to make a decision about whether he is uncomfortable or not; he has to make this decision in the unfamiliar surroundings of a laboratory after a limited exposure time. The results may then be applied to a population at its normal place of work. This ignores the fact that a person's judgement may be very dependent on context. For instance, the radiant asymmetry provided by direct sunshine is far higher than the level which is regarded as satisfactory from a radiant heating system, yet people seek out and welcome sunshine. While complaints of draughts are common in modern offices, a gentle walking pace produces an air speed over the body of greater than 1 m/s, which would normally be regarded as very draughty, yet no one complains of draught discomfort while walking. The response to a stimulus depends on the general surroundings and expectation of the person.

A particular example is the range effect. When an observer experiences a range of stimuli and is asked to rate them on a category scale, he tends to rate them by putting the stimuli from the middle of the range into the central categories of the rating scale. This has been clearly demonstrated in experiments on the acceptability of noise. Subjects exposed to a range of sound levels tend to place the boundary between acceptable and unacceptable noise at the centre of the range of noise which they have been exposed. Thus people who are exposed to high noise levels will apparently tolerate more noise than people who have only been exposed to low noise levels. The range effects do not apply only to the range of stimuli provided by the experimenter. People carry their own standards with them, based on their general experience, with which they compare a new stimulus. Thus, the meaning of the words comfortable or uncomfortable will not have an absolute value, but will be relative to his experience and expectation. When Gagge et al. (1967) put young men in an environmental chamber at 48°C, the subjects rated the environment as slightly uncomfortable. There is little doubt that the equivalent environment in an office would be regarded as intolerable. However, the subjects knew they were in a physiological laboratory, were expecting to sweat, and did not object strongly to the experience.

It is clear, however, that their comfort rating cannot be transferred to a different situation. The standards of acceptability are set by the range of stimuli that people are used to. Poulton (1977) points out that this implies that the goal of providing a universally acceptable environment may be ever receding. If people do make judgements of acceptability on the basis of their own experience, then the maximum acceptable level will fall as the general level falls. If the noise level in a district is reduced, the level at which a noise becomes unacceptable will also be reduced and so the loudest noise will always be too loud. Air conditioning engineers are often heard to complain that standards of expectation rise as fast as the standard of air conditioning, so that the level of complaints stays constant.

Words and Expressions

uninspiring [ʌnin'spaiəriŋ] a. 平凡的
challenge ['tʃæləndʒ] n. 异议,质问,需要
draught [drɑ:ft] n. 吹风
thermally neutral 热中性状态
non-uniformity 不均匀性
radiant asymmetry 辐射不对称
subject ['sʌbdʒikt] v. 受验者
trade off 交替使用
plot [plɔt] v. 测绘
presentation [prezən'teiʃən] n. 表达
paradigm ['pærədaim] n. 范例
range effect 量级分布效果
environmental chamber 环境实验室
recede [ri'si:d] v. 失去重要性
stay constant 不变的

4.6 Compressor Failure

Many compressors fail because of one or more of the following conditions: (1) slugging, (2) liquid flooding, (3) loss of lubricating oil, (4) contamination, (5) bad piping practices, (6) improper thermostatic expansion valve superheat setting, and (7) flooded starts.

Slugging

Slugging usually occurs on compressor startup and lasts for only a short time. However, it can occur while the compressor is running during a rapid change in the system operating conditions. It is associated with a clattering noise much like an automobile engine under a heavy strain. This noise is created by the compressing of the liquid refrigerant and/or oil. Compressors are designed to compress vapor only and not liquid. When liquid is compressed by the compressor a hydraulic pressure that may exceed 1 000 psig (6 890 kPa) is created in the cylinder.

Slugging can result in blown head and/or valve plate gaskets, broken valve reeds, broken pistons, and damaged piston wrist pins. If any of these conditions are found, the conditions that cause slugging should be checked and if found corrected.

Liquid flooding

Liquid flooding is the constant flow of liquid refrigerant droplets to the compressor. When liquid refrigerant enters the compressor, it goes into the crankcase, where the oil is diluted. Liquid refrigerant is an excellent cleaning agent and will wash oil from the compressor surfaces. In most cases the oil will foam, reducing its lubricating value and resulting in overheating of the bearing surfaces. This condition is more likely on air-cooled compressors than on refrigerant-cooled compressors.

In cases of severe liquid floodback, damage to the pistons, valves, and rings is probably due to the lack of lubrication. Also, there may be broken parts which show very little wear. Usually, liquid flooding is indicated by more wear on the parts farthest from the oil pump.

Loss of lubricating oil

The loss of lubricating oil will result in damage to the compressor. The wearing surfaces will be galled, overheated, and as a result, ruined. The compressor motor will be overheated and will possibly burn out. As the quantity of oil drops in the crankcase, the temperature of the remaining oil increases. Compressor oil starts vaporizing at 310 to 320°F (136.66 to 142.22°C), which reduces the amount of lubrication the cylinders receive, resulting in excessive ring and cylinder wear. The oil breaks down completely at 350°F (158.89°F), causing contaminants and a complete loss of lubricating qualities.

Contamination

The contaminants in a system include air, moisture, dirt, and other foreign matter. These contaminants cause several system malfunctions, such as high discharge pressure, poor system performance, moisture freezing in the flow control device, oil contamination, and acid.

Bad piping practices

Bad piping practices can also contribute to oil leaving the compressor. When unnecessary traps are allowed to remain in the system, oil will settle in them and cause the compressor to operate short of oil. Sizing of the suction line is extremely important for proper oil return. If an accumulator is used, it must be of the proper size for the system. Accumulators should be capable of holding approximately one-half of the total refrigerant charge on smaller systems. It is generally desirable to check with the accumulator and equipment manufacturers for their recommendations. Also, an accumulator will not protect the compressor from refrigerant floodback during the off cycle.

Improper thermostatic expansion valve superheat setting

When checking and adjusting thermostatic expansion valve superheat settings, the procedure should be to start at the evaporator coil. If there is more than one expansion valve, they must all be set to maintain the same superheat setting. If they are set to maintain different superheat settings, oil logging is quite possible, especially on low-temperature applications.

Flooded starts

A flooded start generally is caused by refrigerant migration to the compressor during the off cycle. The refrigerant moves into the compressor crankcase and mixes with the oil when the compressor is colder than the remainder of the system. When the compressor starts, the liquid refrigerant quickly boils off, causing the oil to foam.

The amount of refrigerant absorbed by the oil is determined by the oil temperature and the pressure in the crankcase. The lower the temperature and the higher the pressure, the more refrigerant will be absorbed by the oil. Under certain conditions the refrigerant-oil mixture will separate and stratify, with the liquid refrigerant settling to the bottom of the crankcase where the oil pump will pick it up first. When the compressor starts, the oil pump forces the liquid refrigerant into the bearings and any oil that is there will be washed away.

Words and Expressions

slugging   ['slʌgiŋ]   n. 缓动
lubricating   ['lju:brikeitiŋ]   a. 润滑的

clatter ['klætə] n. v. (机械转动等)(发出)卡搭声
gasket ['gæskit] n. 衬圈,衬垫
reed [ri:d] n. 簧片
bearing ['bɛəriŋ] n. 轴承
wrist pin n. [活塞,曲柄]销
droplet ['drɔplit] n. 微滴
crankcase ['kræŋkeiz] n. 曲轴箱
foam [fəum] n. 泡沫 v. 起泡沫
gall [gɔ:l] v. 咬住,卡死
break down 分解
contaminant [kən'tæminənt] n. 污染物
lubrication [ˌlju:bri'keiʃən] n. 润滑
malfunction [mæl'fʌnkʃən] n. 机能失常,发生故障
accumulator [ə'kju:mjuleitə] n. 贮液器,收集器
check with 与……联系,与……接洽
charge [tʃa:dʒ] v. 注入,装填
setting [setiŋ] n. 定位,调整
coverage ['kʌvəridʒ] n. 有效范围
procedure [prə'si:dʒə] n. 程序,工序
coil [kɔil] n. 蛇[盘,旋,螺]管
logging [lɔgiŋ] n. 阻塞
migration [maig'reiʃən] n. 流动
boil off 汽化,蒸发
stratify ['strætifai] v. 分层
pick up 吸收
thermostatic(al) [ˌθə:mou'stætik(əl)] a. 恒温(器)的

4.7 Operation and Maintenance of the Air – conditioning Plant

Hand-over and documentation

Designers and contractors can help to ensure adequate maintenance by stressing its importance to the client. The client should be advised about the personnel required and provided with the requisite information for maintenance.

For plant to continue working properly throughout its life it is necessary for the maintenance and operating staff to be familiar with the principles and methods of running the plant. In addition to a full set of record drawings, two manuals should be available, one for the operating staff (e.g. office manager, caretaker) and another for the maintenance staff. The former should describe such things as the design principles, the method of operation, details of alarms and safety precautions. The latter, larger service manual, should contain the information listed by BS 5 720: 1 979 and reproduced below.

List of documentation required for system maintenance engineer

- the designer's description of the installation, including simplified line flow and balance diagrams for the complete installation;
- as fitted installation drawings and the designer's operational instructions;
- operation and maintenance instructions for equipment, manufacturer's spare parts lists and spare ordering instructions;
- schedules of electrical equipment;
- schedules of electrical equipment;
- test results and test certificates as called for under the contract, including any insurance or statutory inspection authority certificate;

• copies of guarantee certificates for plant and equipment;

• list of keys, tools and spare parts that are handed over.

British Standard 5 720: 1 979 provides further advice regarding the organization and content of maintenance manuals. These should be available in draft form for checking at the commissioning stage, in addition to as fitted drawings. This will assist those concerned in setting the plant to work efficiently and, at the same time, the manual can be revised to suit any operational changes that may have been necessary, before they are issued to the client.

Before the plant is handed over, it is necessary that the staff responsible for operating the plant are given verbal instruction and demonstrations on the principles and operation of the systems. Any such verbal instructions should be given in addition to the documentation.

Maintenance organization

Once the client has accepted an installation from the contractor, the maintenance of a plant of any complexity should be organized to ensure continued efficient operation of the plant, aiming to protect the capital investment at a minimum economic cost.

The basis of any planned maintenance scheme is a filing system whereby the checks and services to be carried out on any piece of plant come to light at the appropriate time. This can be done by a card index system or by using a computer. When staff complete a piece of maintenance they ought to note down anything which they see to be in need of attention or likely to be in need of attention in the near future, such as bearing running hot which would eventually fail. This enables the repair to be carried out at a convenient time, rather than in a period when everything seems to fail at once.

Contract maintenance by specialist firms is often used as an alternative to directly employed labour, either for a part or the whole of the service.

Frequency of servicing

Routine maintenance includes inspections, cleaning, water treatment, adjustment and overhaul. The frequency at which these should be made is normally given in the manufacturers' manuals but these are average values which are best modified by the actual site conditions and in the light of operating experience.

The frequency at which plant is serviced depends on the following:
- plant and system efficiency and hence efficient energy consumption;
- effect on reliability of service;
- routine maintenance costs;
- fault repair costs;
- safety inspection;
- hours of system operation.

As part of the routine maintenance inspections, standby and emergency plant must be checked but not necessarily brought on-line for long operating periods.

Following shut-downs for repairs and plant modifications it may be necessary to recommission the system or part thereof, in which case the appropriate procedures should be followed.

It is particularly important to include insurance inspections of pressure vessels and the testing of fire alarms in routine maintenance.

Fault-finding

Fault-finding procedures may be included in the service-manual. Though these procedures for individual plant items will often be available from manufacturers, they should also relate to the system in which the plant item is placed.

Maintenance support

In support of maintenance, it is recommended that consideration be given to the following:
- engineer's office;
- workshop with appropriate tools;
- equipment spare parts;
- maintenance materials;
- instruments;
- site tools.

Words and Expressions

hand-over n. 移交,交接
documentation [ˌdɔkjumen'teiʃən] n. 提供的条件;文件(或证书等的)提供;文件(或证书等的)利用
client ['klaiənt] n. 委托人,买方,顾客
requisite ['rekwizit] a. 需要的,必不可少的 n. 必需品
caretaker ['kɛəteikə] n. 看管人
statutory ['stætjutri] a. 法定的,规定的
comissioning [kə'miʃəniŋ] n. 试运转,使用
demonstration ['deməns'treiʃən] n. 示范
complexity [kɔmp'leksiti] n. 复杂性,复杂的物
filing [failiŋ] n. (文件的)整理汇集
filing system 档案制度
whereby [hwɛə'bai] ad. 由此,从而
come to light 被人发现
note down 记录下,摘下
overhand [əuvəhænd] n. vt. 大修,仔细检查

in the light of 依据,按照
effect on 操作
standby ['stændbai] n. 备用设备 a. 备用的
on-line n. (与主机)联机,在线,机内
modification [ˌmɔdifi'keiʃən] n. 更改,改装,修改
thereof ['ðɛər'ɔf] ad. 关于它的
fault-finding n. a. 检查故障(的)

4.8 Air-coditioning cycle equipment

The major pieces of equipment required to complete the air-conditioning cycle are listed as follows: ①Fan. ②Supply ducts. ③Supply outlets. ④Space to be conditioned. ⑤Returnoutlets. ⑥Return ducts. ⑦Filter. ⑧Heating coil(Combustion chamber) or cooling coil.

The purpose and function of each of these components are covered in the following sections.

Fan

The fan moves air to and from an enclosed space. In an air-conditioning system, the fan moves air that consists of: ①All outdoor air. ②All indoor or room air(This is also called recirculated air). ③A combination of outdoor and indoor air.

The fan pulls air from the outdoors and from the room at the same time. Since the drafts in the room cause discomfort, and poor air movement slows the tody heat rejection process, it is necessary to regulate the amount of air supplied by the fan. To accomplished this regulation, a fan is selected that can deliver the correct amount of air. By controlling the speed of the fan, the air stream in the room can be regulated to provide good circulation without drafts.

Supply duct

The supply duct directs the air from the fan to the room. The supply duct should be as short as possible and has a minimum number of turns to insure that the air can flow freely.

Supply outlets help to distribute the air evenly in a room. Some outlets fan the air and otner outlets direct the air in a jet stream. Still other outlets combine these actions. As a result of these actions, the outlets are able to exert some control on the direction of the air delivered by the fan. This directional control plus the location and the number of outlets in the room contribute greatly to the comfort or discomfort resulting from the air pattern.

Room space

The room or the space to be conditioned is one of the most important parts of the air cycle. The dictionary states that a room is an enclosed space set apart by partitions. If an enclosed space does not exist, then it is impossibel to complete the air cycle. This is due to the fact that the conditioned air from the supply outlets simply flows into the atmosphere. In fact, the material and the quality of workman-ship used to enclose the space are also important since these factors helps to control the loss of heat or cold that is confined in the enclosed space.

Return outlets

As stated previously, return outlets allow room air to enter the return duct. The main function of the return outlet is to allow air to pass from room. These outlets are usually located on the opposite wall from the supply outlet. For example, if the supply duct is on the floor or on the wall near the celling, then the return duct may be located on the floor or on the wall near the floor.

Filters

Filters clean the air by removing dust and dirt particles. Filters are located within the return air duct. These devices are made of many materials including spun glass and composition plastic. Other filter materials maintain an electrostatic charge, and attract and capture dust and dirt particles from the air flowing through them.

Cooling coil and heating coil or combustion chamber

The cooling coil and the heating coil, or combustion chamber, are located either ahead of or after the fan. In all installations, however, these devices are placed after the filter. Such an arrangement prevents excessive dust and dirt particles from covering the coil surface.

Winter operation (Heating coil or combustion chamber) During winter operation, the airconditioning cycle adds heat to the air. The return air from the room is passed over the surface of a heating coil or over the surface of a combustion chamber. The air is heated to the required temperature. It is then delivered to the room through the supply duct. The air loses its heat to the room and passes through the return duct to the coil or chamber. The cycle is repeated as long as the heated air is required. If the room air is too dry, moisture can be added by installing shallow pans in the bonnet above the combustion chamber or in the ductwork after the coil. The pans are automatically filled with water to a preset level. Thus, moisture is added to the air by the process of evaporation as the air passes over the pans.

Summer operation (cooling coil) For summer operation, the airconditioning cycle cools the air. The return air from the room passes over the surface of the cooling coil. The air is cooled to the required temperature. If there is too much moisture in the room air (high humidity), it is removed automatically as the air is cooled by the coil.

Words and Expressions

hydronic　[hai'drɔnik]　*adj*. 液体循环加热(或冷却)的
condensate　[kɔn'denseit]　*n*. 冷凝物
humidity　[hju:'miditi]　*n*. 湿气,潮湿,湿度
ventilation　[venti'leiʃən]　*n*. 通风,流通空气
diffuser　[di'fju:z]　*n*. 散布者,扩散体
exhaust　[ig'zɔ:st]　*vt*. 用尽,耗尽　*vi*. 排气　*adj*. 用不完的
filter　['filtə]　*n*. 滤波器,过滤器,筛选　*vt*. 过滤,渗透
regulate　['regjuleit]　*vt*. 管制,调节,校准
bonnet　['bɔnit]　*n*. 烟囱帽,阀帽

5

Boiler

5.1 Boiler and Its Development

The steam generating system, frequently called the boiler, is a system that transfers the heat from the products of combustion to water and produces hot water or steam. The combustion is accomplished in a furnace. Heat is transferred in the furnace mainly by radiation to water-cooled walls, which constitutes the evaporation section of the steam generation system. After leaving the furnace, the gases pass through a superheater in which steam receives heat from the gases and has its temperature risen above the saturation temperature. Since the temperature of the gases leaving the superheater section is still high, modern steam generators often employ additional heat transfer surfaces to utilize the thermal energy of the gases. These include the surfaces of reheaters, economizers, and air preheaters.

Boilers may be classified into three categories according to their applications. These include industrial, marine, and central electric power station. Generally, the industrial boilers produce saturated steam or hot water. The pressure condition is frequently low. The marine boilers are much larger and usually produce superheated steam. The boilers for electric power generation stations are quite different in terms of steam conditions and generation rates. The steam pressure may be either supercritical or subcritical and the temperature is frequently around 538℃.

Boilers may also be classified according to the relative positions of products of combustion. In one type boiler, called the fire-tube boiler, the products of combustion flow through tubes surrounded by water. This type of boiler is frequently used in most steam locomotives, in small factories, and sometimes, in heating buildings. In another type of boiler, called the water-tube boiler, the products of combustion flow over water-filled tubes. Both ends of the water tubes are connected to the headers or the boiler drums. In the drum the steam is separated from the saturated water. Then, the saturated steam usually goes to the superheater in which the steam temperature is increased. All high-pressure and large boilers are of the water-tube type. The small tubes in the water-tube boiler can withstand high pressure better than the large drums of a fire-tube boiler.

Boilers are operated by firing various fuels. These fuels include bituminous coal, lignite, anthracite, natural gas, and oil. Different fuels result in different boiler designs and operations.

To attain high system efficiency, the steam generator usually, consists of the evaporation section, superheaters, reheaters, economizers, and air preheaters. In power plant system design one steam generator is frequently used to match one turbine unit. Because of this, steam generator unit size increases as turbine unit size increases.

Since the general introduction of pulverized coal-fired boilers in the 1950s there has been a considerable increase in unit size. The rapid increase in size at one stage resulted in some cases of excessive extrapolations from earlier designs with a consequent loss in the standard of reliability. To counter this a program of extensive testing was embarked upon on, units in stations. This program provided information, which resulted in the attainment of higher standards of plant reliability.

On-going development and improved manufacturing techniques led to the introduction of further design changes. Important changes can be summarized as follows:

(1) As a result of design and manufacturing development, steam drum internals have been modified to improve steam/water separation and to allow interchange of components between drums.

(2) Changes were made to the superheater and reheater tube thicknesses and materials to give increased design life and improve corrosion allowances. Platen designs were altered due to operational experience and constructional changes recognized improved manufacturing methods and practices. Because of the difficulty of fabrication, a change was made from reheater outlet drums to a system of headers with a steam outlet at each end of the headers. This also gave better steam distribution to the hot reheat lines.

(3) Changes to furnace internals, were made to give better heat transfer characteristics and to simplify construction procedures.

(4) Boiler tubes have been subjected to 100% ultrasonic examination to comply with more stringent specification requirements and case histories have been prepared relating to all pressure parts. A complete record of the design, manufacture and quality aspects of each component is thus provided which gives confidence in the long-term operation of pressure parts.

(5) Operational experience on a number of power stations demonstrated that a 2-speed motor on forced draught (FD) fans and induced draught (ID) fans was of limited advantage and, because of a

potential trip on changeover, tended always to be operated in the high speed mode. Consequently it was decided that single speed motors should be fitted.

Words and Expressions

water-cooled wall　水冷壁
category　['kætigəri]　n. 种类,类型
marine　[mə'riːn]　adj. 船舶的,海的
locomotive　[ˌləukə'məutiv]　n. 机车
header　['hedə]　n. 联箱,母管
drum　[drʌm]　n. 汽包,汽鼓
bituminous　[bi'tjuːminəs]　adj. 烟煤
lignite　['lignait]　n. 褐煤
anthracite　['ænθrəsait]　n. 无烟煤
match　[mætʃ]　n. 匹配,使协调
extrapolation　[ˌekstrəpəu'leiʃən]　n. 外推,推断
attainment　[ə'teimənt]　n. 达到
internals　[in'təːnls]　n. 内部部件
modify　['mɔdifai]　vt. 更改,改变
platen　['plætən]　n. 屏
comply with　照做
specification　[ˌspesifi'keiʃən]　n. 说明书
forced draught　送风机
induced draught　引风机
trip　[trip]　vi. 解扣,跳闸

5.2　Stokers

Water-cooled vibrating-grate stokers

　　Several manufacturers build spreader stokers with aircooled vibrating or oscillating grates. An entirely different design of stoker is the water-cooled vibrating-grate hopper-feed type, Fig. 5.1. An adaptation of an original European design used successfully with many of the low ranking lignite and brown coals found in Central Europe, this type of stoker is equally successful in burning the better grades of coal. Since introduction to the American market in the middle fifties, it has found steadily increasing acceptance because of simplicity, inherent low flyash carry-over characteristics and very low maintenance.

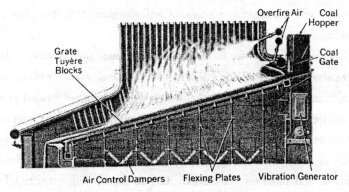

Fig. 5.1 Wter-cooled vibrating-grate stoker

The water-cooled vibrating-grate stoker consists of a tuyere grate surface mounted on, and in intimate contact with, a grid of water tubes interconnected with the boiler circulation system for positive cooling. The entire structure is supported by a number of flexing plates allowing the grid and its grate to move freely in a vibrating action that conveys coal from the feeding hopper onto the grate and gradually to the rear of the stoker. Ashes are automatically discharged to either a shallow or basement ash pit.

Vibration of the grates is intermittent, and the frequency of the vibration periods is regulated by a timing device. Timing is regulated by the automatic combustion control system to conform to load variations, synchronizing the fuel feeding rate with the air supply.

Furnace design

The water-cooled vibrating-grate stoker is suitable for burning a wide range of bituminous and lignite coals. Even with coals having a high free-swelling index, the gentle agitation and compaction of the fuel bed tends to keep the bed porous without the formation of large clinkers generally associated with low ash-fusion coals. A well distributed, uniform fuel bed is maintained without blow holes or thin spots.

The furnace design for this stoker should include water-cooled walls to prevent slag formation adjacent to the stoker. A rear arch extending over approximately one third of the stoker length directs the gases forward to mix with the rich volatile gases released in the ignition zone. A short front arch is adequate for most bituminous fuels. The use of high pressure air jets-from 27 to 30 in. of water (gage)-through the front arch provides turbulent gas mixing and promotes combustion. In rare cases, with extremely low-volatile fuels, some refractory facing of the front water-cooled arch may be desirable to increase the temperature over the ignition section.

Burning rates of these stokers vary with different fuels but, in general, the maximum heat release rate should not exceed 400 000 Btu/sq ft, hr. In this range, fly-carbon carry-over is held to a minimum.

Water cooling of the grates makes this stoker especially adaptable to multiple-fuel firing, as a shift to oil or gas does not require special provision for protection of the grates. A normal bed of ash left as a cover gives adequate protection from furnace radiation.

The strategic placement of burners in this type of furnace configuration may, in many cases, permit operation with a bare grate without exceeding safe metal temperature limits.

Chain-grate and traveling-grate stokers

Traveling-grate stokers, including the specific type known as the chain-grate stoker, have assembled links, grates, or keys joined together in endless belt arrangements that pass over the sprockets or return bends located at the front and the rear of the furnace. Coal, fed from the hopper (Fig. 5.2), onto the moving assembly, enters the furnace after passing under an adjustable gate to regulate the thickness of the fuel bed. The layer of coal on the grate, as it enters the furnace, is heated by radiation from the furnace gases and is ignited together with the hydrocarbon and other combustible gases driven off by distillation. The fuel bed continues to burn as it moves along, with the bed growing progressively thinner as combustion continues. At the far end of the travel, ash is discharged from the end of the grate into the ash pit. Although there are structural differences, the operation of the chain-grate and other traveling-grate types are quite similar. Generally these stokers used furnace arches (front and/or rear) to improve combustion by reflecting heat onto the fuel bed.

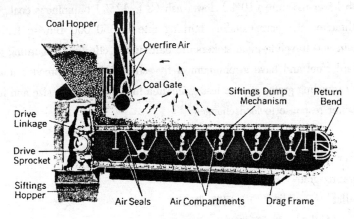

Fig. 5.2 Chain-grate stoker (Courtesy Laclede Stoker Co.)

The front arch also serves to break up and mix rich streams of volatile gases that might otherwise travel through the unit unburned.

In 1954, a chain-grate stoker was developed, which eliminated the need of a front arch (Fig.5.2). Two rows of overfire-air jets, located in the front wall, are particularly effective in completing the combustion of the rich, volatile gases over the first two compartments, which are blasted more heavily than is permissible with an arch.

Chain- and traveling-grate stokers can burn a wide variety of fuels. Almost any solid fuel-peat, lignite, subbituminous, free-burning bituminous, anthracite and coke breeze-of suitable size can be burned on these stokers. When burning anthracite and coke breeze, which are low in volatile constituents, rear arches are used to deflect and direct incandescent fuel particles and combustion gases toward the front of the stoker, where they assist in the ignition of the incoming raw fuel.

Chain- and traveling-grate stokers are offered for a maximum continuous burning rate of 425 000 Btu/sq ft, hr with high-moisture (20%), high-ash (20%) bituminous coal, and 500 000 Btu/sq ft, hr with lower-moisture (10%), lower-ash (8 to 12%) bituminous coal. For anthracite, the corresponding burning rate is 350 000 Btu/sq ft, hr. Chain-and traveling-grate stokers are particularly effective in burning low-volatile fuel and have a minimum of fly-ash carry-over. Spreader stokers with traveling grates require less grate area for a given boiler size and have a better response to load changes.

Words and Expressions

stoker ['stəukə] n. 层燃炉,司炉,加煤机
vibrating-grate 振动炉排
oscillat ['ɔsileit] v. 摆动,振动
flex [fleks] v. 弯曲.
bituminous [bi'tju:minəs] u. 烟煤的

arch [aːtʃ]　n. 拱门,弓形结构
chain-grate　链条炉排
anthracite　[ˈænθrəsait]　n. 无烟煤
breeze　[briːz]　n. 灰渣,焦炭屑

5.3　Boiler Circulation

An adequate flow of water and water-steam mixture is necessary for steam generation and control of tube metal temperatures in all the circuits of a steam-generating unit. At supercritical pressures, this flow is produced mechanically by means of pumps. At subcritical pressures, circulation is produced either naturally by the action of the force of gravity, by pumps, or by a combination of the two.

The force of gravity available to produce flow in natural circulation comes from the difference between the densities (lb/cu ft) of the fluids in the downcomer (downflow) and riser (upflow) portions of the circuit (Fig. 5.3). Maximum pumping effect occurs if the fluid in the downcomers is water at or slightly below saturation temperature and free of steam bubbles. Heat-absorbing risers at saturation temperature convey to the boiler drum a water-steam mixture of less density than that of the water in the downcomers. This difference in density establishes the force available for circulation.

The flow in the various circuits of boiler units designed for forced circulation at subcritical pressures, is produced by mechanical pumps. There are two general types of forced-circulation systems, a "once-through" system and a "recirculating" system.

The "once-through" forced-circulation type receives water from the feed supply, pumping it to the inlet of the heat-absorbing circuits. Fluid heating and steam generation take place along the length of the circuit until evaporation is complete. Further progress through the heated circuits

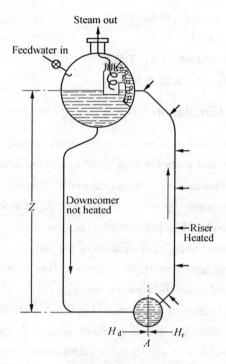

Fig. 5.3　Simple natural-circulation circuit (diagrammatic) including primary steam separator in drum

results in superheating the vapor. Conventionally this type of forced circulation requires no steam-and-water drum. A modification of the "once-through" type evaporates to partial dryness (90% quality) removing the excess water in a separator.

The "recirculating" forced-circulation-type unit has water supplied to the heat-absorbing circuits through a separate circulating pump. The water pumped is considerably in excess of the steam produced and, like a natural-circulation boiler, a steam-and-water drum is required for steam separation. The separated water together with feedwater from the feed pump is returned through downcomer circuits to the circulating pump for another "round trip."

In the recirculating type of forced circulation there is a net thermal loss for the boiler unit because of the separate circulating pump. While practically all the energy required to drive the pumps reappears in the water as added enthalpy, this energy originally came from the fuel at a conversion-to-useful-energy factor of less than 1.0. If an electric motor drive is used, the net energy lost, referred to the fuel input in a plant with 33% thermal efficiency, is about twice the energy supplied to the pump motor.

Natural circulation

In a natural-circulation system, circulation increases with increased heat input (and increased steam output) until a point of maximum fluid flow is reached. Beyond this point, any further increase in heat absorption results in a flow decrease. The form of the curve, shown in Fig. 5.4, is produced by two opposing forces. An increase in flow results

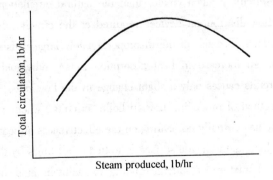

Fig. 5.4 Typical relationship between circulation in a boiler circuit (at a given pressure) and amount of steam produced (scale arbitrary)

from the increasing difference in the densities of the fluids in downcomers and risers as the heat absorption increases. At the same time, the friction and other flow losses in both downcomers and risers also increase. When the rate of increase in these losses (caused primarily by the increase in specific volume in the riser circuits) becomes greater than the gain from increasing density difference, the flow rate begins to drop. A proper objective, therefore, is to design all the circuits to operate in the region of the rising part of the curve, to the left of the peak in Fig. 5.4.

When design conditions are limited to the rising portion of the circulation curve, a natural-circulation boiler tends to be self-compensating for the numerous variations in heat-absorption conditions encountered in an operating unit. These include sudden overloads, change in heat-absorbing-surface cleanliness, nonuniform fuel bed or burner conditions, and even the inability to forecast precisely actual conditions over the operating lifetime.

No similar compensating effect is inherent in a forced-circulation unit operating at subcritical pressures, since a large part of the total resistance of the riser circuits, much greater than the natural circulation effect, is caused by flow-distribution devices required at the circuit inlets. Under these conditions, because of the disproportionately large resistance of the distributors, an increase in heat absorption to an individual circuit or group of circuits causes only a slight change in the flow rate.

The method of producing flow in boiler circuits, whether natural or mechanical, has virtually no bearing on the effectiveness of heat-absorbing surfaces as long as the inside surface is wetted at all times by the water in a water-steam mixture of suitable quality to maintain nucleate boiling. Provided this fundamental requirement is met, the water-film resistance to heat flow is negligibly small, and the overall heat conductance depends on gas-side and tube-wall resistances. Within the nucleate boiling regime, boiler heat-absorbing surface in the furnace or convection portion of the unit absorbs substantially the same amount of heat per sq ft regardless of whether the circulating flow is produced by natural methods or by pumps. With either type of circulation, any departure from the nucleate boiling regime requires special consideration of the forced-convection steam-film heat transfer coefficient and its relation to permissible metal temperatures.

Forced or natural circulation

Under certain conditions forced circulation can be usefully applied to steam generation. Mechanical means to move the fluid within the circuits are employed for boilers designed to operate above or near the critical pressure (3 208.2 psia.) There are instances, also, in the process and waste-heat fields where temperature control or consolidating heat pickup from widely separated points can be economically effected by the use of pumps. The conditions where forced circulation can be applied to advantage are quite specific.

Natural circulation is most effectively employed when large changes in density occur as the result of heat absorption. Therefore, natural circulation is usually restricted to subcritical pressure designs where there is a considerable difference in density between steam and water. At pressures above 2 900 psi a natural-circulation system becomes increasingly large and costly, and a pump may be more economical to assure positive flow. The forced-circulation principle, however, is equally operable in both the supercritical and subcritical pressure ranges. The selection of the identifying name "Universal-Pressure" boiler reflects the broad applicability of the once-through forced-circulation principle. Its choice, as opposed to the retention of natural circulation in the subcritical range, is essentially determined by the economics of the installation.

The differential in densities of steam and water for the range of 14.7

to 3 208.2 psia is noted in Fig. 5.5. A substantial differential persists well up toward the critical pressure. As long as the maximum effectiveness of this differential is maintained by the efficient separation of the steam from the water in the circulating system, as with the use of the cyclone steam separator, mechanical aid to circulation is not essential.

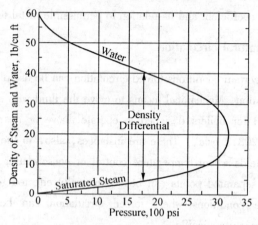

Fig. 5.5　Densities of steam and water at saturated steam temperature for pressures from atmospheric to critical

Words and Expressions

circulation　[ˌsəːkjuˈleiʃən]　n. 循环
density　[ˈdensiti]　n. 密度,浓厚
downcomer　[daunˈkʌm]　v. 下降管
modification　[ˌmɔdifiˈkeiʃən]　n. 修改,减少,变形,缓和
enthalpy　[enˈθælpi]　n. 焓,热量
compensate　[ˈkɔmpenseit]　v. 抵消,弥补,补偿
coefficient　[ˌkəuiˈfiʃənt]　n. 系数
subcritical　[ˈsʌbˈkritikəl]　a. 亚临界的,低于临界的
installation　[ˌinstəˈleiʃən]　n. 安装,设备

Boiler 119

5.4 Fossil-fuel Boilers for Electric Utilities

Selection of steam generating equipment

Most of the electric power used in the U.S. is produced in steam plants using fossil fuels and high-speed turbines.

Each steam generating unit must satisfy the user's specific needs in the most economical manner. Achieving this requires close cooperation between the designer and the user's engineering staff or consultants.

Before the specifications for a steam generator can be written, the user or plant designer must conduct a cost evaluation of the entire electric generating plant. In areas where fossil-fuel costs are high, it may be necessary to evaluate both nuclear and fossil units to determine which best satisfies the user's needs.

The cost of electricity from a steam plant has three principal elements: (1) capital equipment, (2) fuel, and (3) other operating and maintenance costs.

The capital cost survey must include the steam generator, steam turbine and electric generator, condenser, feedwater heaters and pumps, fuel handling facilities, buildings and real estate costs. The fuel cost survey must include the costs of the various fuels which may be used, and the probable changes in cost of these fuels during plant lifetime. There is a direct relation between plant efficiency and fuel used, and an important interrelation between plant efficiency and equipment cost.

Other important items are the location of the electric generating plant with respect to fuel supply and the areas where electricity is used. In some cases it is more economical to transport electricity than fuel, and some large steam generating stations are being built at the coal-mine mouth to generate electricity which is used several hundred miles away. If the user is a member of a grid system, the probable requirements of other grid members may be an important factor. Anticipated costs of operation and maintenance must also be included in the evaluation.

Considerable time and effort are required to establish sufficiently accurate basic data with comprehensive consideration of engineering factors, judgment in planning for future expansion or changes, and evaluation of the tangibles and intangibles, so that the experience and craftsmanship of the boiler manufacturer and other suppliers can be applied to the full benefit of the plant designer and the owner. The user should, at the outset, decide who is to prepare this data. If he lacks personnel with the necessary qualifications, the services of consulting engineers should be utilized. A thorough discussion with the boiler manufacturer will provide many details which will aid the user in making correct decisions.

Before the equipment can be selected, the basis of operation and arrangement of the entire steam plant must be planned. Ultimately the available data must be translated into the form of equipment specifications so that the manufacturers of various components can provide apparatus in accordance with the user's requirements. After equipment selection, construction drawings must be prepared for the foundations, building, piping and walkways. The construction work must be coordinated utilizing modern schedule and control techniques for effective management and completion of erection.

Boiler designer's requirements

Most important to the boiler designer are the amount of steam required, the fuel to be used, and the steam conditions which are specified as a result of the user's cost evaluation. These steam conditions include temperature and pressure of the primary and reheat steam.

The boiler designer needs all data pertinent to steam generation to enable him to produce the most economical steam-generating equipment to satisfy the needs of the user. This requires close cooperation between the boiler designer and the user's engineering staff or consultants.

The requirements and conditions that form the basis for the designer's selection of equipment can be outlined as follows:

1. Fuel(s)—sources presently available, analyses, costs, and future trends.

2. Steam requirements

(a) Pressure and temperature—at points of use, at outlet of steam generating units, allowable temperature variations.

(b) Rate of heat delivery (or steam flow)—to points of end use, to boiler house auxiliaries and feed water heating, to blowdown, from outlet of steam generating unit, variations (minimum, average and maximum), and predictable future requirements.

3. Boiler feedwater—source and analysis, and temperature entering steam generating unit.

4. Space and geographical considerations—space limitations, relation of new equipment to existing boiler house equipment, environmental requirements and restrictions of local laws, earthquake and wind requirements, elevation above sea level, foundation conditions, climate, and accessibility for service and construction.

5. Kind and cost of energy for driving auxiliaries.

6. Operating personnel—experience level of workmen for operation and maintenance, and cost of labor.

7. Guarantess.

8. Evaluation basis—for unit efficiency, auxiliary power required, building volume, and various fixed charges.

With this information, the boiler designer is able to analyze the user 's specific needs and coordinate the many components that make up a steam generator into the most economical design, by balancing first cost charges with long-term savings.

Design practice

The boiler designer usually works with standardized (pre-engineered) components. Detailed engineering of these components has been completed, hence shop fabrication is expedited and operating experience is proved. Examples of these are fuel burners, pulverizers, furnace sections, steam drums, and pressure parts. These components can be transformed readily into units of various capacities and dimensions. This results in lower costs, more rapid delivery schedules and improved availability of equipment in service.

There has been little standardization of complete unit designs for utility application primarily because of the distinctive nature of each user's conditions. The variables are not so much steam capacity, pressure and temperature as the types of fuels that are fired and the user's plans for utilizing the steam generating unit within his system. Variations of this type require changes in detail and overal arrangement of components. This, together with ever-changing costs of money, fuel, materials and labor, has made full unit standardization impracticable.

Words and Expressions

utility [juˈtiliti] n. 实用,公用事业
staff [stəːf] n. 全体职员
tangible [ˈtændʒəbl] a. 确实的,实质的
qualification [ˌkwɔlifiˈkeiʃən] n. 限定,条件
schedule [ˈskedʒul] n. 时刻表,进度
erection [iˈrekʃən] n. 建筑,安装
pertinent [ˈpəːtinənt] a. 相关的,有关系的

guarantee　[ˌgærən'tiː]　　n. 保证,保证书
hence　　[hens]　　adv. 从此,今后,因此
expedite　　['ekspidait]　　v. 使加速,迅速完成
dimension　[di'menʃən]　　n. 尺寸

5.5　Spreader Stoker

Grates for spreader stoker

　　Spreader-stoker firing is old in principle and based on many experiments conducted over the years. It became practical in the early 1930's when specially designed highresistance air-metering grates were coupled with adequate spreader-feeder mechanisms. The first of these metering grates was a stationary type, with the ash removed manually through the front doors. This limited application to boilers of 20 000 to 30 000 lb of steam per hr capacity.

　　Stationary grates were soon followed by dumping-grate designs in which grate sections are provided for each feeder, and the undergrate air plenum chambers are correspondingly divided. This permits the temporary discontinuance of fuel and air supply to a grate section for ash removal without affecting other sections of the stoker.

　　Introduction of the continuous-ash-discharge traveling grate of the air-metering design in the later 1930's brought the spreader stoker into immediate and widespread popularity. Since there are no interruptions for removing ashes, and because of the thin, fast-burning fuel bed, average burning rates were increased approximately 70% over the stationary and dumping grate types. This type stoker is generally competitive in sizes up to about 525 sq ft of grate area, corresponding to steam capacity somewhat over 400 000 lb of steam per hr. The furnace width required for stokers above this size usually results in increased boiler costs as compared to pulverized-coal-or Cyclone-Furnace-fired units with narrower and higher furnaces.

Although continuous-cleaning grates of reciprocating and vibrating designs have also been developed, the continuous-ash-discharge traveling-grate stoker is preferred for large boilers because of its higher burning rates.

The normal practice of all continuous-ash-discharge spreader stokers is to remove the ashes at the front or feeding end of the stoker. This permits the most satisfactory fuel distribution pattern and provides maximum residence time on the grates for complete combustion of the fuel.

The traveling-grate spreader stoker has selfadjusting air seals at both the front and rear of the grate. These effectively reduce leakage and stratification of air along the front and rear furnace walls, where it cannot be efficiently utilized in the combustion process.

Furnace design

An example of good furnace design is shown in Fig. 5.6 which also illustrates the fly-carbon reinjection system, discussed later in this chapter. This unit has water-cooled walls which are actually a necessity for traveling or continuous-cleaning spreader-stoker grates where slag or clinker formation adjacent to the stoker would interfere with movement of the fuel bed. Furnaces with refractory walls are sometimes installed with stationary or intermittent dumping-grate spreader stokers, but the high maintenance cost of such refractories makes this application questionable. The water walls are usually vertical, or nearly so, as arches are not desirable.

An overfire air system, with pressures from 27 to 30 in. of water (gage), is essential to successful suspension burning. It is customary to

Boiler 125

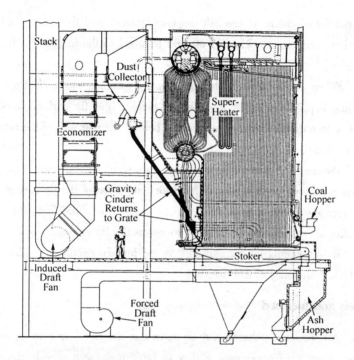

Fig. 5.6 Spreader-stoker installation with gravity fly-carbon return

provide at least two rows of evenly spaced high-pressure-air jets in the furnace rear wall and one in the front wall. This air mixes with the furnace gases and creates the turbulence required to complete combustion.

Fly-carbon collection and reinjection systems

Partial suspension burning results in a greater carry-over of particulate matter in the flue gas than with other types of stokers. Dust collectors are consequently required with spreader stokers.

The collector generally used with spreader stokers is a cyclone-type precipitator with a selective feature so that the fines are deposited in a hopper for discharge to the ash disposal system, and the coarse carbon-bearing particles are skimmed off and returned to the furnace for further burning.

When plant physical layout permits locating the collecting and settling hopper outlets at a sufficient height, the fly carbon flows by gravity to a distributing hopper directly behind the rear wall of the furnace (Fig. 5.6).

Pneumatic systems, using high pressure air as the conveying medium, have been extensively used for reinjection of the fly carbon into the furnace in the high temperature zone just above the fuel bed. The overfire-air system may be adapted to return the fly carbon.

Reintroducing the fly carbon into the furnace results in an increase in boiler efficiency of 2% to 3%.

Fuels and fuel bed

All spreader stokers, and in particular the traveling-grate spreader type, have an extraordinary ability to burn fuels with a wide range of burning characteristics, including coals with caking tendencies. High-moisture, free-burning bituminous and lignite coals are commonly used, and some low volatile fuels, such as coke breeze, have been burned in a mixture with higher volatile coal. Anthracite coal, however, is not a satisfactory fuel for spreaderstoker firing.

Coal size segregation is a problem with any type of stoker, but the spreader stoker can tolerate a small amount of segregation because the feeding rate of the individual feeder-distributors can be varied. Size segregation, where fine and coarse coal are not distributed evenly over the grate, produces a ragged fire and poor efficiency.

The ideal fuel and ash bed for coal-fired spreader stokers is evenly distributed and from 2 to 4 inches thick. Maximum heat release rates are from 450 000 Btu/sq ft, hr on stationary or dumping grates, to 750 000 Btu/sq ft, hr on traveling—grate spreader stokers. Higher releases are practical with certain of the waste fuels, such as pulpwood bark.

The ash moisture content in bituminous coals are factors to be considered in the selection of the grate type. If the ash content of the coal exceeds 10% (as-fired basis), stationary or dumping grates should not be considered unless heat release rates are reduced at least 25%, Traveling grates have no limits for maximum ash content.

Residue handling

With stationary grates, the ash is removed from the grates one section at a time by hoe or rake through suitable doors at the grate level. Intermittent-dumping-grate stokers discharge the ash to pits. These may be shallow for firing-floor cleanout in the absence of basement space.

The practical maximum net length or length open to air flow for a stationary grate is about 9 ft. With a dump grate arranged for floor cleaning, the net length should be held under 12 ft. In the case of an arrangement with a basement ash pit this dimension may be 15 ft.

Traveling-grate continuous-ash-discharge stokers usually require either a basement ash pit or elevation of the firing level to obtain equivalent ash storage space.

The recommended maximum net length of reciprocating and vibrating grates for spreader stokers is 15 feet, while for traveling grates it is about 18 feet with current designs.

Ashes may be removed from the ash pits for final disposal by means of any of the conventional ash-transport systems such as pneumatic conveyors and sluices.

Words and Expressions

plenum ['pli:nən] *n.* 充满,充实

interruption　［ˌintəˈrʌpʃən］　n. 中断,妨碍,障碍物
grate　［greit］　n. 炉架;壁炉
reciprocate　［riˈsiprəkeit］　v. 回报,回信,互换
illustrate　［ˈiləstreit］　v. 举例说明,显示,说明
adjacent　［əˈdʒeisənt］　a. 接近的,邻近的,附近的
suspension　［səsˈpenʃən］　n. 悬浮,暂停
skim　［skim］　v. 掠去,掠过,浏览
pneumatic　［njuːˈmætik］　a. 空气的,气体的,气动的
vibrate　［vaiˈbreit］　v. 使振动,使摇摆

5.6　Economizers and Air Heaters

In a boiler operating at subcritical pressure, the temperature of the gases leaving the steam generating surfaces of the boiler is essentially determined by the saturation temperature of the boiling water. The higher the steam pressure the higher will be this saturation temperature. The flue gases must be at a still higher temperature level, usually from 700 to 1 000°F, to permit transfer of heat from the gases to the steam generating surfaces. If the flue gases were exhausted to the atmosphere at such temperatures, the resultant loss in boiler efficiency could be intolerable. Feedwater on its way to the boiler at temperatures substantially below saturation, or air on its way to the furnace offers opportunity to absorb much of the residual, low-grade heat in the gases leaving the boiler with substantial improvement in overall efficiency. Historically, when this heat was absorbed by feedwater, the heat exchange device was logically called an "economizer." It served to improve the economy in the use of fuel.

Subsequently, it was found desirable and profitable to recover some or all of this low-grade heat in air heaters which raised the temperature of the air supplied for combustion. This not only improved boiler efficiency by lowering stack temperatures but it also improved the combustion conditions in the furnace. Higher heat release rates and higher furnace tempera-tures improved the economics of the boiler installation. Air heaters and economizers are consequently often called "heat traps." Modern boilers make full use of these devices for lowering the cost and improving the reliability of steam supply.

Economizers

The early economizers were installed in boiler units operating on natural draft. They generally utilized tubes of equal or larger diameter than the boiler tubes, and widely spaced to reduce resistance to gas flow.

Cast iron proved to be an acceptable material for economizers because of its inherent resistance to corrosion, both internal and external. Cast iron fins were used in some designs of economizers to give extended heat transfer surface on the gas side and to minimize the effects of external corrosion.

Steel was early adapted to successful use in boilers but at first could not be used in economizers because of the corrosive effects of free oxygen. In the boiler, most of the dissolved oxygen in the feedwater was driven off in the steam drum with the steam, and the corrosive effect on the boiler tubes was accordingly reduced. In the economizer, as the temperature of the feedwater rose, the oxygen was gradually driven out of solution and attacked the inside of the tubes. Also the temperature of the water in the boiler, at saturation temperature, was above the dew point of the flue gases, while in the economizer, the feedwater, often entering at a temperature as low as 100°F, cooled the surrounding flue gases so much that moisture condensed on the outside of the tubes. This moisture, with some of the sulfur dioxide and sulfur trioxide from the flue gas, caused corrosion. The moisture also formed a bond for the collection of ash on the tubes, restricting the gas passages and reducing the heat transfer. Cleaning apparatus had to be used to remove this deposit. Early economizers of cast iron were equipped with mechanical scrapers. Cast iron economizers of this type are still in use with some low pressure boilers.

When feedwater temperatures were increased by the introduction of stage bleeding of turbines and extraction feed heating, the minimum operating temperature for the economizer was increased, thus eliminating gas-side condensation with its attendant corrosion and fouling. Feedwater was treated and oxygen removed by deaeration to reduce internal corrosion. These improvements made it possible to use steel for economizers tubes, thus permitting the use of economizers at high pressures. Soot blowing was developed to keep gas-side surfaces clean. Induced and forced draft replaced natural draft, allowing more compact and economical surface arrangements.

One of the earliest straight-tube steel economizers of B & W design was built to ASME standards in 1915. A successful two-drum bent-tube type of economizer was developed early in 1917. A later version of this type applied to a Radiant boiler is illustrated. An integral-type bent-tube economizer with separate lower drum and with the upper ends of the tubes connected to the rear top drum of a storing boiler is occasionally built. The two-drum type, however, is preferred (if drums are to be used) because there is less limitation on size, location and shape. In either case, the tube diameters and spacing can be the same as for the boiler, or they can be modified to improve heat absorption, draft loss, water velocities and the conditions for external cleaning. Water is fed into the lower drum and flows up through the tubes to the upper drum. Gases flow either along the tubes, preferably entering at the top and flowing down counter to the water flow, or across the tubes in single or multiple passes.

Smaller tube economizers (2-in. OD) were introduced about 1920 and, since that time, have come to be widely used. The small-tube economizer requires less space, is easier to manufacture, and uses less steel for tubes and casing than the larger tube units. It is particularly suitable for high pressures.

The early 2-in. tube economizers were generally made with straight horizontal tubes rolled into horizontal square headers. Handhole fittings were provided in the headers opposite the ends of the tubes so that every tube could be inspected and mechanically cleaned internally. Water fed into the bottom header flowed up through the tubes from header to header and then from the top header into the boiler. Gas entered the top of the economizer and flowed down across the staggered tubes, leaving at the bottom. This type of economizer was used with the first 650 psi boiler units in 1922, and with coal-fired high-pressure units shortly afterward.

An improved design of the horizontal steel tube economizer, frequently used when it was necessary to clean the inside of the tubes mechanically, was also developed during the 1920's. The 2-in. OD tubes were bent through 180 degrees at one end. The other end was equipped with a special flanged and bolted return-bend fitting.

Air heaters

The air heater in a steam generating unit reclaims some heat (which would otherwise be lost) from the flue gas and adds that heat to the air required for the combustion of the fuel.

As in the case of economizers, air heaters originated in Europe before they were used in the United States. Early patent files reveal the invention of air heaters long before the industry had developed to the stage where they could be used economically.

The first air heater to be installed in a commercial boiler unit in the United States was built in 1922. Flat parallel steel plates formed alternate gas and air passages. It was necessary that the passes be completely separate from each other, since any air leakage into the gas stream not only reduced the efficiency of the air heater but increased the load on the forced and induced draft fans. Plate air heaters (recuperative type) are still in use but are not as suitable as tubular or regenerative heaters for the higher gas and air pressures which are now common practice.

Placing its first tubular air heater in service early in 1923, B & W built a total of 50 air heaters during 1923 and 1924. The demand at that time arose as a result of increases in boiler pressure and size. Before 1922 the highest pressures commonly used in power generation ranged from 350 to 400 psi. In 1922 units of 650 psi were developed to generate more kilowatt-hours per pound of steam. The increase in steam pressure made large units possible. The larger units and higher pressures made extraction steam feedwater heating economical, and the higher feed pressures and temperatures in turn made the addition of air heaters economical.

Before 1920 practically all coal used in the production of steam was burned on stokers or grates. Furnace walls were generally all refractory or, in a few instances, partly water cooled. Hot air supplied to the fire improved stoker performance by raising the temperature level in the combustion zone, although this increased maintenance costs of stoker parts and furnace surface. The development of water-cooled furnace walls that could withstand high combustion temperatures contributed greatly to the effective use of air heaters in boiler units.

In the early 1920's there was a tremendous increase in the

development and use of pulverized-coal firing in central stations. For this type of firing, hot air was ideal for drying, transporting and burning the coal in suspension. Demand for air heaters was thus established.

Words and Expressions

intolerable ［in'tɔlərəbl］ a. 不能容忍的,难堪的 adv. 非常地,无法忍受地
logical ［'lɔdʒikəl］ a. 逻辑的,必然的,合理的
inherent ［in'hiərənt］ a. 内在的,固有的,根本的
dissolve ［di'zɔlv］ v. 解散,结束,溶解,消失
scraper ［'skreipə］ n. 刮刀
eliminate ［i'limineit］ v. 削减,除去
handhole ［hændhəul］ n. 手孔
reclaim ［ri'kleim］ v. 收回,要求,归还
commercial ［kə'mə:ʃəl］ a. 大量生产的,商业的
feedwater ［fi:d'wɔ:tə］ n. 给水,补水
tremendous ［tri'mendəs］ a. 巨大的,可怕的

5.7 Selection of Coal-burning Equipment

The selection of the most suitable equipment for a particular job consists of balancing the investment, operating characteristics, efficiency, and type of coal to give the most economical installation.

Almost any coal can be burned successfully in pulverized form or on some type of stoker. Cyclone-Furnace firing has special advantages for certain coals for which it is suited.

The capacity limitations imposed by stokers have been overcome by the development of pulverized-coal and Cyclone-Furnace firing. These improved methods of burning coal also provide:

1. Ability to use any size of coal available.

2. Improved response to load changes.

3. Increase in thermal efficiency because of lower excess air for combustion and lower carbon loss than with stoker firing.

4. A reduction in manpower required for operation.

5. Improved ability to burn coal in combination with oil and gas.

Experience shows that stoker firing is more economical for steam generating units of capacity less than 100 000 lb of steam per hr, where the lower efficiency of a stoker can be tolerated. In larger plants, where fuel cost is a larger fraction of the operating cost, pulverized-coal or Cyclone-Furnace firing is more economical except in special cases.

Operating characteristics may be of controlling significance in the choice of firing methods. For example, where unit size is suitable for pulverized-coal, Cyclone-Furnace, or stoker firing, an extremely wide load range may make stoker firing preferable. Where rotary kilns and industrial furnaces are fired by coal, pulverized-coal firing is generally used.

The type of coal influences the choice of the method of firing for boiler furnaces with the primary considerations as follows:

Pulverized-coal firing: grindability, rank, moisture, volatile matter, and ash.

Stoker firing: rank of coal, volatile matter, ash, and ashsoftening temperature.

Cyclone-Furnace firing: volatile matter, ash, and ash viscosity.

Convenient approximations for the selection of bituminous coals for the firing of boilers are given in Table 5.1.

Table 5.1 Coal characteristics and the method of firing

	Stoker	Pulverized Coal	Cyclone Furnace
Max. total moisture* (as fired), %	15~20	15	20
Min. Volatile matter (dry basis), %	15	15	15
Max. total ash (dry basis), %	20	20	25
Max. sulfur (as fired), %	5	—	—

Pulverized-coal systems

The function of a pulverized-coal system is to pulverize the coal, deliver it to the fuel-burning equipment, and accomplish complete combustion in the furnace with a minimum of excess air. The system must operate as a continuous process and, within specified design limitations, the coal supply or feed must be varied as rapidly and as widely as required by the combustion process.

A small portion of the air required for combustion (15 to 20% in current installations) is used to transport the coal to the burner. This is known as primary air. In the direct-firing system, primary air is also used to dry the coal in the pulverizer. The remainder of the combustion air (80 to 85%) is introduced at the burner and is known as secondary air.

The two basic equipment components of a pulverized coal system are:

1. The pulverizer which pulverizes the coal to the fineness required.
2. The burner which accomplishes the mixing of the pulverized-coal-

---

* These limits may be exceeded for lower rank, higher inherent-moisture-content coals, i.e., subbituminous and lignite.

primary-air mixture with secondary air in the right proportions and delivers the mixture to the furnace for combustion.

Other necessary requirements are:

3. Hot air for drying the coal for effective pulverization.

4. Fan (s) to supply air to the pulverizer and deliver the coal-air mixture to the burner (s).

5. Coal feeder to control the rate of coal feed to each pulverizer.

6. Coal and air conveying lines.

Two principal systems-the bin system and the direct-firing system-have been used for processing, distributing and burning pulverized coal. The direct-firing system is the one being installed almost exclusively today.

Bin system

The bin system is primarily of historical interest, although a large number of units of this type remain in operation. Its use was required before pulverizing equipment had reached the stage of development where it could be relied upon for uninterrupted operation, flexibility and consistent performance.

In this system the coal is processed at a location apart from the furnace, and the end product is pneumatically conveyed to cyclone collectors which recover the fines and clean the moisture-laden air before returning it to the atmosphere. The pulverized coal is discharged into storage bins and later conveyed by pneumatic transport through pipelines to utilization bins which may be as far as 5 000 ft from the point of preparation.

For the coal-air transport system, a differential-pitch screw pump, is provided to feed pulverized coal continuously into a pipeline, where coal is aerated or fluidized at the entrance so that it flows through the pipe somewhat like a viscous fluid. Through a system of two-way valves the coal can be distributed to any number of bins. The system may be arranged for manual, remote or automatic control. These air-transport systems are built in sizes from 1 to 100 tons of coal per hour. For successful operation, the surface moisture in the pulverized coal must not exceed 3%, and the fineness should not be less than 90% through a 50-mesh sieve.

Although bin systems installed in older plants are still operating quite satisfactorily, this system is no longer competitive with the direct-firing system. Furthermore, the drying, transportation and storage of pulverized coal, other than anthracite, involves a fire hazard from spontaneous combustion.

Direct-firing system

The bin system has been superseded by the direct-firing system because of improvements in safety conditions, plant cleanliness, greater simplicity, lower initial investment, lower operating cost, and less space requirement.

The pulverizing equipment developed for the directfiring system permits continuous utilization of raw coal directly from the bunkers where coal is stored in the condition in which it is received at the plant. This is accomplished by feeding the raw coal directly into the pulverizer, where it is dried as well as pulverized, and then delivering it to the burners in a single continuous operation.

Components of the direct-firing system are as follows:

1. Raw-coal feeder.

2. Source (steam or gas air heater) to supply hot primary air to the pulverizer for drying the coal.

3. Pulverizer fan, also known as the primary-air fan, arranged as a blower (or exhauster).

4. Pulverizer arranged to operate under pressure (or suction).
5. Coal-and-air conveying lines.
6. Burners.

There are two direct-firing methods in use-the pressure type, which is more commonly used, and the suction type. The principal differences between the two methods are summarized in Table 5.2.

Table 5.2 Comparative features of direct-firing pressure and suction systems

System	Pressure	Suction
Type of fan	Blower	Exhauster
Location of fan	Pulverizer inlet	Pulverizer outlet
Fan construction	Standard	Explosion-proof
Fan handles	Air only	Pulverized coal and air
Relative fan efficiency	High	Low
Fan wear	Low to none	High
Pulverized coal distribution to burners	Good	Distributor required

In the pressure method, the primary-air fan, located on the inlet side of the pulverizer, forces the hot primary air through the pulverizer where it picks up the pulverized coal, and delivers the proper coal-air mixture to the burners. Where a separate air heater is provided, the fan operates on cold air, forcing the air first through the air heater and then the pulverizer. In either event, the coal is delivered to the burners by a fan operating entirely on air, so that no entrained dust passes through the fan. One pulverizer generally furnishes the coal for several burners. With the pressure method, it is usual to supply each burner with a single conveying line direct from the pulverizer, thus eliminating the expense of a distributor.

In the suction method, the air and entrained coal are drawn through the pulverizer under negative pressure by an exhauster located on the outlet side of the pulverizer. With this arrangement the fan handles a mixture of coal and air, and distribution of the mixture to more than one burner must be obtained by a distributor beyond the fan discharge.

The feeding of coal and air to the pulverizer is controlled by either of two methods: (1) The coal feed is proportioned to the load demand, and the primary-air supply is adjusted to the rate of coal feed; or (2) the primary air through the pulverizer is proportioned to the load demand, and the coal feed is adjusted to the rate of air flow. In either case, a predetermined air-coal ratio is maintained for any given load.

The direct-firing system, in addition to eliminating separately fired dryers and storage facilities for pulverized coal, permits the use of inlet air temperatures to the pulverizer up to 650°F and higher for drying high-moisture coals (total moisture 20%, surface moisture 15%) or high-moisture lignites (20 to 40% total moisture) in the pulverizer.

The direct-firing system has one minor disadvantage. The operating range of a pulverizer is usually not more than 3 to 1 (without change in the number of burners in service) because the air velocities in lines and other parts of the system must be maintained above the minimum values to keep the coal in suspension. In practice most boiler units are provided with more than one pulverizer, each feeding multiple burners. Load variations beyond 3 to 1 are generally accommodated by shutting down (or starting up) a pulverizer and the burners it supplies.

Words and Expressions

investment ['in'vestmənt] n. 投资,投资额
rotary ['rəutəri] a. 旋转的,转动的
grindability [ˌgraində'biliti] n. 可磨性,磨削性
rank [ræŋk] n. 等级
volatile ['vɔlətail] a. 挥发性的,易变的

pulverize ['pʌlvəraiz] v. 将……弄碎,磨碎
convey [kən'vei] v. 传送,输运
uninterrupted ['ʌnˌintə'rʌptid] a. 不间断的
bin [bin] n. 仓,箱
anthracite ['ænθrəsait] n. 无烟煤,白煤,硬煤
hazard ['hæzəd] n. 危险,机会,偶然
raw-coal 原煤,未加工的煤

5.8 Oil and Gas Burning Equipment

The burner is the principal equipment component for the firing of oil and gas. Burners are normally located in the vertical walls of the furnace. Burners, together with the furnaces in which they are installed, are designed to burn the fuel properly in accordance with the principles of combustion outlined.

The burners introduce the fuel and air into the furnace to sustain the exothermic chemical reactions for the most effective release of heat. That effectiveness is judged by the following:

1. The rate of feed of the fuel and air shall comply with the load demand on the boiler over a predetermined operating range.

2. The efficiency of the combustion process shall be as high as possible with the minimum of unburned combustibles and minimum excess air in the products.

3. The physical size and complexity of the furnace and burners shall be as small as possible to minimize the required investment and to meet the limitations on space, weight, and flexibility imposed by the service conditions.

4. The design of the burners, including the materials used, shall provide reliable operation under specified service conditions, and shall assure meeting accepted standards of maintenance for the burners and the

furnaces in which they are installed.

5. Safety shall be paramount under all conditions of operation of burners, furnace and boiler, including starting, stopping, load changes, and variations in the fuel.

The normal use of a steam generator requires operation at different outputs to meet varying load demands. The specified operating range or "load range" for a burner is the ratio of full load on the burner to the minimum load at which the burner must be capable of reliable operation. For example, with a boiler of 100 000 lb/hr capacity (steam delivered), a load range of 4 to 1 on the burners means that the unit can be operated from 100 000 lb/hr down to 25 000 lb/hr without changing the number of burners in operation, and with complete combustion.

Combustion air is generally delivered to the burners by fans. It is necessary to supply more than the theoretical air quantity to assure complete combustion of the fuel in the combustion chamber (furnace). The amount of excess air provided should be just enough to burn the fuel completely in order to minimize the sensible heat loss in the stack gases. The excess air normally required with oil and gas, expressed as percent of theoretical air.

Continuity of service is enhanced by designing the furnace and arranging the burners to minimize slagging and fouling of heat-absorbing surfaces for the normal range of fuels burned.

Maintenance costs of the burner are minimized by (1) the least exposure to furnace heat, and (2) provision for replacement or repair of vulnerable parts while the unit continues in operation.

Safety precautions

The handling and burning of any fuel is potentially hazardous. Some fuels ignite more readily than others. Safe handling and operation demand knowledge of the characteristics of the fuel and careful observance of necessary precautions.

Because of the rapid diffusion of gas, any leak of fuel gas into an enclosed space may result in an explosive mixture of air and gas. Oil normally is not in a form where it will disperse readily in air and may have a higher ignition temperature. However, because of the volatile components in fuel oil, explosive mixtures may exist in oil tanks in the space above the oil or in empty tanks, unless they are blanketed with inert gas, which is not normally practicable. Oil tank vents are therefore equipped with a flame-arresting screen to prevent the passage of a flame.

One of the requirements for good combustion is intimate mixing of fuel and air. In the case of gaseous fuels and oil (and most other fuels) such mixtures are potentially explosive and can be expected to ignite from a single spark. Therefore these mixtures must never be allowed to exist except inside the combustion chamber at the burner, and then only when the burner is lighted.

This fundamental principle forms the basis for safety precautions and burner lighting and operating sequences. Three rules are of prime importance, whether in a manual or automatic system:

1. Never allow oil or gas to accumulate anywhere, other than in a tank or lines which form part of the fuel supply system. The slightest odor of gas should be cause for alarm. Steps should be taken immediately to ventilate the area thoroughly and then locate the source.

2. Purge the furnace and setting completely before introducing any light or spark, or before relighting after all flame has been extinguished. On a multiple-burner unit, burners may be ignited without a purge if one or more are in service already.

3. Have a lighted torch or spark-producing device in operation before introducing any fuel into a furnace. To prevent a backfire or

flareback of flame into the fireroom or forced air supply system (depending on the installation) the torch or ignitor must be properly placed with respect to the burner and must provide a flame or spark of adequate size continuously until stable ignition of a main burner is accomplished.

Other items essential to safe burner operation are:

4. Maintenance of a positive air flow through the burners, into the furnace, and up the stack.

5. Maintenance of adequate oil pressure and temperature for atomization, and also adequate steam or air pressure in the case of steam or air atomizers.

Compliance with these rules, particularly the first one, requires good housekeeping throughout the plant and an operating staff alert to any abnormal conditions.

To observe the last four rules, automatic control installations may include:

(a) Purge interlocks, e.g., requiring a specified minimum air flow for a specific time period sufficient to purge the setting before the fuel trip valve can be opened.

(b) Flame detector-Each burner should have its own flame detector connected to an alarm and interlocked to shut off the fuel to the burner it serves upon flame failure.

(c) Closed-position switches for burner shut-off valves, requiring that all shut-off valves be closed to permit opening the fuel trip valve.

(d) Shut-off of fuel on failure of forced or induced draft fan.

(e) Shut-off of fuel in the event of low fuel pressure (and low steam or air pressure to oil atomizers, where appropriate).

(f) Shut-off of fuel in event of low oil temperature.

(g) Shut-off of fuel in gas-fired units in event of excessive fuel-gas pressure.

Sealing off air intakes to boiler rooms is a safety violation in plants where combustion air for the burners is supplied from inside the building. In some of these plants, where the air flow is substantial, the boiler room may become uncomfortable for personnel, particularly in extremely cold weather. Personnel comfort should not be provided by reducing air supply to the boiler room, since limiting air supply to the burners causes burner pulsations.

Any of the commonly used fuels can be burned with safety when using the proper equipment with operating skill. The hazard is introduced when, through carelessness or misoperation of a piece of equipment, the fuel is no longer burned in a safe manner. While a malfunction should be corrected promptly, there should be no panic. Investigations of explosions of boiler furnaces equipped with good recording equipment, reveal that the conditions leading to the explosion in most cases had existed for a considerable time-long enough for someone to have taken unhurried corrective action before the accident happened. The old concern that malfunctions of safety equipment cause frequent, unnecessary, unit trips is not consistent with the facts. False trips are infrequent and are becoming less.

Words and Expressions

burning ['bə:niŋ] a. 燃烧的 n. 燃烧
sustain [səs'tein] v. 支持,维持,证明
furnace ['fə:nis] n. 火炉,炉膛
flexibility [,fleksə'biliti] n. 易曲性,适应性
paramount ['pærəmaunt] a. 最重要的,首位的
vulnerable ['vʌlnərəbl] a. 难防守的,易受伤的,脆弱的
hazardous ['hæzədəs] a. 碰运气的,危险的
precaution [pri'kɔ:ʃən] n. 预防,防备

ignition　[ig'niʃən]　　n. 点火,点火装置,燃烧
intimate　['intimit]　　a. 亲密的,本质的
purge　[pə:dʒ]　　n. 清洗,净化
intake　['inteik]　　n. 入口,吸入,进风量
malfunction　[mæl'fʌŋkʃən]　　n. 障碍,故障,疾病

5.9　Furnace

　　A boiler furnace is constructed to encompass the enclosure that surrounds the space needed for combustion and radiation heat transfer to the water-steam mixture. A boiler furnace also collects a portion of the coal ash at the furnace bottom and removes it. There are two types of furnace bottoms, depending whether the ash is in liquid or solid form. When the gas temperature in the furnace is higher than the ash fusion temperature, the ash is in a molten state, moving downward and eventually being trapped in the slag pool. In this arrangement, frequently called the wet-bottom furnace, about 50% of the total ash is trapped within the furnace. The remainder of the ash will leave the furnace. When the gas temperature in the furnace is lower than the ash fusion temperature, the ash remains in a solid state, falling into the bottom of the furnace. In this dry-bottom furnace, the ash is collected in a refractory-lined hopper. The hopper surface is cooled by placing water tubes on the refractory material. The dry-bottom furnace generally collects about 20% of the coal ash, thus comparatively more fly ash for the precipitators that are required for all boiler installations.

　　The furnace wall is protected by water-filled tubes, which are formed into a solid wall and are backed by refractory material. These tubes constitute almost the entire heat absorbing surfaces in the furnace. These surfaces receive heat from the products of combustion mainly by radiation. The amount of heat received depends on the quantity of energy released and the volume of the furnace. A large heat absorption means a large temperature reduction in the furnace, resulting in a low gas exit temperature. This furnace exit temperature plays an important role in boiler design. When the exit gas temperature exceeds the ash fusion, the ash becomes melted and the slag begins to build up on the boiler convective heat transfer elements such as the superheater and reheater. These slag deposits will adversely affect the performance of these elements and require periodic surface cleanings. On the other hand, low exit gas temperature will result in a large reduction of temperature differential for subsequent heat transfer elements and lead to an increase in the number of heating surfaces. In design, the temperature of the gas leaving the furnace should be a little lower than the fusion temperature of the coal fired. Regulation of this gas temperature is accomplished by controlling the amount of energy released and the size of the furnace. Experiences indicate that the heat release per unit area of heat absorbing surface is an important parameter. As the heat release increases, the gas exit temperature will increase.

Radiation heat transfer in the boiler furnace is complex, and accurate prediction of the gas temperature at the furnace exit is difficult. Many variables can affect the furnace radiation. These include at least the surface characteristics, and the composition of the combustion products. The surface characteristics are dependent not only on the tube material, but also the tube surface conditions such as the thickness of the slag and the ash deposits. The products of combustion contain various gases, water vapor, and solid particles. The exact composition depends on the type of fuel fired and the amount of excess air used. Some components including carbon dioxide, carbon monoxide, water vapor, and solid particles are the participating media, emitting and absorbing the radiation energy in the furnace. Other components such as oxygen and nitrogen are nonparticipating media, being transparent to thermal radiation. In addition, the furnace radiation heat transfer is affected by the furnace geometry complex and by variation in operating conditions. Evidently, a theoretical model for predicting the radiation and the furnace exit gas temperature is impossible, at the present time. We now present an approximate method to solving this complex problem.

Double-Arch FW Furnace

For a reheat unit supplied by Foster Wheeler, it is top supported, and vertical burners located on the arches are fed a fuel/air mixture by conduits issuing from ball-mill pulverizers located at ground level. The reliable FW ball-mill was selected in view of the low grind ability of the high-ash fuel, and the fineness required throughout the mill load range. Hot drying air is provided to the mills through tubular primary air heater by primary air fans. Secondary air fans, followed by regenerative secondary air heaters, supply air to the front and rear walls below the arches.

In the lower furnace, a W-shaped flames' pattern forms. Combustion continues as gases rise in the upper furnace, up to its exit vertical plane, tangent to the tip of the furnace nose. Gases cross the vestibule, then turn down and split into the two separate convection surface passes of the heat recovery area. One of these passes contains the entire reheater surface, for control of reheat steam temperature by proportioning of gases. The front pass encompasses the convection primary superheater and uppereconomizer. Ash is collected and extracted from the ash pit underneath the furnace, and from the hoppers below the flues and the electro-static precipitator.

Words and Expressions

encompass [inˈkʌmpəs]   *vt*. 围绕,包围

enclosure ['in'kləuʒə] n. 围绕,封人
bottom ['bɔtəm] n. 底部,炉底
fusion ['fju:ʒən] n. 熔化
molten ['məultən] adj. 熔化的
trap [træp] n. 捕捉,搜集
wet-bottom furnace 液态排渣炉膛
dry-bottom furnace 固态排渣炉膛
refractory [ri'fræktəri] adj. 耐火材料;耐火的,耐热的
medium ['mi:djəm] n. 介质,方法
arch [a:tʃ] n. 拱,拱顶
conduit ['kɔndit] n. 管道,管路
issue ['isju:] n. 排出,流出
grindability [ˌgraində'biliti] n. 可磨性
REGENERATIVE [ri'dʒenərətiv] adj. 再生式,回热式,蓄热式
tip [tip] vt. 端点,端头
vestibule ['vestibju:l] n. 前厅,通廊
pit [pit] n. 沟,槽
flue [flu:] n. 烟道,风道

5.10　Gas and Fuel Oil-fired Furnaces

The conditions of combustion of natural gas and fuel oil have much in common, and therefore, both fuels can be burned in furnaces of the same design. In most cases, such furnaces are designed primarily for fuel oil with natural gas as the auxiliary fuel. The combustion characteristics of fuel oil and natural gas are similar in the following respects:

1. Both fuels contain practically no adventitious moisture and form roughly the same volumes of combustion products; therefore, the blowers of a steam boiler can efficiently operate irrespective of whether fuel oil or natural gas is being burned in the boiler furnace.

2. Burning of fuel oil and natural gas occurs in the vaporized state following the laws of branched chain reactions. The intensity of burning in both cases is determined by the conditions of intermixing, and the highest allowable heat release rates of the furnace volume are rater close to each other ($300kW/m^3$ for fuel oil and $350kW/m^3$ for natural gas). Thus, for the same steam output of a boiler, the furnace dimensions for these two kinds of fuel can be taken to be practically the same.

3. Both fuels form almost no ash on combustion (the ash content of fuel oil A^d is less than 0.3%), which avoids clinkering of the water walls in the furnace and makes slag-handling facilities unnecessary. In view of this, furnaces for both fuels are made with a horizontal or slightly inclined bottom, with manholes provided for repairs.

4. Since the fuel is in the gaseous (or vaporized) state, it can be more easily intermixed with air, which ensures virtually complete combustion at a high heat release rate and low excess air ratio $a_l'' = 1.02 - 1.05$, For both fuels, air can be preheated to the same temperature ($t_{ha} = 250 \sim 300°C$), which makes it possible to employ combined gas-fuel oil burners with close values of the volume flow rate of air and almost the same resistance.

With intensive burning, both fuels form a relatively short flame core zone near the burners. In fuel oil combustion, this zone is characterized by a rather high temperature level and an extremely intense heat flux radiated onto the water walls. This may lead to the overheating of the tube metal and the appearance of high-temperature corrosion, resulting in a high concentration of nitrogen oxides in the flame core.

In the vertical section, gas and fuel oil furnaces may be open, with restriction or with cyclone primary furnace. Most industrially made gas and fuel oil-fired boilers are provided with conventional furnaces of prismatic shape with a single-front or double-front (opposite) arrangement of burners. In the single-front arrangement, burners are mounted in several (three or four) tiers. This arrangement is less expensive and more convenient in operation, but cannot ensure uniform filling of the furnace space by the flame and is inapplicable in furnace of a short depth (less than 6m), since temperature and heat absorption of the rear water wall would then increase intolerably.

In an opposite arrangement of burners, the water walls of the furnace operate under more favourable conditions. The flame is concentrated in the central high-temperature zone of the furnace space. The opposite motion of the flames creates unfavourable conditions for turbulization and better fuel burn-up in the tail portions of the flames and, under identical conditions, results in an increase in the heat release rate in the flame core zone by $20 \sim 30\%$. A constriction in the furnace can increase flow turbulization in the flame core zone and in the zone where fuel afterburning occurs at the outlet from the combustion chamber.

In an experimental series of steam boilers for 300-MW monobloc units, a new proposal is to organize combustion in opposite cyclone-type primary furnaces in order to decrease the itensity of heat flows onto the furnace water walls. The high turbulization of flow in the cyclone primary furnace enables $85 \sim 90\%$ of the fuel to be burned. Cyclone primary furnaces are covered with pinfinned tubes with carborundum refactory facing. This design, however, leads to a high temperature of the flame and a higher heat flow onto the water walls, making it not the best solution for some kinds of fuel.

Gaseous fuels are known to produce flames of a lower emissivity than fuel oil, so that when a boiler is changed from fuel oil to natural gas firing, heat absorption by the furnace space decrease, while the temperature of combustion products at the outlet from the furnace becomes higher. In open furnaces at the rated load, this temperature difference may be as high as 100℃, which inevitably changes the temperature conditions of subsequent heating surfaces, primarily that of superheater. In open furnace with multi-tier single-front burner arrangement, the temperature of the gas at the furnace outlet is equalized in such cases by changing the pattern of the flame core: when burning natural gas, only two or three lowermost burner tiers are in operation, for a change from gas to fuel oil, burners of the upper tiers are fired; in later designs, the gases are recirculated into the furnace to accomplish the same purpose.

Recently, it has been proposed to diminish local heat flows on furnace water walls by arranging the burners in the bottom of an open furnace and by controlling the whirling of the secondary air flow. In fuel oil combustion, the degree of whirling is decreased, so that the flame extends to a greater height in the furnace and thus noticeably decrease local heat flows onto the water walls, while the temperature of gases at the furnace outlet rise substantially. When burning natural gas, the degree of whirling is increased to make the flame wider and shorter.

Words and Expressions

auxiliary [ɔːgˈziljəri] a. 辅助的, 附加的
facility [fəˈsiliti] n. 设备, 装置, 机构
horizontal [ˌhɔriˈzɔnt] n. 水平面, 水平的物体
incline [inˈklain] v. 倾斜
flux [flʌks] n. 流动, 流量
turbulization [təːbjulaiˈzeiʃən] n. 湍流, 紊流, 涡流
proposal [prəˈpəuzəl] n. 建议, 计划
carborundm [ˌkaːbəˈrʌndəm] n. 金刚砂, 碳化硅
emissivity [imiˈsiviti] n. 发射率, 发射性, 辐射系数
local [ˈləukəl] a. 地方的, 当地的

5.11 Boiler Design

A boiler may be a unit complete in itself without auxiliary heat absorbing equipment, or it may constitute a rather small part of a large steam generating complex in which the steam is generated primarily in the furnace tubes, and the convection surface consists of a superheater, reheater, steaming economizer and air heater. In the latter case, it is possible to consider that a drum-type boiler comprises only the steam drum and the screen tubes between the furnace and the superheater. However, the furnace water-wall tubes, and usually a number of side-wall and support tubes in the convection portion of the unit, discharge steam into the drum and therefore effectively form a part of the boiler.

In the case of the Universal-Pressure boiler, there is no steam drum, but rather an arrangement of tubes in which steam is generated and superheated. Whether the boiler is a drum-or once-through type, whether it is an individual unit or a small part of a large complex, it is necessary in design to give proper consideration to the performance required from the total complex of the steam generating unit. Within this framework, the important items which must be accomplished in boiler design are the following:

1. Determine the heat to be absorbed in the boiler and other heat transfer equipment, the optimum efficiency to use, and the type of fuel or fuels for which the unit is to be designed. When a particular fuel is selected, determine the amount of fuel required, the necessary or preferred preheated air temperature and the quantities of air required and flue gas to be generated.

2. Determine the size and shape required for the furnace, giving consideration to location, the space requirements of burners of fuel bed, and incorporating sufficient furnace volume to accomplish complete

combustion. Provision must also be made for properhandling of the ash contained in the fuel, and watercooled surface must be provided in the furnace walls to reduce the gas temperature leaving the furnace to the desired value.

3. The general disposition of convection heating surfaces must be so planned that the superheater and reheater, when provided, are located at the optimum temperature zone where the gas temperature is high enough to afford good heat transfer from the gas to the steam, yet not so high as to result in excessive tube temperatures or excessive fouling from ash in the fuel.

While there is flexibility in the location of saturation or boiler surface, there must be enough total convection surface either before or after the superheater to transfer the heat required to heat the feedwater to saturation temperature and to generate the remainder of the steam required which is not generated in the furnace. This can be accomplished without an economizer, or an economizer can be provided to heat the feedwater to saturation temperature or even to generate up to 20% of the full-load steam requirement.

The foregoing must be accomplished in a design that provides for proper cleanliness of heating surfaces without buildup of slag or ash deposits and without corrosion of pressure parts.

4. Pressure parts must be designed in accordance with applicable codes using approved materials with stresses not exceeding those allowable at the temperatures experienced during operation.

5. A tight boiler setting or enclosure must be constructed around the furnace, boiler, superheater, reheater and air heater, and gastight flues or ducts must be provided to convey the gases of combustion to the stack.

6. Supports for pressure parts and setting must be designed with adequate consideration for expansion and local requirements, including

wind and earthquake loading.

Combustion data

In most areas there are several fuels available and their availability and cost may be expected to change during the lifetime of the plant, with the result that the unit must be designed to burn more than one fuel. It is usually possible to determine which fuel is the most difficult from the standpoint of combustion and ash handling, and the unit is therefore designed for the most difficult fuel which will be used.

After the steam requirements-steam flow, steam pressure and temperature-and boiler feedwater temperature are determined, the required rate of heat absorption, q, is determined from the equation:

$$q = w'(h'_2 - h'_1) + w''(h''_2 - h''_1) \qquad (5.1)$$

where:

q = rate of heat absorption, Btu/hr

w' = primary steam or feedwater flow, lb/hr

w'' = reheat steam flow, lb/hr

h'_1 = enthalpy of feedwater entering, Btu/lb

h'_2 = enthalpy of primary steam leaving superheater, Btu/lb

h''_1 = enthalpy of steam entering reheater, Btu/lb

h''_2 = enthalpy of steam leaving reheater, Btu/lb

To determine unit efficiency, it is necessary to know the temperature of the flue gas leaving the unit. This temperature may be set at the point where further addition of heating surface to reduce gas temperature would not be justified by the increased economy obtained. In the case of sulfur-bearing fuels, flue gas temperature is usually kept above the dew point to avoid sulfur corrosion of economizer or air heater surfaces.

The efficiency of combustion is 100 minus the sum of the heat losses expressed in percent. For a fuel with known characteristics and a given flue gas temperature, heat losses are evaluated by methods. The fuel input rate is then determined from equations (5.2).

$$w_F = q/(Q_H \times \text{eff}) \qquad (5.2)$$

where:

w_F = fuel input rate, lb/hr

Q_H = high heat value of fuel, Btu/lb

eff = efficiency

From the quantity of fuel to be burned per hr, the corresponding weight of air required and the weight of combustion gases produced are determined.

Furnace design

When pulverized-coal or Cyclone-Furnace firing is used, the wall(s) in which the burners or cyclones are located must be designed to accommodate them and the necessary fuel- and air-supply lines. Minimum clearances, established by experience, must be maintained between burners to avoid interference of the fuel streams from the various burners with each other. Minimum clearances must also be provided between burners and side walls and between each burner and the opposite wall to avoid flame impingement on furnace walls with consequent possible overheating of wall tubes or excessive deposits of ash or slag.

Where fuel is burned on stokers or hearths, the size of the furnace is usually set by providing a plan area based on a specified release of heat per sq ft of grate area per hr. These fuel burning rates are based on experience and vary for different types of stokers.

The furnace must also be proportioned so that combustion is completed with due regard to the factors of temperature, turbulence and time.

Adequate combustion temperature is partly a function of burner (or other fuel-burning equipment) design, i. e. , the burner equipment must be designed to provide the proper mixing of air and gas, and it must be sized for the job to be done so that the burner is not over-or underloaded. Likewise, there must not be too much cooling surface in the furnace in proportion to the fuel to be burned. Preheated air is beneficial in obtaining adequate combustion temperature, and is required for pulverizedcoal and Cyclone-Furnace firing, as well as for residual or heavy oils.

Turbulence is primarily a function of the fuel-burning equipment, and its importance lies in supplying air, not only to individual fuel particles but also to any unburned or partially burned gases until combustion is completed.

The time factor is fulfilled primarily by providing sufficient furnace volume so that the combustion gases remain in the furnace long enough to assure completeness of combustion.

Water-cooled walls. Most modern boiler furnaces have all walls water-cooled. This not only reduces maintenance on the furnace walls, but also serves to reduce the gas temperature entering the convection bank to the point where slag deposit and superheater corrosion can be controlled by sootblowers.

Furnace wall tubes are spaced on close centers to obtain maximum heat absorption. Tangent tube construction, used on earlier units, has been replaced with "membrane walls" in which a steel bar or membrane is welded between adjacent tubes. This construction, used on both natural- and forced-circulation units for all types of firing, consists of flat wall sections composed of panels of single rows of tubes on centers wider than a tube diameter connected by means of a membrane bar securely welded to the tube on its centerline. This results in a continuous wall surface of rugged, pressuretight construction capable of transferring a maximumamount of heat to the tube. The individual panels are of a width and length suitable for economical manufacture and assembly, with bottom and top headers attached in the shop prior to shipment for field assembly. Membrane walls with refractory lining are used in the lower furnace walls of cyclone-fired units.

Handing of ash. In the case of coal and, to a lesser extent with oil, an extremely important consideration is the presence of ash in the fuel. If this ash is not properly considered in the design and operation, it can and does deposit not only on furnace walls and floor, but through the convection banks. This not only reduces the heat absorbed by the unit, but increases draft loss, corrodes pressure parts, and eventually can cause shutdown of the unit for cleaning and repairs. With certain fuels the proper handling of ash constitutes an overriding consideration in the design of furnaces, boilers, and other heat transfer equipment.

In coal-fired furnaces the ash problems are more severe. There are two approaches to the handling of ash, namely, the dry-ash furnace and the slag-tap furnace. *Dry-ash furnace*. In the dry-ash furnace, which is particularly applicable to coals with high ash fusion temperatures, the furnace is provided with a hopper bottom and with sufficient cooling surface so that the ash impinging on furnace walls or hopper bottom is solid and dry and can be removed essentially as dry particles. When pulverized coal is burned in a dryasy furnace, about 80% of the ash is carried through the convection banks; most of this fly ash is normally removed by particulate-removal equipment located just ahead of the stack.

Slag-tap furnace. With many coals having low ash fusion temperatures, it is difficult to utilize a dry-bottom furnace because the slag is either molten or sticky and tends to cling and build up on furnace walls and bottom. The slag-tap furnace has been developed to handle coals of these types. The most successful form of the slag-tap furnace is that used in coniunction with Cyclone-Furnace firing. The furnace comprises a two-stage arrangement. In the lower part of the furnace, gas temperature is maintained highenough so that the slag drops in liquid form onto a floor where a pool of liquid slag is maintained and tapped into a slag tank containing water. In the upper part of the furnace, the gases are cooled below the ash fusion point so that ash carried over into the convection banks is dry and does not adhere.

Convection boiler surface

The gas temperature leaving the furnace or entering the boiler depends mainly on the ratio of the heat released to the amount of furnace-wall cooling surface installed. Because the cost of furnace-wall cooling surface is relatively higher than that of boiler surface, the furnace size and surface are limited to the amount required to lower the gas temperature entering the convection tube banks sufficiently to avoid ash deposits.

The first few rows of tubes in the convection bank may be boiler tubes widely spaced to provide gas lanes wide enough to prevent plugging with ash and slag and to facilitate cleaning. These widely spaced boiler tubes are known as the slag screen or boiler screen. In many large units they are used to support the furnace rear wall tubes. These screen tubes receive heat by radiation from the furnace, and by radiation and convection from the combustion gases passing through them.

In the larger current units, the superheater generally replaces the boiler screen or, if not , is located immediately beyond it, The gas temperature entering the superheater must be high enough to give the superheat desired with a reasonable amount of heating surface and the use of economical materials. The arrangement . shows two or three rows of boilerscreen tubes ahead of superheater tules on close spacing. However it may also be necessary to locate several rows of superheater tubes on wide spacing.

Design of boiler surface after the superheater will depend on the particular type of unit selected, desired gas temperature drop, and acceptable gas pressure drop (draft loss) through the boiler surface.

The object in the design of convection heating surfaces is to establish the combination of tube diameter, tube spacing, length of tubes, number of tubes wide and deep, and gas baffling that will give the desired gas temperature drop with the pressure drop permissible.

Heating surface and pressure drop are directly interrelated since both are primarily dependent on gas massvelocity. If either heating surface or pressure drop is increased, the other must decrease in order to maintain the desired gas temperature drop (heat transfer). Hence there is an optimum gas mass velocity which results in the optimum combination of heating surface and gas pressure drop.

For a given gas mass velocity (lb of gas per hr per sq ft of gas flow channel) or for a given gas velocity, a considerably higher gas film conductance, heat absorption, and draft loss result when the gases flow at right angles to the tubes (crossflow) than when they flow parallel to the tubes (longitudinal flow). Gas turns between tube banks generally add draft loss with little or no benefit to heat absorption and should be designed for easy flow.

From a long record of experience, given sets of conditions for each fuel to be burned have been effectively established as the conditions of economic practice. While these conditions vary as improvements occur over a period of years, at any particular time competitive economics acts to hold most of the variables involved within a fairly limited range.

Design of pressure parts

Boilers have achieved the safety and reliability which they now have through the use of sound materials and safe practices for determining acceptable stresses in tubes, drums and other pressure parts. Boilers are always designed to applicable codes. Most stationary boilers in the U. S. are designed to the ASME Code. In each case, the stress allowable depends on the maximum temperature to which the part is subjected, and therefore it is important that pressure parts be so designed that design temperatures are known and are not exceeded in operation. In boilers, the material temperatures are normally designed to be only a few degrees above the saturation temperature corresponding to the boiler pressure. In boiler tubes, this is accomplished by providing sufficient water to avoid the occurrence of a DNB, or departure from nucleate boiling. This means that an adequate supply of water must be provided for each tube, and this is particularly important in furnace and screen tubes where heat input it high. Because steam drums have thick walls, it is necessary to limit the heat flow through them to avoid excessively high thermal gradients. Where the drum is penetrated by a number of tube holes, the flow of water through these holes serves to cool the ligaments between. Where the heat input through a drum would be too high, because of high gas temperature or velocity, insulation may be provided on the outside of the drum. This is particularly necessary where there are no tube peretrations to provide cooling.

In a drum-type boiler, equipment is provided in the steam drum for the reduction of moisture and solids in the steam to acceptable values. In once-through boilers, all moisture is evaporated in the tubes where boiling and superheating occur sequentially. In boilers of this type, steam purity depends on maintaining adequate purity of the feedwater.

The boiler safety valve constitutes a very important item in the safety of modern boilers. By law, the boiler design pressure for which the pressure parts must be designed cannot be less than the safety-valve relief pressure. As a practical matter, to avoid unnecessary losses and maintenance from frequent action of the safety valves, the first safety valve should be set to relieve at not less than the desired boiler operating pressure plus about 5%. The operating pressure in the boiler steam drum, in turn, depends on the pressure required at the point of use and the intervening pressure drop. As an example, where the steam is used in a turbine, the boiler operating pressure is determined by adding to the turbine throttle pressure and pressure drop through the steam piping, nonreturn valve, superheater, and drum internals at maximum steam flow.

Boiler supports

Boiler and furnace wall tubes are usually supported by the drums or headers to which they are connected. In the design of proper supports the following considerations are important:

1. The tubes must be so arranged that they will not be subject to excessive bending-moment stresses in carrying the weight of the tubes, drums, other parts which they support, and contained water. When the unit is bottom supported, the tubes must satisfy column requirements.

2. The holding strength of the tube seats must not be exceeded.

3. Provision must be made to accommodate the required expansion of the pressure parts. For a top-supported unit, the hanger rods must be designed to swing at the proper angle, and they must be long enough to take the movement without excessive stresses in either the rods or the pressure parts. Bottom-supported boilers should be anchored only at one point, guided along one line, and allowed to expand freely in all other directions. To reduce the frictional forces and resultant stresses in the

pressure parts, roller saddles or mountings are desirable for bottom-supported heavy loads.

Words and Expressions

water-wall tube   水冷壁管
Univer-Pressure boiler   常压锅炉
flexibility   [ˌfleksə'biliti]   n. 弹性,适应性,机动性
economizer   [i(:)'kɔnəmaizə]   n. 省煤器
pulverizedcoal   煤粉
Cyclone-Furnace firing   旋风炉
handing of ash   灰的处理

5.12　Superheaters and Reheaters

Early in the eighteenth century, it was demonstrated that substantial savings in fuel could be experienced when steam engines were run with some superheat in the steam. In the late 1800's, lubrication problems were encountered with reciprocating engines, but once these were overcome, development of superheaters continued.

Commercial development of the steam turbine hastened the general use of superheat. By 1920 steam temperatures of 650 °F, representing superheats of 250 °F, were generally accepted. In the early 1920's the regenerative cycle, using steam bled from turbines for feedwater heating, was developed to improve station economy without going to higher steam temperatures. At the same time, superheater development permitted raising the steam temperature to 725 °F. A further gain in economy by still higher temperature was at that time limited by allowable superheater tube-metal temperature. This led to the commercial use of reheat, where the steam leaving the high-pressure stage of the turbine was reheated in a separate reheat superheater and returned at higher temperature and enthalpy to the low-pressure stage.

The first reheat unit for a central station was proposed in 1922 and went into service in September, 1924. It was designed for 650 psi and operated at 550psi and 725 °F. Exhaust steam from the high-pressure turbine was reheated to 725 °F at 135 psi.

Amuch higher-pressure reheat unit, designed in 1924 for 1200 psi and 700 °F primary steam temperature with reheat at 360 psi and 700 °F, went into service in December, 1925.

Advantages of superheat and reheat

When saturated steam is utilized in a steam turbine, the work done results in a loss of energy by the steam and consequent condensation of a portion of the steam, even though there is a drop in pressure. The amount of work that can be done by the turbine is limited by the amount of moisture which can be handled by the turbine without excessive wear on the turbine blades. This is normally somewhere between 10 and 15%. It is possible to increase the amount of work done by moisture separation between turbine stages, but this is economical only in special cases. Even with moisture separation, the total energy that can be transformed to work in the turbine is small compared to the amount of heat required to raise the water from feedwater temperature to saturation and then evaporate it. Thus moisture constitutes the basic limitation in turbine design.

Because a turbine generally transforms the heat of superheat into work without forming moisture, the heat of superheat is essentially all recoverable in the turbine. This is illustrated in the temperature-entropy diagram of the ideal Rankine cycle. Where the heat added to the right of the saturated vapor line is shown as 100% recoverable. While this is not always entirely correct, the Rankine cycle diagrams indicate that this is essentially true.

The foregoing discussion is not specifically applicable at steam pressures in the vicinity of the critical point. The term "superheat" is not really appropriate in defining the temperature of the working fluid at or above the critical point. However, even at pressures exceeding 3 208 psia, heat added at temperatures above 705 °F is essentially all recoverable in a turbine.

The benefits of superheat are illustrated graphically in Fig. 5.7, which shows the reduction in cycle heat rate by increasing the steam temperature from 900 to 1 100 °F at pressures from 1800 to 3 500 psi.

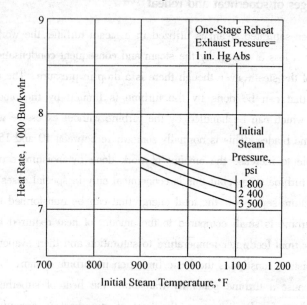

Fig. 5.7 Effect of changes in steam temperature and pressure on performance of ideal Rankine cycle with one-stage reheat.

Superheater types

The original and somewhat basic type of superheater and reheater was the convection unit, for gas temperatures where heat transfer by radiation was very small. With a unit of this type the steam temperature leaving the superheater increases with boiler output because of the decreasing percentage of heat input that is absorbed in the furnace, leaving more heat available for superheater absorption. Since convection heat transfer rates are almost a direct function of output, the total absorption in the superheater per lb of steam increases with increase in boiler output (see Fig. 5.8). This effect is increasingly pronounced the further the superheater is removed from the furnace, i. e. , the lower the gas temperature entering the superheater.

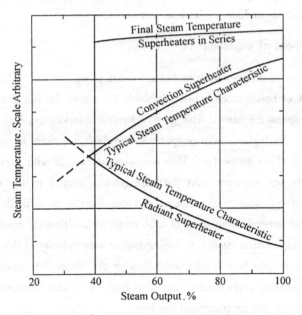

Fig. 5.8 A substantially uniform final steam temperature over a range of output can be attained by a series arrangement of radiant and convection superheater components.

On the other hand, the radiant superheater receives its heat through radiation and practically none from convection. Because the heat absorption of furnace surfaces does not increase in direct proportion to boiler output but at a considerably lesser rate, the curve of radiant superheat as a function of load slopes downward with increase in boiler output.

In certain cases the two opposite-sloping curves have been coordinated by the combination of radiant and convection superheaters to give flat superheat curves over wide ranges in load, as typically indicated in Fig. 5.8. A separately fired superheater has the characteristic that it can be fired to produce a flat superheat curve.

Development of superheaters

The early convection superheaters were placed above or behind a deep bank of boiler tubes in order to shield them from the fire or from the higher temperature gases. The greater heat absorption required in the superheater for higher steam temperatures made it necessary to move the superheater closer to the fire. This new location brought with it problems which were not apparent with the superheaters located in the original lower-gas-temperature zone. Steam- and gas-distribution difficulties and instances of general overheating of tube metal were ultimately resolved by improved superheater design, including higher mass velocity of the steam. This increased the heat conductance through the steam film, resulting in lower tube-metal temperatures, and also improved steam distribution by increasing pressure drop through the tubes.

Steam mass velocity in modern super-heaters ranges from as low as 100 000 to 1 000 000 lb/sq ft, hr or higher depending on pressure, steam and gas temperatures, and the tolerable pressure drop in the superheater.

The fundamental considerations governing super-heater design apply also to reheater design. However, the pressure drop in reheaters is critical because the gain in heat rate with the reheat cycle can be completely nullified by too much pressure drop through the reheater system. Hence, steam mass flows are generally somewhat lower in the reheater.

Tube sizes. Plain cylindrical tubes of 2-in. or $2\frac{1}{2}$-in. outside diameter predominate in superheaters and reheaters in stationary practice. Smaller diameters (1-in. or $1\frac{1}{4}$-in.) are used to conserve weight and space in marine units. Steam pressure drop is higher and alignment more difficult with the smaller diameters. Larger diameters bring about higher pressure stresses.

Recent designs have called for greater spans between supports for horizontal superheater tubes, and for wider tube spacing or fewer tubes per row to avoid slag accumulation. The $2\frac{1}{2}$-in. tube has met these new conditions with a minimum sacrifice of the smaller-tube advantages, and 3-in. tubes are used to advantage in some cases. When steam temperatures increase, the allowable stresses may force a return to the smallerdiameter thinner-wall tube.

Plain tubes are used almost exclusively in modern superheater practice. Extended surface on superheater tubes in the form of fins, rings, or studs not only makes gas-side cleaning difficult, but the added thickness increases metal temperature and thermal stress beyond tolerable limits.

Relationships in superheater design

Effective superheater design calls for the resolution of several factors. The outstanding considerations are:

1. The steam temperature desired.

2. The superheater surface required to give this steam temperature.

3. The gas temperature zone in which the surface is to be located.

4. The type of steel, alloy, or other material best suited to make up the surface and the supports.

5. The rate of steam flow through the tubes (mass velocity), which is limited by the permissible steam pressure drop but which, in turn, exerts a dominant control over tube-metal temperatures.

6. The arrangement of surface to meet the characteristics of the fuels anticipated, with particular reference to the spacing of the tubes to prevent accumulations of ash and slag or to provide for the removal of such formations in their early stages.

7. The physical design and type of superheater as a structure.

A change in any one of the first six items will call for a counterbalancing change in all other items.

The steam temperature desired in advanced power station design is the maximum for which the superheater designer and manufacturer can produce an economical structure. Economics in this case requires the resolution of two interrelated factors-first, or investment cost and the later cost of upkeep for minimum operating troubles, outages, and replacements. A higher first cost is warranted if the upkeep cost is thereby reduced sufficiently to cover , in a reasonable time, the extra initial cost. The steam temperature desired is, therefore, based on the complete coordinated knowledge available for the optimum evaluation of the combination of the other five items and the necessities of the particular project. Operating experience in recent years has resulted in the use of approximately 1 000 °F steam temperature both for primary superheat and reheat in nearly all large units purchased for installation in the U. S.

After the steam temperature desired is actually set or specified, the next consideration is the amount of surface necessary to give this superheat. The amount of superheater surface required is dependent on the four remaining items and, since there is no single correlation, the amount of surface must be determined by trial, locating it in a zone of gas temperature that is likely to be satisfactory. In the so-called standard boilers, the zone is fairly well established by the physical arrangements and by the space preempted for superheater surface.

Steam mass velocity, steam pressure drop, and super-heater tube-metal temperatures are calculated after the amount of surface is established for the trial location and the trial tube spacing. The proper type of material is then selected for the component tubes, headers, and other parts. It may be necessary to compare several arrangements to obtain an optimum combination that will:

1. Require an alloy of lesser cost.

2. Give a more reasonable steam pressure drop without jeopardizing the tube temperatures.

3. Give a higher steam mass velocity in order to lower the tube temperatures.

4. Give a different spacing of tubes that will provide more protection against the ash accumulations with uncertain types of fuel.

5. Permit closer spacing of the tubes, thereby making a more economical arrangement for a fuel supply that is known to be favorable.

6. Give an arrangement of tubes which will reduce the draft loss for an installation where draft loss evaluation is crucial.

7. Permit the superheater surface to be located in a zone of a higher gas temperature, with a consequent saving in surface, that will compensate for deviation from a standard arrangement.

It is possible to achieve a practical design with optimum economic and operational characteristics and with all criteria reasonably satisfied, but a large measure of experience and the application of sound physical principles are required for satisfactory results.

Relationships in reheater design

The same general similarity exists between superheater and reheater considerations, but the reheater is limited in ruggedness of design by the permissible steam pressure drop. Steam mass velocities in reheater tubes should be sufficient to keep the steam-film temperature drop below 150 °F. Ordinarily this may be done with less than 5% pressure drop through the reheater tubes. This allows another 5% pressure drop for the reheater piping and valves without exceeding the usual 10% total allowable.

Metals for tubes

Oxidation resistance, maximum allowable stress, and economics determine the choice of materials for superheater and reheater tubes. The use of carbon steel should be extended as far as these considerations permit. Beyond this point, carefully selected alloy steels should be used.

Words and Expressions

superheater ['sju:pəhi:tə] n. 过热器
reheater ['ri:'hi:tə] n. 再热器
exhaust [ig'zɔ:st] vt. 取出,弄空
temperature-entropy diagram 温熵图
saturated vapor 饱和蒸汽
upkeep ['ʌpki:p] n. 保养,维修,维持
installation [ˌinstə'leiʃən] n. 安装,设置,装置
accumulation [əkju:mju'leiʃ(ə)n] n. 积聚,堆积物

6

Turbine

6.1 Steam Turbine

A turbine is a rotary engine which is driven by a stream of fluid (liquid or gas) directed on to the blades of the rotor. In a steam turbine this fluid is steam. Part of the heat and pressure energy of steam are changed into mechanical energy by imparting rotary motion to turbine blade wheels. In turbines the rotary motion is obtained by direct action of the steam on the blade wheels or rotors. The speed of the flow of the fluid, which in water turbines is produced by a fall in level, in steam turbines is produced by a fall in pressure of the steam from the boiler. The steam is expanded from a higher to a lower pressure in nozzles or in the blading, and then increases its speed at the expense or in the of its heat and pressure. The speed of the steam is then reduced by doing work on the moving blades.

The great advantages of the turbine are freedom from vibration and noise, smooth and uniform rotary force, and ability to handle large quantities of fluid-in this case steam. Its simplicity and reliability type of engine for driving pumps, blowers, and other equipment. In these cases the turbine's most efficient speed is usually much higher than that of the machine it is driving, so a speed reduction gear usually has to be used. Steam turbines do not work very efficiently in small sizes.

Very large steam turbines in conjunction with speed reduction gears are used for driving ships; in fact, a steam turbine is the only practicable kind of engine for driving ships. It is in large electrical power stations that the steam turbine reaches its highest development, and some new power stations are being equipped with steam turbines producing more than 600 000 horsepower each.

The steam turbine consists of the following essential parts:

1. A casing usually divided at the horizontal centerline, with the halves bolted together for ease of assembly and disassembly, and containing the stationary blade system.

2. A rotor with the moving blades on wheels, and with bearing journals on the ends of the rotor.

3. A bearing box in the casing, supporting the shaft.

4. A governor and valve system for regulating the speed and power of the turbine by controlling the steam flow, and an oil system for lubrication of the bearings and a set of safety devices.

5. A coupling of some sort to connect with the driven machine.

6. Pipe connection to a supply of steam at the inlet, and to an exhaust system at the outlet of the casing.

Fig.6.1 shows a simple form of impulse turbine. In this the steam issues from a stationary nozzle (or nozzles) which is curved so as to direct the jet on to a ring of blades attached to a rotating wheel or disc. These blades are shaped to 'catch' the steam from the nozzle smoothly, and they are curved so that they change the direction of the jet and in so doing receive an impulse which pushes them forward.

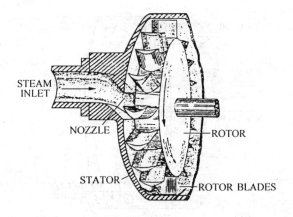

Fig. 6.1   Diagram of an impulse turbine
The steam, directed on to the blades, gives them
an impulse which rotates the rotor

If, instead of using fixed nozzles and a separate wheel, we were to mount the nozzle itself on a wheel, the reaction of the issuing jet would drive it in the opposite direction to the impulse wheel. The very first steam turbine was a pure reaction turbine of this type, but for various reasons it is never used nowadays.

There is another kind of turbine (Fig. 6.2) which combines the principles of impulse and reaction but is usually referred to simply as a 'reaction' turbine. An essential characteristic of a nozzle is that the passage narrows from the inlet onwards, and consequently the fluid which enters at a relatively low speed must come out at a much higher speed. The increase in speed is produced by a drop of pressure, the pressure of the fluid being higher as it enters the nozzle than as it leaves. The casing in Fig. 6.2 carries a complete ring of nozzles which, as in the impulse turbine, are curved and direct the steam on to the moving blades at the most effective angle. The moving blades are also nozzles, similar to the stationary nozzles but facing the other way, and in addition to catching and

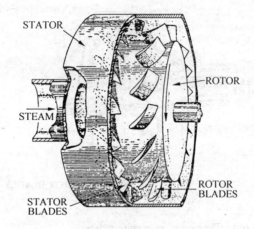

Fig.6.2 Diagram of a reaction turbine

The stator blades form nozzles through which the steam is accelerated and directed on to the nozzles formed by the rotor blades

deflecting the steam issuing from the stationary nozzles, they also accelerate it, the drive coming half from an impulse and half from a reaction force. The jet speed in this type of turbine is half what it is in an impulse turbine having the same blade speed. In either case the steam leaves the moving blades more or less at right angles to the direction of motion of the blades.

The simplest type of steam turbine has one stage; that is , one row each of stationary and of moving blades. Such turbines are commonly used for power outputs of a few hundred horse-power at most, with moderate inlet pressures and temperatures, and for an atmospheric or higher pressure at the exhaust. Under these conditions it is possible to use the steam with adequate efficiency in a single stage.

To obtain as much power as possible from each pound of coal burned in the boiler it is necessary to work with a high steam pressure and temperature at the inlet to the turbine and as low a pressure as possible at the exhaust. By condensing the exhaust steam in a separate condenser, using a large quantity of cooling water, a very low exhaust pressure can be maintained and the condensed steam pumped back to the boiler as pure feed water. If the steam were allowed to expand from boiler pressure to condenser pressure in one step, the jet velocity from the nozzle would be so great that it would be impossible to build a turbine to run fast enough to utilize such a high jet speed efficiently-indeed, a single stage steam turbine normally has a very low efficiency. For large power output, and for the high inlet pressures and temperatures and low exhaust pressures which are required for good thermal efficiency, both with impulse and reaction turbines, a single stage is not adequate. Steam under such conditions has high available energy and for its efficient utilization the turbine must have many stages in series. Also, under these conditions the exhaust volume flow becomes large, and it is necessary to have more than one exhaust stage; for example, a large turbine may have three are alternately rows of stationary blades carried in the casing and rows of blades attached to the rotor, arranged so that the steam is directed to enter each row of stationary and moving blades at the proper angle. The stationary blades are always nozzles, the rotor blades are also nozzles in the case of a reaction turbine but only guide channels in the case of an impulse turbine.

The successive stages are normally arranged side by side along a horizontal axis, constituting what is called an "axial flow" turbine. The steam enters at one end and leaves at the other, or, if the flow is very big, the steam may enter at the middle and leave at both ends, an arrangement called "double flow". The casing consists of a bottom half, which usually carries the bearings that support the rotor, and a top half, which is bolted to the bottom half at the horizontal joint after the rotor has been placed in position.

When the stages are very numerous it has proved most practicable to use two or more casings or cylinders, usually arranged in line and with the shafts coupled together.

Modern turbines are supplied by the boiler with steam that is highly superheated. As the steam passes through the turbine, its pressure and temperature fall until at a certain stage all the superheat is lost, and thereafter drops of water are formed by condensation of some of the steam. These drops can damage the blades and reduce the turbine efficiency, and this is one reason why the steam, after passing through the high-pressure turbine, is sometimes re-superheated before entering the medium-pressure turbine.

Words and Expressions

rotary ['rəutəri] a. 旋转的,转动的
blade [bleid] n. 叶片,刀片
rotor ['rəutə] n. 转子,旋转部
blading ['bleidiŋ] n. 叶片(装置)
nozzle ['nɔzl] n. 喷管,喷嘴
reliability [rilaiə'biliti] n. 可靠性
blower ['bləuə] n. 鼓风机
lubricate [lu:bri'keit] v. 润滑
inlet ['inlet] n. 入口,插入物,注入
cylinder ['silində] n. 气缸,圆筒
superheat n. v. 过热
medium-pressure a. 中压的
by imparting to 通过把……给与
in conjunction with 与……相结合
in series 串联地,多级地
side by side 并排地

6.2 Gas Turbine

This is a form of internal combustion engine in which air, heated by burning fuel, expands, and in doing so is made to turn a specially shaped wheel (the turbine wheel) directly, instead of pushing pistons up and down as in the reciprocating engine.

Because of the continuous, smooth nature of its internal processes, the gas turbine, like the steam turbine, is almost completely free from vibration; and this, together with its essential simplicity, makes it more reliable and easier to maintain. It is lighter and less bulky than the piston engine, and it can be built in larger sizes to give higher powers from single power units. For all these reasons, the use of gas turbines is increasing for all forms of transport, on land, sea, and in the air. It may be wondered, in view of all these advantages, why the gas turbine engine was not introduced sooner, especially since the general idea of a gas turbine is not a new one. Indeed, the idea of using the energy in hot gases to turn a wheel directly is perhaps a more obvious one than the more complicated system employed in piston engines. In fact, the turbine principle is more difficult to apply in practice. The first small and relatively inefficient gas turbines were operated by the exhaust gases from piston engines, and these were used to drive superchargers. It was not until the 1930's that successful self-operating gas turbines were made, and used for aircraft propulsion. About the same time that aircraft turbines were being achieved, gas turbines had been developed for stationary use and as power units for railway locomotives.

The gas turbine consists essentially of an air compressor, a combustion chamber, and a turbine wheel.

Compressors Two basic types of compressors are used in gas turbines: axial and centrifugal. In a few special cases a combination type known as a mixed wheel, which is partially centrifugal and partially axial, has been used. The axialflow compressor is the most widely used because of its ability to handle large volumes of air at high efficiency. For small gas turbines in the range of 500 hp. and less, the centrifugal replaces the axial.

Combustors Combustors, sometimes referred to as combustion chambers, for gas turbines take a wide variety of shapes and forms, for example, the annular, can-type or cannular. The gas turbine combustor components are fuel nozzle, combustion section and transition section to turbine inlet. Air for the combustion chamber is forced into the engine by a compressor . Fuel is mixed with the compressed air and burned in combustors . The heat energy thus released is changed by the turbine into totary energy . Because of the high initial temperature of the combustion products, excess air is used to cool the combustion products to the turbine inlet design temperature.

Turbine wheels Two types of gas turbine wheels are used: radial-inflow, and axial-flow. Small gas turbines use the radialflow wheel. For large volume flows, axial turbine wheels are used almost exclusively. Although some of the turbines used in the small gas turbine plants are of the simple impulse type, most high performance turbines are neither pure impulse nor pure reaction. The high performance turbines are normally designed for varying amounts of reaction and impulse to give optimum performance.

The compressor and the turbine wheel are on the same shaft and rotate together. The hot gases from the combustion chamber strike the turbine blades, driving the shaft and thus rotating the compressor. Air from the atmosphere is sucked into the inlet ports of the compressor and flows forward through each blade stage (the axial-flow compressor). As the air pressure increases, its volume decreases until maximum compression is reached at the last stage. The highly compressed (and the high temperature) air is then discharged into the duct leading to the combustion chamber. This unit has one or more fuel nozzles, through which the fuel is sprayed to mix with the moving air. In starting , the fuel spray is ignited by using of spark plugs. Once ignited, the fuel-air mixture burns continuously, so that the ignition can be switched off.

Instead of the single combustion chamber, which is the annular form of the chamber, a number of separate chambers, known as can-type or cannular chambers, are often used. Thus in a typical aircraft gas turbine, eight to ten can-type chambers, each with its own fuel nozzle, are employed.

The products of combustion leave the chamber through a duct and fixed guides or nozzes to enter the turbine. Here the gases flow axially, falling in both temperature and pressure as they transmit most of their energy to the turbine wheel.

Fig. 6.3 illustrates diagrammatically the basic principles of this type of engine, and makes clear the technical difficulties which delayed the development of successful gas turbines. (A) is the air intake through which air passes to the compressor (B), and then into the combustion chamber (C), at a high pressure and hotter than it was owing to the compression (to at least 50 lb. per square inch). Fuel is injected into the compressed air, and burned with high efficiency in the combustion chambers. The combustion raises the temperature to 850°C. or more, and this expands the air. The resultant gases at high pressure and temperature blow continuously on to the turbine wheel (D) which drives the compressor. After they leave D, the gases, still at a fairly high pressure and temperature and still expanding, can be used in two ways. On the gas turbine proper, and in turbo-prop aircraft engines, the issuing gases drive a further turbine wheel (or series of wheels) (E), which is fixed to the

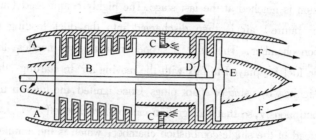

Fig.6.3 Diagram of a Gas Turbine
A. Air intake. B. Compressor. C. Combustion chambers. D. Turbine wheel driving compressor. E Turbine wheel driving propeller. F. Tailpipe through which gases escape. G. Propeller shaft. The large arrow shows the direction of flight, the smaller ones the direction of air and burnt gases

power shaft. This shaft may drive a propeller, as in turbo-prop engines or, for example, a motorcar gear-box, as in a gas turbine car.

In the pure jet engine, on the other hand, the issuing gases pass straight out into the air through a tail pipe, forming a high-speed jet which pushes the engine forward on the reaction principle, like a rocket. In the 'by-pass' jet aircraft engine there is a low-pressure and a high-pressure compressor. Some of the air from the first by-passes the second and the combustion chamber, giving a cooler, slower, heavier jet of air in the tail pipe, more suitable for slower jet aircraft.

The material of the turbine wheels is continuously exposed to the very hot gases, and the demands made on the metals used for the blading of a gas turbine are very heavy-even more than for a steam turbine. Another problem concerns the efficiency of the air compressor; if this is inefficient, it will absorb too much power itself, and so much of the available energy of the gases will be used up in the turbine wheel (D) that there will be little left to deliver as thrust, or as useful power from the second wheel (E). Gas turbines therefore, could not be developed until very efficient air compressors had been evolved, well as steels or other metals metals able to resist high temperatures.

For some purposes, the piston type of engine is still preferable to the gas turbine. Its fuel consumption is usually appreciably lower for a given power output, but the gas turbine is lighter. Also it is not easy to make satisfactory gas turbines of low power output, suitable, for example, for road vehicles although efforts are being made to solve this problem.

The gas turbine has special advantages for aircraft propulsion, owing to its low weight and small size, and it has found in aviation its first important application and the greatest stimulus for its development. As an aero-engine it is used either for pure jet propulsion or to drive a conventional propeller.

Jet-propulsion engines are most efficient at high altitudes and high airspeeds and are particularly suited for high-performance military aircraft. Modern military jet-propulsion engines are capable of producing tremendous power. In emergencies this can be augmented still further with the aid of an afterburner, which adds heat to the gases just before they enter the exhaust nozzle. This afterburning increases their velocity and adds to the forward thrust or the engine.

Another gas-turbine application for aircraft is the turboprop. In this application the gas turbine has two purposes: it drives a conventional propeller, and it produces additional thrust by means of the reactive force of the jet leaving the exhaust nozzle of the engine. The advantage of short takeoff inherent in propeller-driven aircraft is thus combined with the faster and higher flying capabilities of the conventional jet-propulsion engine.

Intermediate between the conventional jet-propulsion engine and the turboprop is a later development called the turbofan engine. It differs from the ordinary jet-propulsion engine in that a fan is located at the inlet that takes in a great deal more air than actually passes through the core of the engine. The fan compresses this air slightly and then delivers most of it though a bypass duct around the engine, where , it is accelerated and released with a higher velocity than it had at intake, thus adding to the thrust of the engine. The remainder of the air flows through the core of the engine, where it is compressed, heated and expanded through the turbine and exhaust nozzle as in a conventional jet.

The ratio of air bypassed through the duct surrounding the core of the engine to that passing through the core is called the bypass ratio. This varies widely according to application. Bypass ratio as high as 8 to 1 are common in large turbofan engines. In general, high bypass ratios and high compression ratios result in improved fuel economy.

The turbofan engine has a number of advantages. The added thrust of the engine eliminates the need for carrying heavy additional loads of water sometimes employed for injection to increase the thrust of conventional engines during take off on warm days. When operating within the proper speed and altitude range, fuel savings of the order of 20 percent can be realized. These advantages have made this type of engine the favourite for commercial use on very large jet aircraft.

In the field of electric-power generation, the gas turbine, as compared with the diesel engine and steam turbine, are limited in capacity by the fact that the pressure involved is low, making it necessary to employ large turbines and compressors in order to handle the huge volumes of air required. For this reason no serious attempt has been made to design a gas-turbine-gas-power plant in the modern central-station to replace steam power plant in which single units as large as 1 200 000 kilowatts have been built.

Three applications deserve special mention: (1) operation in combination with steam power plants as a means of increasing the overall efficiency; (2) for standby and peakload service; and (3) for portable power plants. A promising combined steam-turbine-gas-turbine power plant is one in which high temperature exhaust gases from a conventional gas turbine are employed to supply oxygen to the furnace of a steam boiler in place of preheated combustion air. This combination is feasible because the gases exhausted from a gas turbine still contain about 80 percent of the oxygen in the air supplied to the compressor inlet. Such an arrangement is capable of increasing substantially the overall efficiency of the plant. It also offers savings in size and weight of the boilers required, less building volume, quicker starting of the boiler, and elimination of the forced and induced draft fans normally required by the boiler.

Other ways in which the gas turbine can be employed to improve the efficiency of a steam power plant are to use the exhaust gases for feedwater heating or for the generation of steam in an exhaust-heat boiler.

The gas turbine offers an attractive means for providing additional peak-load and standby power. It can often be installed for this purpose at lower cost than additional steam or hydroelectric capacity. Furthermore, it offers the advantages of virtually automatic operation, simplicity, small space requirements, and minimum maintenance. Another similar application is for end-of-the-line voltage-booster service on long distance transmission lines. A third application is for portable power plants. Here the gas turbine can be mounted on railroad cars or barges for emergency use.

Words and Expressions

piston ['pistən] n. 活塞
supercharge ['sju:pətʃa:dʒə] n. 增压器
propulsion [prə'pʌlʃən] n. 推进(装置),推力
locomotive ['ləukəməutiv] n. 机车 a. 运动的

chamber ['tʃeimbə] n. 室,容器
centrifugal [sen'trifjugəl] a. 离心的
combustor [kəm'bʌstə] n. 燃烧室
annular ['ænjulə] a. 环形的
optimum ['ɔptiməm] n. 最佳值 a. 最佳的
resultant [ri'zʌltənt] a. 总的,生成的 n. 合力,组合
gear-box n. 变速箱
by-pass n. 旁路,支流 a. 旁通 v. 分流
propeller [prə'pelə] n. 螺旋浆,推进器
turbofan n. 涡轮风扇(发动机)
kilowatt ['kiləwɔt] n. 千瓦(特)
peakload ['piːk'laud] n. 峰值负荷
straight out 直接地
is preferable to 优于
of the order of 大约,约为

6.3 Compressor

The most important way in which gases differ from liquids and solids is that they can easily be compressed, or squeezed to occupy a smaller volume. A machine for doing this is known as a compressor, of which the ordinary bicycle pump is the simplest example. There are two main classes of compressor—reciprocating and rotary.

Reciprocating compressors are the type used in the liquefaction of gases, and also to provide a source of power for the familiar pneumatic road drill. They can compress a gas up to 30 000 1b per square inch and more, but they are not suitable for handling large volumes of air at pressures below 50 1b. per square inch.

The reciprocating compressor consists essentially of a cylinder, a piston (p), connecting rod(R), and crankshaft (cs) arranged much the same as in an internal combustion engine. Except at very high pressures, the valves in compressors are not worked mechanically, but are simply thin metal flaps opened and closed by the air itself. As the piston travels downward, it sucks open the inlet valve (v_1), and gas is drawn into the cylinder. On the return stroke the gas in the cylinder is forced out through the delivery valve (v_2), while the pressure in the cylinder holds the inlet valve closed.

The delivery pipe is smaller than the inlet pipe because the gas, being at a higher pressure, occupies a smaller volume. As gas gets hot when compressed, high-pressure compressors must be cooled, either by blowing air or by circulating cooling water in a jacket round the cylinder. A common arrangement is a two-cylinder compressor in which the gas delivered by the first cylinder is cooled before being passed to the second cylinder and further compressed. The gas takes up less room after it has been compressed by the first cylinder and so the second cylinder need not be so large.

The two most important types of rotary compressor are the blade type, and the "positive displacement" type. Until recently, blade—type compressors—of which the ordinary ventilating fan is a simple example—were used only for very low pressures, but now the compressors incorporated into the modern gas turbine can compress air up to 50 lb. per square inch and more. Blade compressors—both ventilating fans and compressors for gas turbines work on either the radial or axial flow principle; in each case the blades are surrounded by a casing in which the compressed air is collected.

With radial-flow compressors the air enters at the centre of the whirling blades and is flung outwards. For higher efficiencies and pressures, however, axialc-flow compressors are used. These work on the same principle as propellers—the blading "screws" the air up to the required pressure, and the air travels through the blades from end to end. They can handle much larger quantities of air for a given overall size of machine, but they must run at high speed and must, therefore, be very carefully manufactured and balanced. The ordinary household electric fan is a simple form of axialflow compressor.

Positive displacement rotary compressors are so called because, as in a reciprocating compressor, the air is pushed through the machine mechanically. A type which is designed for supercharging internal combustion engines consists of a barrel-shaped casing, inside which a rotor with four vanes is mounted out of the centre with the barrel. Air enters at inlet port, is trapped by the vanes as the rotor rotates, and is compressed as the space between the rotor and casing diminishes. The compressed air is delivered at the outlet port.

Words and Expressions

squeeze ['skwi:z] v. 挤,压,使缩减
reciprocate [ri'siprəkeit] v. 往复移动
liquefaction [ˌlikwi'fækson] n. 液化(作用),熔解
pneumatic [nju:'mætik] a. 空气的,气体的,气动的
drill [dril] n. 钻床
crank-shaft n. 曲轴
flap [flæp] n. 风门片
ventilate ['ventileit] v. 使通风,使换气
fling [fliŋ] v. 抛,猛冲
super-charge v. 对……增压
vane [vein] n. 叶片,翼
take up 占据
out of the centre 偏心地

6.4 Gas Turbine Plants

Introduction

A gas turbine plant (Fig. 6.4) consists of a turbo-compressor, combustion chamber (or heat exchanger) and turbine. The plant is started by rotating the compressor-turbine assembly by a starting motor or any other device. When the compressor develops enough pressure to support combustion of the fuel in the combustion chamber, the hot gases can themselves drive the gas turbine, and the plant becomes self-sustaining. The turbine should develop enough power to be able to drive the compressor and load (if any). The output of the plant is the difference between the turbine work and the compressor work. The actual output at the generator terminals will be much less than this.

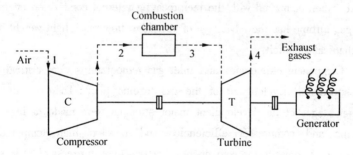

Fig.6.4 A simple open circuit gas turbine plant

A majority of aircraft gas turbine plants use kerosene or gasoline where as other plants can use natural gas, bunker oil and blast furnace gas. Coal or gasified coal can also be used in electric power generating gas turbine plants.

If the gas turbine plant is used as an aircraft engine, the net output at the turbine shaft is used to drive a propeller in a turbo-prop engine, whereas in a turbo-jet engine the turbine output equals the power required to drive the compressor. The output of such a plant is the energy in the exhaust gases which is used for jet propulsion.

The shaft power of a gas turbine plant can also be used for driving electric generators, draft fans, compressors and other industrial devices.

As will be discussed later, the combustion chamber in a large number of industrial applications is replaced by a heat exchanger.

Gas turbine plants can be compared with steam turbine plants; the chief distinguishing features of the gas turbine plants are their high inlet gas temperatures ($t_{max} > 1\ 500$ K) and lower pressures. The exhaust gas pressures of the gas turbine plants are nowhere near the considerably lows pressures (≈ 22.5 m bar) employed in the condensing steam plants. This explains why it is not necessary to employ large low pressure cylinders and multiple exhaust even in large terrestrial gas turbine plants. On the other hand, when compared with the reciprocating internal combustion engine, the gas turbine has the advantage of very high flow rate, light weight and mechanical simplicity.

Component efficiencies and inlet gas temperatures were critical for the successful development of the gas turbine plant. Therefore in the earlier stages of its development major attempts were made to improve turbine and compressor efficiencies and develop high temperature materials. At present, the component efficiencies are in excess of 85% and the turbine blade cooling has enabled the employment of gas temperatures as high as 1 600 K at the inlet.

Open and Closed Circuit Plants

In the simple open circuit gas turbine plants (Fig.6.4) atmospheric air is continuously compressed in the compressor and delivered to the combustion chamber at a high pressure. The hot gases from the combustion chamber pass out to the atmosphere after expanding through the turbine. In this arrangement since the working fluid is not restored (at station 1 in Fig.6.4) to its initial state, technically speaking such a plant does not execute a cycle.

A cycle can only be executed in the closed circuit gas turbine plant shown in Fig 6.5. Here the same working fluid (air or any other gas) circulates through its various components. Heat cannot be supplied to the working fluid by internal combustion; instead, it is supplied externally by employing a heat exchanger which replaces the combustion chamber of the open circuit plant.

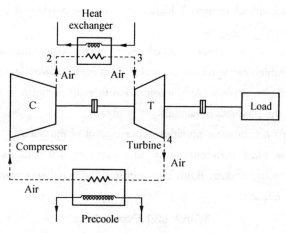

Fig.6.5 A simple closed circuit gas turbine plant

A pre-cooler is included between the turbine exit and the compressor entry. This decreases the specific volume of the air or gas entering the compressor. The lower value of the specific volume reduces the compressor work ($\int v dp$) and its size.

The closed circuit gas turbine plant with its separate external combustion system and precooler looks like a condensing steam plant.

Some advantages of the closed circuit gas turbine plant are given below.

1. Since the working fluid does not leave the plant, fluids with better thermodynamic properties other than air can be employed to derive some aero-thermodynamic advantages. For example, the velocity of sound is higher in helium which permits higher peripheral speeds of the rotor. It is inert and has a higher specific heat and thermal conductivity, resulting in a smaller heat exchanger.

2. By employing high density working fluids, the plant size for a given power can be reduced. In large plants this is a great advantage in terms of mechanical design. A higher density also provides a higher heat transfer rate.

3. The air in a conventional open circuit plant brings its own impurities which cause additional problems of blade erosion and filtration. In a closed circuit plant blade erosion due to solid particles in the air as well as in the products of combustion is absent.

4. This arrangement provides better control of the plant.

5. The chief disadvantage of this plant is that heat is supplied externally to the working fluid. This requires additional equipment besides being less efficient.

Words and Expressions

combustion　[kəm'bʌsʃən]　n. 燃烧,氧化
chamber　['tʃeimbə]　n. 室,房间,箱
kerosene　['kerəsi:n]　n. 煤油
gasoline　['gæsəli:n]　n. 汽油
bunker　['bʌŋkə]　n. 燃料舱,煤箱
terrestrial　[ti'restriəl]　a. 地球上的,陆地的
helium　['hi:ljəm]　n. (化)氦
peripheral　[pə'rifərəl]　a. 周界的,边缘的

impurity　[im'pjuəriti]　n. 杂质
erosion　[i'rəuʒən]　n. 腐蚀,磨蚀
filtrate　['filtreit]　v. 过滤

6.5　Classification of Steam Turbines

Steam turbines may be classified into different categories depending on their construction, the process by which heat drop is achieved, the initial and final conditions of steam used and their industrial usage as follows.

1. According to the number of pressure stages:

(1) Single-stage turbines with one or more velocity stages usually of small-power capacities;

(2) Multistage impulse and reaction turbines; they are made in a wide range of power capacities varying from small to large.

2. According to the direction of steam flow:

(1) Axial-turbines in which the steam flows in a direction parallel to the axis of the turbine;

(2) Radial-turbine in which the steam flows in a direction perpendicular to the axis of the turbine; one or more low-pressure stages in such turbines are made axial.

3. According to the number of cylinders (casings):

(1) Single-cylinder turbines;

(2) Double-cylinder turbines;

(3) Three-cylinder turbines;

(4) Four-cylinder turbines.

Multicylinder turbines which have their rotors mounted on one and the same shaft and coupled to a single generator are known as single shaft turbines; turbines with separate rotor shafts for each cylinder placed parallel to each other are known as multiaxial turbines.

4. According to the method of governing:

(1) Turbines with throttle governing;

(2) Turbines with nozzle governing;

(3) Turbines with bypass governing in which steam besides being fed to the first stage is also directly led to one, two or even three intermediate stages of the turbine.

(4) Turbines with sliding pressure governing in which steam pressure varies with the speed or load of turbine;

5. According to the principle of steam turbine:

(1) Impulse turbines;

(2) Reaction turbines;

6. According to the heat drop process:

(1) Condensing turbines with regenerators: in these turbines steam at a pressure less than atmosphere is directed to a condenser; besides, steam is also extracted from intermediate stages for feed water heating. Small-capacity turbines of earlier designs often do not have regenerative feed heating.

(2) Condensing turbines with one or two intermediate stage extractions at specific pressures for industrial and heating purposes.

(3) Back pressure turbines, the exhausted steam from which is utilized for industrial or heating purposes.

(4) Topping turbines: these turbines are also of the back pressure type with the difference that the exhausted steam from these turbines is further utilized in medium-and low-pressure condensing turbines. These turbines, in general, operate at high initial conditions of steam pressure and temperature, and are mostly used during extension of power station capacities, with a view to obtain better efficiencies.

(5) Back-pressure turbines with steam extraction from intermediate stages at specific pressures; turbines of this type are meant for supplying

the consumer with steam of various pressure and temperature conditions.

(6) Low-pressure (exhaust-pressure) turbines in which the exhausted steam from reciprocating steam engines, power hammers, presses, etc, is utilized for power generation purpose.

(7) Mixed-pressure turbines with two or three pressure stages, with supply of exhausted steam to its intermediate stages.

The turbines enumerated under "b" or "e" usually have extractions for regenerative feed-heat, in addition to the extraction of steam at specific pressures for other purposes.

7. According to the steam conditions at the inlet of turbines:

(1) Low-pressure turbines, using steam at pressures of 0.12 to 0.2 MPa.

(2) Medium-pressure turbines, using steam at pressures of up to 3.9 MPa.

(3) High-pressure turbines, utilizing steam at pressures of 16.8 MPa and higher and temperatures of 535°C and higher.

(4) Turbines of supercritical pressures, using steam at pressures of 22.2 MPa and above and temperatures of 538°C and above.

8. According to their usage in industry:

(1) Stationary turbines with constant speed of rotation primarily used for driving alternators.

(2) Stationary steam turbines with variable speed meant for driving turbo-blowers, air circulators, pumps, etc.

(3) Non-stationary turbines with variabe speed; turbines of this type are usually employed in steamers, ships and railway locomotives (turbo-locomotives).

All these different types of turbines described above depending on their speed of rotation are either coupled directly or through a reduction gearing to the driven machine.

Words and Expressions

initial condition of steam　蒸汽初参数
final condition of steam　蒸汽终参数
single-stage　单级
multistage　['mʌltisteidʒ]　adj. 多级
power capacity　容量,功率
axial-turbine　轴流式透平,轴流式汽轮机
radial-turbine　辐流式透平,辐流式汽轮机
parallel to　平行于
perpendicular to　垂直于
casing　['keisiŋ]　n. 汽缸,气缸,机匣,机壳
single-cylinder turbine　单缸汽轮机
multicylinder turbine　多缸汽轮机
singe shaft turbine　单轴汽轮机
multiaxial turbine　多轴汽轮机
throttle governing　节流调节
nozzle governing　喷嘴调节
bypass governing　旁路调节
sliding pressure governing　滑压调节
intermediate stage　中间级
heat drop process　热力过程
condensing turbine　凝汽式汽轮机
back pressure turbine　背压式汽轮机
topping turbine　前置式汽轮机
with a view of　为了……的目的
steam extraction　抽汽
power hammer　汽锤
enumerate　[i'nju:məreit]　vt. 数,计点,枚举,计算
railway locomotive　火车机车

reduction gearing 减速齿轮

6.6 Current Practice and Trends of Turbine

The earlier years of steamturbine history are replete with designs of unorthodox machines. Perhaps the most unusual departure from modern practice was the vertical turbine. It was arranged with its shaft disposed in a vertical direction, and many units of this type were built. Today the horizontal turbine is universally used. Another characteristic of earlier turbines was the frequent and generous use of the velocity-compounded stage, today called the two-row-wheel. This type of stage, consisting of a nozzle and two moving rows of buckets, with a turning vane between the moving rows, was inferior in efficiency but extremely flexible in its characteristics. Many turbines were built using several such stages in series. Modern turbines still use this type of stage for the widely varying requirements of the first stage in a multistage turbine, though usualy only one such stage is used in a given machine. Experience has shown that the multivalve, multistage horizontal turbine is by far the most acceptable from every standpoint, and we shall be concerned entirely with this type.

One of the most outstanding tendencies from early history to the present time has been to increase the speed of operation of turbines and generators. Whereas the early units operated at 1 200 r/min in the large sizes, modern large turbines are being constructed for the maximum permissible speed in a 60-cycle electrical system, that is ,3 600 r/min. The chief effect of the trend to higher speeds has been the reduction of weight of units, so that designers are able to cope with higher pressures and temperatures, because of the reduced diameters which accompany the higher speeds. Since the peripheral velocities of the elements in the turbine generators are no less than they were in the older slow-speed machines, the stresses are not reduced.

Capacities of larges units are lower at the higher speeds than at the lower speeds, because they are economically limited by the size of the last-stage bucket which can be built. The economic capacity of a steam turbine is roughly proportional to the projected area of the active length of the last-stage bucket. At twice the speed, the diameters are approximately 1/2 as large, and the bucket heights are approximately 1/2 as great, so that the area is approximately 1/4 as great. For this reason, the permissible rating of 3 600 r/min units is roughly 1/4 the permissible rating in 1 800 r/min units. Of course, one may double the capacity of a given turbine by using a "double-flow" exhaust, but this same arrangement could also be used in the slower-speed type. It will later be seen that the economic size of turbine becomes larger as the initial steam conditions become higher, so that, since the 3 600 r/min turbine may properly be credited with permitting higher steam conditions, its maximum rating per last stage is considerably greater than 1/4 the maximum rating of an 1 800 r/min machine.

Both pressures and temperatures have steadily increased from the earliest days of steam turbines. Most of the increases in temperature have been permitted by the discovery of better steel alloys and better knowledge of the materials used in turbines. Outstanding among these is molybdenum, which has permitted construction of turbines up to 950 °F, and higher, with no unusual problems. It may safely be said that progress beyond the 750 °F level was made possible solely by the use of molybdenum in turbine steel.

The data in Table 6.1 are interesting because they indicate how relatively recent is our progress into the higher pressure and temperature range.

Table 6.1 Progress in pressure and Temperature

Pressure	First year of use	Temperature	First year of use
540 psig	1924	750 °F	1926
1 200 psig	1926	825 °F	1933
2 300 psig	1941	900 °F	1936
		950 °F	1938
		1 050 °F	1948

The data in Tabel 6.2 indicate the extremely rapid trend to high temperatures and pressures which has occurred over two successive four-year periods, as indicated by the orders of one major manufacturer.

Table 6.2

Year(inclusive)	Initial conditions	Kilowatts as per cent of total
1940 ~ 1943	1 200 psi and higher	32
	800 ~ 900 psi	40
	900 ~ 1 000 psi	76
1944 ~ 1947	1 200 psi and higher	36
	800 ~ 900 psi	45
	900 ~ 1 000 °F	86

Increase in units for over 800 psi from 72% to 81%.

Increase in units for 900 °F and higher from 76% to 86%.

In the 1920's, a trend to an initial pressure of about 400 psig and initial temperature of 750 °F became evident. This was soon superseded by a new pressure and temperature level in the larger central stations, which may be generalized at about 600 psi-825 °F. The next plateau at which steam conditions leveled off was approximately 850 psi-900 °F, with some competition from the 1 200 psi-900 °F steam conditions. Almost universal adoption of these higher pressures and temperatures in new plants led to the formulation of preferred-standard steam conditions.

Words and Expressions

replete ［ri'pli:t］ a. 充满的
unorthodox ［'ʌn'ɔ:θədɔks］ a. 非正统的,异端的
horizontal ［ˌhɔri'zɔntl］ a. 水平的,卧式的
multistage ［'mʌltisteidʒ］ a. 多级的
peripheral ［pə'rifərəl］ a. 周界的,边缘的
alloy ［'ælɔi］ n. 合金
molybdenum ［mɔ'libdinəm］ n. 钼
plateau ［'plætəu］ n. 平稳段,平稳状态

6.7 The Modern Steam Power Plant

A power plant, of whatever variety, consists of three essential elements: the heat source, the heat utilizer, and the waste heat reservoir or refrigerator. To generate power or produce useful work it is required that heat be supplied to a working fluid, from the heat source. The utilizer is required to convert a portion of the heat supplied to the working fluid into useful power. Since, by the second law of thermodynamics, not all the heat can be converted to useful power, a refrigerator is required to dispose of the remainder of the heat.

Fig.6.6 is a diagram of a modern steam plant, showing most of the essential elements. It may be divided into two main halves. One half consists of the boiler (or heat source) and its auxiliaries; the other, the turbine cycle, consists of turbine, generator, condenser, pumps and feedwater heaters. The turbine cycle, which includes not only the heat utilizer but also the refrigerator, will occupy the major part of our attention in this text.

Considering first the boiler half of the cycle, feedwater is supplied

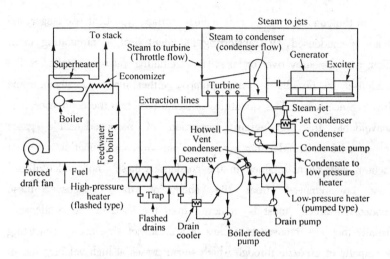

Fig.6.6 Flow diagram of a typical steam power plant

through an economizer to the boiler drum. The economizer reclaims part of the heat in the stack gases and transfers it to the feedwater, thus decreasing the heat to be supplied in the boiler while reducing the temperature of the stack gases. In the boiler drum, the water is boiled and converted to dry and saturated steam, which enters the superheater where the heat of superheat is added. The major part of the steam leaving the superheater is taken to the steam turbine. In many plants some of the steam is bled off for use in a steam-jet air-ejector, discussed below. Steam passing through the steam turbine produces mechanical power on the turbine shaft, which drives the alternator, where electrical energy is generated for distribution. In passing through the turbine in the modern regenerative cycle, some of the steam is bled from the turbine at a series of three or four openings (more or less), for use in feedwater heaters. Approximately 70 to 75% of the steam supplied to the turbine at the throttle continues all the way through the turbine to the exhaust hood, whence it passes to the condenser.

In the condenser, which is a large surface-type heat exchanger, the steam is condensed, by transferring its latent heat to circulating water taken from a nearby river or lake. The circulating water is supplied to the condenser by circulating water pumps, either motor or steamturbine driven. Since tremendous quantities of steam pass into the condenser, it is unavoidable that a certain proportion of non-condensable gases accompanies it. In order that a very low pressure, approximating a perfect vacuum, may be maintained in the condenser, these "noncondensables" must be removed from the shell of the condenser, these "noncondensables" must be removed from the shell of the condenser. Usually they are removed by means of a steam-jet air-ejector, consisting principally of a nozzle through which steam passes at high velocity and in which the non-condensable vapors are entrained. The steam passing through the nozzle (motive steam) and the non-condensable gases mechanically entrained in it are then taken to a heat-transfer device known as an after-condenser, where the steam is condensed at atmospheric pressure and the non-condensable vapors are vented to atmosphere. The steam-jet air-ejector, built in either one or two stages, is essentially a compressor for raising the pressure of the non-condensable vapors from an almost perfect vacuum to atmospheric pressure, to dispose of them.

The main steam, having been condensed in the condenser, is now in the form of liquid water at a very low pressure and approximately saturation temperature. This water drains by gravity to the bottom of the condenser, where it enters a hotwell. Usually the level of the water in the hotwell is maintained by a control applied to the hotwell pump. The hotwell pump removes the water from the hotwell and pumps it through the lower part of the feedwater heating system to another pump, the boiler feed pump. The water discharged from the hotwell pump is taken first to a low-pressure heater in which heat is supplied by the lowest pressure extraction. The low-pressue heater shown in Fig. 6.6 is equipped with a drain pump, the duty of which is to remove the drains (formed by the condensing steam) from the heater and to pump them into the main condensate line, beyond the beater. This type of heater is known as a pumped heater.

From the low-pressure heater the condensate passes to a deaerating heater. The deaerating heater, a direct contact type, serves as a means of boiling the condensate to eliminate any entrained oxygen. Removal of oxygen in the deaerating heater is based on the principle that solubility of non-condensable gases in water is greatly reduced as the temperature of the water approaches the boiling point. Steam extracted from the turbine supplies the heat required to raise to the boiling point the temperature of the condensate entering the deaerator. The non-condensable gases discharged from the surface of the water must be removed. Normally the deaerator is operated at a pressure higher than atmospheric, so that these gases may be vented through a vent condenser. Usual practice is to cool the vent condenser with incoming condensate, to cool the non-condensable gases, and simultaneously to condense the steam, some of which unavoidably escapes from the deaerator with the gases. By proper design of the vent condenser, the steam may be condensed and permitted to drain back into the deaerator, while the non-condensable gases are vented to atmosphere through an orifice.

Occasionally in the original design it may be planned that the deaerator operate at pressures below atmospheric. Even when the fullload design pressure is considerably higher than atmospheric, it is found that at the lighter loads the pressure becomes subatmospheric. It is then essential that the non-condensables continue to be removed from the deaerator, and a steam-jet ejector is necessary for accomplishing this result. The expense and complication in operation occasioned by such an installation make it undesirable. For this reason it is common practice to provide for the shifting of extraction stages at light loads so that the deaerator steam supply is furnished by the next-hight loads so that the deaerator steam supply is furnished by the next-higher extraction point. A simple arrangement is to install a crossover pipe containing a controlling valve, with a check valve in the lower-pressure extraction line before its junction with this crossover pipe. In such an installation opening of the valve in the crossover line automatically supplies higher-pressure steam to the deaerator, and the check valve closes, preventing backflow to the lower extraction stage.

In many power plants a surge tank containing reserve stored water is connected in parallel with the deaerator. The function of the surge tank is to serve as an emergency supply of distilled water, in the event of failure of other sources, or as a reservoir for excess water during load changes, etc. Normally the storage capacity of the deaerator is sufficient to operate the power plant for several minutes, but most designers consider it wise to augment this storage capacity with a large surge tank.

In the majority of large power plants the boiler-feed pump is connected to the discharge of the deaerator. Since the water in the deaerator is at its boiling point, it is essential that the boiler-feed pump be located a considerable distance (usually 20 ft or more) below the deaerator, to avoid flashing of the water in the boiler-feed pump suction. Water leaving the deaerator goes to the boiler-feed pump suction and is pumped into the next higher heater. In Fig. 6.6 this heater is shown as a drain cooler heater, that is, a heater the drains from which pass through a heat exchanger (drain cooler), giving up heat to the incoming condensate. After leaving this heater, the condensate goes to the top or high-pressure heater, in which the condensate is heated to the final feedwater temperature. In Fig. 6.6 the top heater is shown as a flashed heater, so called because its drains are permitted to pass through a controlling orifice or trap to the next-lower heater where part of the saturated water flashes into steam. This arrangements eliminates the use of drain pumps and drain coolers, but it causes a considerable thermodynamic loss. The final feedwater temperature leaving the top heater is in the order of 300 to 450 °F in large modern power plants, and occasionally higher.

Illustrated in Fig. 6.6 are examples of the four types of heater, namely the flashed heater, the drain-cooler heater, the deaerating or contact heater, and the pumped heater.

To provide the uninitiated reader with a few data which give a perspective of the quantities involved in a modern power plant, the following typical data are cited. In modern large steam-turbine practice the pressure at the turbine inlet is typically from 800 to 1 200 psig. Occasionally pressures lower than these are used in the larger turbines (30 000 kW and higher), but today they are the exception rater than the rule. These pressures have been arrived at by power-plant designers, through long practice, as being the ones that give the greatest return on the investment under average conditions.

Temperatures at the inlet to large modern steam turbines range from 825 to 1 050 °F, these temperatures also having been established by usage as those that yield the greatest return on the investment, all things considered. Exhaust pressures for steam turbines in central stations are determined to a large extent by the cooling-water temperature available. These exhaust pressures range from 3/4 in. Hg in the northern parts of the United States to approximately 2.5 in. Hg in the southern parts, or higher-particularly where cooling towers are required because of inadequate water supply. A reasonable national average seems to be about 1.5 in. Hg.

Condensate-pump discharge pressures normally range from 50 to 150 psig. Boiler-feed pump discharge pressures are normally from 10 to 25% higher than the drum pressure in the boiler. Pressure drops in the extraction lines between turbines and heaters are usually about 5% of the pressure existing at the turbines. Pressure drops between the superheater discharge and the turbine inlet are normally from 5 to 10% of the pressure at the superheater discharge. Deaerating heater pressures range from subatmospheric values to approximately 55 or 60 psig, 30 ~ 40 psig representing a reasonable average full-load value.

The number of feedwater heaters used in modern power plants varies from as few as one in the smaller plants having cheap fuel to as many as 8 or 10 in the larger plants having expensive fuel or where the designer is seeking the lowest possible fuel consumption. Although the higher number of heaters gives better thermal performance, in many plants the fixed charges on the more expensive heater installation make a large number of heaters prohibitive. The choice is always an interesting economic problem and quite easily solved.

In a steam turbine arranged for regenerative feedwater heating, the throttle steam rate of the turbine is normally about 15% higher than in a plant arranged for "straight-condensing" operation (without extraction for feedwater heating). In the regenerative cycle the condenser flow is normally about 70% to 75% of the throttle flow, 25% to 30% of the throttle flow having been extracted for supply of the feedwater heaters.

Stack gas temperatures from modern boilers range from approximately 300 to 600 °F, the tendency being in the direction of the lower figure, which is necessary to obtain high boiler efficiency. Stack gas temperature may be reduced by means of either air-preheaters of feedwater economizers. A large number of feedwater-heating stages with a high discharge temperature from the high-pressure heater precludes the use of an extensive economizer. In such installations it is necessary to resort to an air-preheater to recover some of the heat in the stack gases. While air-preheat temperature is limited to the lower values in a stoker installation, modern pulverized fuel installations have been designed which use very high air-preheat temperatures, of the order of 500 ~ 600 °F, with higher values distinctly feasible.

Words and Expressions

utilizer ['juːtilaizə] n. 利用装置
reservoir ['rezəvwaː] n. 蓄水池
refrigerator [ri'fridʒəreitə] n. 冷藏器,冷藏间
thermo-dynamics n. 热力学
auxiliary [ɔːg'ziljəri] n. (复)辅助设备
feed-water n. 给水
economizer [i'kɔnəmaizə] n. 省煤器
stack-gas n. 排放的烟气
saturate ['sætʃəreit] v. 使饱和
superheater n. 过热器
alternator ['ɔːltəneitə] n. 交流发电机
throttle ['θrɔtl] n. 节流阀 v. 节流
hood [hud] n. 帽
whence [hwens] ad. 从何处
vacuum ['vækjuəm] n. 真空(度)
entrain [in'trein] v. 带走,夹带,卷吸
hotwell n. 温泉
deaerate [diː'eiəreit] v. 使除去气体
vent [vent] v. 排放出 n. 出口
orifice ['ɔrifis] n. 孔,口,喷管
cross-over n. 交叉
surge-tank n. 备用箱

augment [ɔːgʹment]　v. 增加
air-preheater　n. 空气预热器
preclude [priʹkluːd]　v. 预防,排除
pulverize [ʹpʌlvəraiz]　v. 研磨,使成粉末
bleed off　放出

6.8　Wind Turbines

Wind is air in motion. Windmills or wind turbines convert the kinetic energy of wind into useful work.

It is believed that the annual wind energy available on earth is about 13×10^{12} kW h. This is equivalent to a total installed capacity of about 15×10^5 MW or 1 500 power stations each of 1 000 MW capacity. While the power that could be tapped out from the vast sea of wind may be comparable with hydropower, it should be remembered that it is available in a highly diluted form. Therefore, while dams are built to exploit and regulate hydropower, there is no such parallel on the wind power scene.

Wind had been used as a source of power in sailing ships for many centuries. The force that acted on ship's sail was later employed to turn a wheel like the water wheel which already existed. The wind-driven wheel first appeared in Persia in the seventh century A.D. By tenth century A. D., windmills were used for pumping water for irrigation and by thirteenth century A.D. for corn grinding.

The corn grinding mill was a two-storey structure; the mill stone was located in the upper storey and the lower storey consisted of a sail rotor. It consisted of six or twelve fabric sails which rotated the mill by the action of the wind. Shutters on the sails regulated the rotor speed. In 1592 A.D. the windmill was used to drive mechanical saws in Holland. A large Dutch windmill of the eighteenth century with a 30.5 m sail span developed about 7.5 kW at a wind velocity of 32 kmph.

The energy of flowing water and wind was the only natural source of mechanical power before the advent of steam and internal combustion engines. Therefore windmills and watermills were the first prime movers which were used to do small jobs such as corn grinding and water pumping. It is generally believed that the windmill made its appearance much later than the watermill.

The watermills had to be located on the banks of streams. Therefore, they suffered from the disadvantage of limited location. In this respect windmills had greater freedom of location. If sufficient wind velocities were available over reasonable periods, more important factors in choosing a site for the windmill would be the transportation of corn for grinding and the site for water pumping.

In both wind and water turbine plants the working fluid and its energy are freely available. Though there are no fuel costs involved, other expenditures in harnessing these forms of energy are not negligible. The capital cost of some wind power plants can be prohibitive. As in other power plants, the cost per unit of energy generated decreases as the size of the wind turbine increases.

Medium-sized ($100 \sim 200$ kW, $d \simeq 20$ m) wind turbines are suitable for electric power requirements of isolated areas in hills and small islands where other sources of power may be non-existent of difficult to install and operate. The use of some of an energy storage system can take care of the random nature of the wind energy.

Large wind power plants of capacities of a couple of megawatts can be connected to the main network fed by thermal and hydrostations. In such a system wind energy can be utilized for saving fuel and water.

Compared to other well-established sources of energy, the wind energy at present appears to be insignificant as far as the contribution to the total energy requirement is concerned. However, at a time when mankind is facing an energy crisis every source, however small, should be tapped.

Elements of a wind power plant

A windmill or turbine is an extended turbomachine operating at comparatively lower speeds. A wind turbine power plant consists of principally the propeller or rotor, step-up gear, and electric generator and the tail vane, all mounted on a tower or mast. The actual design will depend upon the size of the plant and its application.

Various elements of a wind turbine power plant are described here briefly.

Rotor

The shape, size and number of blades in a wind turbine rotor depend on whether it is a horizontal or vertical axis machine. The number of blades generally varies from two to twelve. A high speed rotor requires fewer blades to extract the energy from the wind steam, whereas a slow machine requires a relatively larger number of blades.

In horizontal axis machines two-bladed rotors are known to have greater vibration problems compared to three blades.

In wind turbine rotors blades are subjected to high and alternating stresses. Therefore, the blades must have sufficient strength and be light. Thus the strength-to-density ratio of the material used is an important factor.

Wood is widely used for small high-speed machines. It has the required strength-density ratio.

Various metals and their alloys also used. Small blades are cast. Plastic materials are now also making inroads into the manufacture of wind machines. They have high strength-density ratio, offer great ease in manufacture and are also weather resistant.

Step-up gear

On account of the great difference in rotational speeds of the wind turbine rotor (which is generally low) and the machine that is drives, a step-up gear for obtaining the required high speed is generally employed between the driving and driven shafts. This invariably takes the form of a gearing arrangement consisting of one or more gear trains. The entire gearing arrangement must have high efficiency and reliability coupled with light weight.

Belts and chains have not been employed as widely as the gearing.

Speed-regulating mechanism

From aerodynamic considerations, it is desirable to operate a wind turbine at a constant blade-to-wind speed ratio. However, in many applications a mechanism to maintain the speed of the wind turbine constant at varying wind velocities and loads is required.

A propeller type of pump and a hydraulic brake (water paddle for producing hot water) are excellent speed governors themselves. Speed regulation can be obtained for both fixed and variable pitch blades.

The mechanism for variable pitch blades is the same as that used in Kaplan hydroturbines or aircraft propellers. The variable pitch mechanism enables the rotor to operate most efficiently at varying wind velocities and in feathering during gusts.

The centrifugal force acting on the blades at speeds higher than the design is also employed to change the blade pitch. This can also be achieved by a fly-ball governor.

Electric generator

Besides driving pumps and corn grinding mills, wind turbines are now being increasingly used for driving electric generators or "aerogenerators" as they are sometimes called. These aerogenerators are both direct and alternating current machines and are available from a capacity of a few watts to hundreds of kilowatts.

The direct current machines operate in a considerable speed range, whereas the alternating current generator with constant frequency requires constant speed.

For small isolated communities, some kind of energy storage is always required. This is best met by do generators feeding a battery of accumulators during low load and high wind periods.

To minimize weight, aerogenerators must operate at high speeds which depend on the type of the wind turbine (Blade-to-wind speed ratio) and the weight of the step-up gear.

When the speed of the wind turbine is low, multi-pole synchronous alternators are used. But the large number of poles increases the weight of the aerogenerators. However, such a machine is acceptable if it eliminates the speed-up gear by using higher blade-to-wind speed ratios.

When an alternator is directly coupled to an ac network, its speed is nearly constant. Such a generator can be designed for sufficient overload capacity to absorb the wind energy available at high wind velocities.

Orientation mechanism

A horizontal axis wind turbine requires a mechanism which turns the rotor into the wind stream. The working of the vertical axis machines does not depend on the wind direction and, therefore, an orientation mechanism is not required.

In primitive windmills the rotor was turned manually into the wind direction by a pole hanging from the tail. Modern wind turbines have sophisticated automatic mechanisms to obtain the orientation as and when required.

The simplest and most widely used method to orient small windmills in the wind direction is by employing a wind vane.

Another method is to employ an automatic direction finding and orienting mechanism. This is relatively faster.

A fan-tail whose axis of rotation is normal to the axis of the main rotor is also employed to turn the windmill into the wind stream. The cross wind drives the auxiliary rotor which in turn rotates the windmill into the wind through reduction gears. This is a slow mechanism.

Tower

All windmills have to be mounted on a stand or a tower above the ground level. Tower heights of over 250 m have been employed for obtaining high wind velocities and mounting large wind turbine rotors. Increasing the tower height besides increasing the capital cost also increases the maintenance cost. Therefore the gain in the power output due to high wind velocity at a given altitude must be accurately estimated to justify the high costs. Economic and vibration problems are major factors in the design of towers for large wind turbines.

An angle iron tower of a four-sided pyramidal shape is commonly used. A similar structure constructed from metal pipings is also used. Towers have also been constructed from wood, brick and concrete.

Words and Expressions

kinetic ['kai'netik] a. 动力的

hydropower ['haidrə‚pauə] n. 水力发出的电力

dilute [dai'lju:t] v. 稀释,冲淡

megawatt ['megəwɔt] n. 兆瓦(特)

inroad ['inroud] v. 袭击 n. 损害

aero-generator n. 空气发电机

auxiliary [ɔ:g'ziljəri] a. 辅助的

pyramidal [‚pirə'mikəl] a. 金字塔形的,角锥状的

piping ['paipiŋ] n. 笛声,尖叫声

synchronous ['siŋkrənəs] a. 同步的

6.9 The Principle of Steam Turbine

A heat engine is one that converts heat energy into mechanical energy. So the steam turbine is classed as a heat engine, as are the steam and internal-combustion engines. The turbine makes use of the fact that steam when issuing from a small opening attains a high velocity. The velocity attained during expansion depends upon the initial and final heat content of the steam. This difference in heat content represents the heat energy converted into kinetic energy (energy due to velocity) during the process. The kinetic energy or work available in the steam leaving a nozzle is equal to the work that the steam could have done had it been allowed to expand (with the same heat loss) behind a piston in a cylinder.

The fact that any moving substance possesses energy, or the ability to do work, is shown by many everyday examples. A stream of water discharged from a fire hose may break a window glass if directed against it. When the speed of an automobile is reduced by the use of brakes, an appreciable amount of heat is generated. In like manner the steam turbine permits the steam to expand and attain high velocity. It then converts this velocity energy into mechanical energy. There are two general principles by which this can be accomplished. In the case of the fire hose, as the stream of water issued from the nozzle, its velocity was increased, and owing to this impulse it struck the window glass with considerable force. A turbine that makes use of the impulsive force of high-velocity steam is known as an "impulse turbine". While the water issuing from the nozzle of the fire hose is increased in velocity, a reactionary force is exerted on the nozzle. This reactionary force is opposite in direction to the flow of the water. A turbine that makes use of the reaction force produced by the flow steam through a nozzle is a "reaction turbine". Practically in all commercial turbines a combination of impulse and reactive forces is utilized. Both impulse and reaction blading on the same shaft utilize the steam more efficiently than does one alone.

Impulse-turbine nozzles organize the steam so that it flows in well-formed high-speed jets. Moving buckets (blades) absorb the jet's kinetic energy and convert it to mechanical work in a rotating shaft (Fig. 6.7). When the bucket is locked, the jet enters and leaves with equal speed and develops maximum force F but no mechanical work is done. As the bucket is allowed to speed up, the jet moves more slowly and force F shrinks. Fig. 6.8 shows how both force and work done vary with the blade speed. The steam jet does maximum work when the bucket speed is just one-half of the steam speed. In this condition, the moving bucket leaves behind it a trail of inert steam, since all kinetic energy is converted

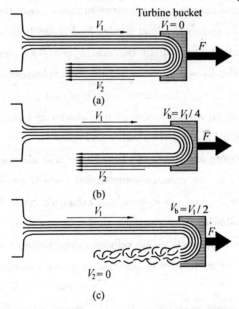

Figure 6.7 Steam flow in moving buckets

to work. The starting force or torque of this ideal turbine is double the torque at its most efficient speed.

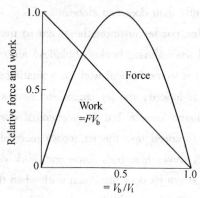

Figure 6.8   Curves of the reactive force and work with bucket speed

For practical reasons, most impulse turbines mount their buckets on the rims of disks (wheels) , and nozzles feed steam from one side (Fig. 6.9). Pressurized steam from the nozzle box flows through parallel converging nozzles formed by vanes or foils. Steam leaves as a broad high-speed jet to flow through the slower moving-bucket passages, which turn the steam flow to an axial direction as they absorb its kinetic energy. The steam leaves with lower internal energy and speed.

Steam pressure and speed vary through the true impulse stage. When the impulse stages are pressure-compounded, which are called Rateau stages, pressure drop occurs in steps and exhausted steam from one-stage flows through following similar impulse stages, where it expands to a lower pressure. If the impulse stages are velocity-compounded, which are called Curtiss stages, steam velocity is absorbed in a series of constant-pressure steps.

In the reaction stage (Fig. 6.10), steam enters the fixed-blade passages; it leaves as a steam jet that fills the entire rotor periphery.

Steam flows between moving blades that form moving nozzles. There it drops in pressure, and its speed rises relative to the blades, which creates the reactive force that does work. Despite the rising relative speed, the overall effect reduces the absolute steam speed through one stage. When the enthalpy drop is about equal in moving and stationary blades, it is called a 50 percent reaction stage.

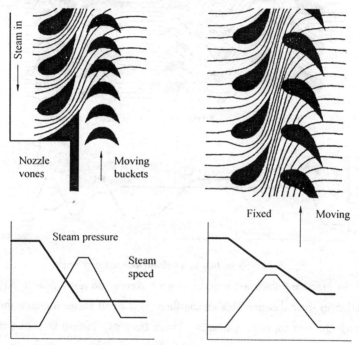

Fig. 6.9   Steam flow in an impulse stage

Fig. 6.10   Steam flow in a reaction stage

Fig. 6.11 shows a velocity-compounded control stage followed by two reaction stages. The high-speed steam jet gives up only part of its kinetic energy in the first row of moving buckets. Then come reversing blades that redirect the slowed-up steam into the second row of moving buckets, where most of its remaining kinetic energy is absorbed. Steam then enters the series of reaction stages.

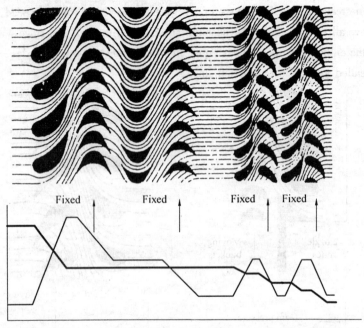

Fig. 6.11 Steam flow in a velocity-compounded stage

In practice, so-called impulse-stage turbines use about 5% to 10% reaction in their design. This means there is a small steam pressure drop through the moving-blade passages. These buckets, instead of taking the symmetrical shape, have a longer tail to form a slightly converging passage at the exit.

Words and Expressions

heat engine 热机
steam engine 蒸汽机
internal-combustion engine 内燃机
issue from 从……喷出,从……流出

heat content 热值
kinetic energy 动能
heat loss 热损
piston ['pistən] n. 活塞
cylinder ['silində] n. 气缸,汽缸
nozzle ['nɔzl] n. 喷嘴,喷管,燃烧器
discharge from 从……排出,从……流出
fire hose 消防水龙头
brake [breik] n. 制动器,刹车
impulsive force 冲击力
impulse turbine 冲击式透平,冲击式汽轮机
reactionary force 反击力
reaction turbine 反击式透平,反击式汽轮机
commercial turbine 商业透平,商业汽轮机
balding ['bɔ:ldiŋ] adj. 叶片,叶栅
jet [dʒet] . 汽流,射流,喷气式发动机,喷气式飞机
moving bucket/blade 动叶
rotating shaft 转轴
shrink [ʃriŋk] vt. 收缩,减小,热套
rim of disk/wheel 轮缘
converging nozzle 渐缩喷嘴
vane [vein] n. 叶片,轮叶,刀片,节气阀
foil [fɔil] n. 叶形饰,翼,薄片
leave behind 遗留,把……丢在后面,超过
nozzle box 喷嘴室
Rateau stages 托拉级,压力级
pressure drop 压降
Curtiss stage 柯蒂斯级,复速级
velocity-compounded stage 复速级

enthalpy drop 焓降
control stage 调节级
give up 释放,放弃,中断
reversing blade 转向导叶片
symmetrical [si'metrikəl] adj. 对称的

7

Environmental Protection, Corrosion and Others

7.1 Ash Removal and Disposal

The problems of ash removal and disposal are significant principally in the case of solid fuels. The amount of ash in fuel oil is small and usually is a problem primarily inside the furnace and boiler setting. However, mechanical dust collectors are occasionally used.

With the early methods of burning coal on grates using natural draft, most of the coal ash remained on the grate and was ultimately discharged into a hopper for disposal. With more modern stokers, such as the spreader stoker, part of the burning is accomplished in suspension and this results in a greater carry-over of particulate matter in the flue gas.

With pulverized-coal firing, all the burning is accomplished in suspension with the result that about 80% of the ash remains in the flue gases in the case of a dry-ash pulverized coal-fired unit. This may be reduced to about 50% with a slag-tap unit with pulverized-coal firing.

With Cyclone-Furnace firing, the fly-ash loading in the flue gases is reduced to 20% to 30% of the ash in the coal. The problem of particulate carry-over in the flue gases is thus reduced by a factor of 3 or 4 for Cyclone Furnace firing as compared with a dry-ash pulverized coal-fired unit. This is important from the standpoint of the cost of equipment required to achieve a given particulate content in the stack gases.

Ash removal from the furnace

Stoker-fired units and dry-ash pulverized-coal-fired units are designed so that the ash settles in hoppers from which it is removed for disposal. Some possible uses for this slag are as land fill, road-base material, granular material for roofing, aggregate for use in concrete blocks and preformed concrete, asphalt mix material, cinders for icy reads, insulation, and grit for sandblasting. Most of these uses apply also to ash removed in dry form from stoker-and pulverized-coal-fired furnaces.

Particulate removal

To meet the objective of a clear stack, some form of particulate-removal equipment is now generally required to remove the fly ash from flue gases from units where fuels are burned in suspension. Several types of particulate-removal equipment are available. These may be classified as electrostatic precipitators, mechanical dust collectors, fabric filters and wet scrubbers. Fly ash removed by equipment of these types may be used for most of the applications listed for ash removed as slag.

Electrostatic precipitators

Electrostatic precipitators produce an electric charge on the particles to be collected and then propel the charged particles by electrostatic forces to the collecting electrodes. The precipitator operation involves 4 basic steps:

1. An intense, discharging field is maintained between the discharge electrode and the collecting electrodes.

2. The carrier gases are ionized by the intense, discharging field. These gas ions, in turn, charge the entrained particles.

3. The negatively charged particles, still in the presence of an electrostatic field, are attracted to the positively (grounded) charged collecting electrodes.

4. The collected dust is discharged by rapping into storage hoppers.

The collection efficiency of the electrostatic precipitator is related to the time of particle exposure to the electrostatic field, the strength of the field, and the resistivity of the dust particle. An efficiency of 99% is obtained at a cost generally favorable in comparison with other types of equipment. Hence, as of 1970, a very high percentage of particulate-removal units installed in commercial boiler plants are electrostatic precipitators.

Mechanical collectors

The operation of mechanical collectors depends on exerting centrifugal force on the particles to be collected by introducing the dust-laden gas stream tangentially into the body of the collector. The particulate matter is thrown to the outside wall of the collector where it is removed. Mechanical collectors operate most effectively in the particle-size range above about 10 microns. Below 10 microns, the collection efficiency drops considerably below 90%. As efficiency requirements continue to increase, the use of mechanical collectors is expected to decline.

Fabric filters

Fabric filters operate by trapping dust by impingement on the fine filters comprising the fabric. As the collection of dust continues, an accumulation of dust particles adheres to the fabric surface. The fabric filter obtains its maximum efficiency during this period of dust buildup. After a fixed operating period, the bags must be cleaned. Immediately after cleaning, the filtering efficiency is reduced until the buildup of collected dust takes place.

The fabric filter can be applied in any process area where dry collection is desired and where the temperature and humidity of the gases to be handled do not impose limitations. At efficiencies of 99% and less, the fabric filter is generally not competitive with the electrostatic precipitator for boiler application. However, for particulate matter, efficiencies above 99% can be achieved with fabric filters, and applications in congested areas may increase.

Wet scrubbers

Wet scrubbers remove dust from a gas stream by collecting it with a suitable liquid. (see Fig. 7.1)

A good wet scrubber is one that can effect the most intimate contact between the gas stream and liquid for the purpose of transferring the suspended particulate matter from the gas to the liquid. Collection efficiency, dust-particle size, and pressure drop are closely related in the operation of a wet scrubber. The required operating pressure drop varies inversely as the dust-particle size for a given collection efficiency; or a given dust-particle size, for a given collection efficiency; or for a given dust-particle size, collection efficiency increases as operating pressure drop increases.

Unlike other particulate collection equipment, the wet scrubber employs a liquid stream to collect particulate matter. For this reason, it can usually perform additional process functions besides dust collection. Gas absorption, chemical reaction, and heat transfer are some of these.

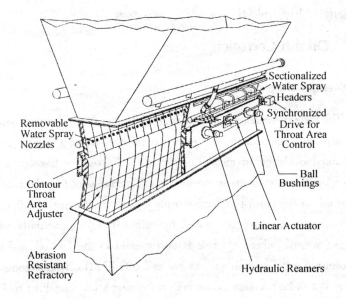

Fig.7.1 Veturi-type wet scrubber

Simultaneous removal of dust and gaseous pollutants by use of a suitable scrubbing liquid can be accomplished with a wet scrubber.

Words and Expressions

ash [æʃ] n. 灰
suspension [səs'penʃən] n. 悬浮,暂停
disposal [dis'pəuzəl] n. 丢掉,处理,布置
scrubber ['skrʌbə] n. 刷子,刷洗工具,擦洗者
precipitator [pri'sipiteitə] n. 除尘器,聚尘器
ionize ['aiənaiz] v. 使离子化 vi. 电离
rap [ræp] v. 叩击,敲击
tangential [tæn'dʒenʃəl] a. 正切的,切线方向的
decline [di'klain] v. 拒绝,倾斜,跌落
trap [træp] v. 用陷阱捕捉,诱捕

humidity [hju:'miditi] n. 湿气,潮湿,湿度

7.2 Oil-ash Corrosion

High-temperature corrosion

The sodium-vanadium complexes, usually found in oil-ash deposits, are corrosive when molten. The corrosion mechanism is probably one of accelerated oxidation of metal brought about by oxygen transfer to its surface by the constituents in the molten ash, accompanied by the removal by the ash of the normal protective oxide coating on the metal surface.

Corrosion can also be caused by sulfate attack, particularly when sodium (or some other) chloride is also present in the fuel oil, and this may occur at metal temperatures as low as 1 000 °F. This type of corrosion is more apt to be encountered on boilers burning a low-vanadium fuel oil but containing several hundred ppm of sodium chloride. Even when the chloride content of the fuel oil is negligible, sulfate corrosion may still be severe when reducing or alternating oxidizing-reducing conditions prevail around the tubes.

A measurable corrosion rate can be observed over a wide range of metal and gas temperatures, depending on the amount and composition of the oil-ash deposit.

The effect of the sodium level in the fuel oil is not quite so clear-cut because combustion conditions and the chloride content of the fuel oil may be controlling. The sodium content does, however, definitely affect the minimum metal temperature at which corrosion will be significant.

At the present time there does not appear to be any alloy that is immune to oil-ash corrosion. In general, the higher the chromium content of the alloy the more resistant it is to attack. This is the main reason for the use of 18 Cr-8Ni alloys for high-temperature superheater tubes. High chromium contents, greater than 30%, give added corrosion resistance but at the expense of physical properties; 25Cr-20Ni has been used as a tube cladding but even this alloy has not provided complete protection. The presence of nickel in high-temperature alloys is needed for strength. High-nickel alloys may be fairly resistant to oil-ash attack under oxidizing conditions but they are liable to sulfide attack brought about by local reducing conditions or by the presence of chloride in the ash deposit. Since it is difficult to avoid such conditions entirely, high-nickel content of alloys may be of limited value. In any event, the higher material cost must be justified by longer life, which is not always predictable.

Low-temperature corrosion

In oil-fired boilers the problem of low-temperature corrosion resulting from the formation and condensation of sulfuric acid from the flue gases is similar to that previously described for coal firing.

Oil-fired boilers are more susceptible to low-temperature corrosion than are most coal-fired units for two reasons:

1. the vanadium in the oil-ash deposits is a good catalyst for the conversion of SO_2 to SO_3 and
2. there is a smaller quantity of ash in the flue gases. Ash particles in the flue gas reduce the amount of SO_3 vapor in the gas. Since oil has considerably less ash than coal, significant differences would be expected. Furthermore, coal ash is more basic than oil ash and tends to neutralize any acid deposited; oil ash generally lacks this capability.

Under certain conditions, oil-fired boilers may emit acidic particulates from their stacks that stain or etch painted surfaces in the neighborhood of the plant. The acidic deposits or smuts are generally caused by metallic surfaces (air heaters, flues and stacks) operating well below the acid dew point of the flue gases or by soot which has absorbed sulfuric acid vapor in its passage through the boiler. Methods that can be used to prevent acid-smut emission include:

1. Minimize SO_3 formation in the flue gases,
2. Neutralize SO_3 in flue gases,
3. Maintain all surfaces in contact with the flue gases above about 250 °F.
4. Completely burn fuel oil to eliminate soot particles.

Methods of control

The methods of control that have been used or proposed to control fouling and corrosion in oil-fired boilers are summarized, but in every instance economics governs their applicability. There is no doubt that reducing the amount of ash and sulfur entering the furnace is the surest means of control, and that minimizing the effects of the ash constituents, once they have deposited on the tubes, is the least reliable. Since the severity of fouling and corrosion depends not only on the fuel-oil characteristics but also on boiler design and operating variables, a generalized solution to these problems cannot be prescribed.

Fuel oil supply

Although fuel selection and blending are practiced to some extent in this country, it is done to provide safe and reliable handling and storage at the user's plant rather than to avoid fouling difficulties. Since the threshold limits of sodium, sulfur and vanadium are not accurately defined for either fouling or corrosion, utilization of these means of control cannot be fully exploited.

Processes are available for both the desulfurization and de-ashing of fuel oils. Water washing of residual fuel oil has been successfully applied to a few marine-type boilers, but it is doubtful that it will be widely used because only sodium and sediment, mainly rust and sand, are removed by the process. Use of low-sulfur, low-ash crudes and desulfurized fuel oil is expected to increase.

Fuel oil additives

The practice of water washing out of service and, to a limited extent, in service has been beneficial in overcoming some of the troubles experienced with present oil fuels. In addition, continued study of the problem has revealed another approach that is effective where the fuel-oil ash is most troublesome. In brief, the method involves adding to the fuel or furnace small amounts of materials that change the character of the ash sufficiently to permit its removal by steam or air sootblowers or air lances.

Additives are effective in reducing the troubles associated with superheater fouling, high-temperature ash corrosion, and low-temperature sulfuric acid corrosion. Most effective are alumina, dolomite and magnesia. Kaolin is also a source of alumina.

The reduction of fouling and high-temperature corrosion is accomplished basically by producing a highmelting-point ash deposit that is powder or friable and easily removed by sootblowers or lances. When the ash is dry, corrosion is considerably reduced.

Low-temperature sulfuric-acid corrosion is reduced by the formation of refractory sulfates by reaction with the SO_3 gas in the flue-gas stream. By thus removing the SO_3 gas, the dew point of the flue gases is sufficiently reduced to protect the metal surfaces. The sulfate compounds formed are relatively dry and easily removed by the normal cleaning equipment.

In general, the amount of additive used should be about equal to the ash content of the fuel oil. In some instances, slightly different proportions may be required for best results, especially for high-temperature corrosion reduction, in which it is generally accepted that the additive should be used in weight ratios of 2 or 3 to 1, based on the vanadium content of the oil.

Several methods have been successfully used to introduce the additive materials into the furnace. The one in general use consists of metering a controlled amount of an additive oil slurry into the burner supply line. The additive material should be pulverized to 100% through a 325 mesh screen (44 microns) for good dispersion and minimum atomizer wear.

For a boiler fired by a high-pressure return-flow oil system, it has been found advantageous to introduce the additive powders by blowing them into the furnace at the desired locations. The powder has to be 100% through a 325-mesh screen for good dispersion.

A third, and more recent method, is to introduce the additive as a water slurry through specially adapted sootblowers or lances. This method offers the advantage of applying the additive in exactly the location desired, with a possible reduction in the quantity required. Some caution should be observed with this system to prevent possible thermal shock (quench-cracking) damage to the hot tubes. The presence of chlorides in the water slurry, from either the water or the additive material, could possibly produce stress-corrosion cracking of austenitic tubing and should be considered.

The choice of the particular additive material depends on its availability and cost to the individual plant and the method of application chosen. For example, alumina causes greater sprayer-plate wear than other materials when used in an oil slury.

The quantity of deposit formed is, of course, an important consideration for each individual unit from the aspect of cleaning. A comparison of the amounts of deposit formed with different additives shows that dolomite produces the greatest quantity because of its sulfating ability, alumina and kaolin form the least, and magnesia is intermediate. However, when adequate cleaning facilities are available, the deposits are easily removed, and the quantities formed should not be a problem.

Excess-air control

As mentioned previously the problems encountered in the combustion of residual fuels-high-temperature deposits (fouling), high-temperature corrosion, and low-temperature sulfuric-acid corrosion-all arise from the presence of vanadium and sulfur in their highest states of oxidation. By reducing the excess air from 7% to 1% or 2%, it is possible to avoid the formation of fully oxidized vanadium and sulfur compounds and , thereby, reduce boiler fouling and corrosion problems.

In a series of tests on an experimental boiler, it was found that the maximum corrosion rate of type 304 stainless steel superheater alloy held at 1 250 °F in 2 100 °F flue gas was reduced more than 75% when the excess air was reduced form an average of 7% to a level of 1% to 2%. Moreover, the ash deposits that formed on the superheater bank were soft and powdery, in contrast to hard, dense deposits that adhered tenaciously to the tubes when the excess air was around 7%. Also, the rate of ash buildup was only half as great. Operation at the 1% to 2% excess air level practically eliminated low-temperatures corrosion of carbon steel at all metal temperatures above the water dew point of the flue gases. However, much of the beneficial effects of low excess-air combustion are lost if the excess air at the burner fluctuates even for short periods of time to a level of about 5%. Carbon loss values for low excess air were approximately 0.5%, which is generally acceptable for electric utility and industrial practice.

A number of large industrial boilers both in this country and in

Europe have been operating with low excess air for several years. As a result, the benefits in reducing low-temperature corrosion are well established for units with steam temperatures of 1 000 °F or less. However the benefits on high-temperature slagging and corrosion are not wholly conclusive. In any event, great care must be exercised to distribute the air and fuel oil equally to the burners, and combustion conditions must be continuously monitored to assure that combustion of the fuel is complete before the combustion gases enter the convection tube banks.

Words and Expressions

corrosion [kə'rəuʒən] n. 腐蚀,腐蚀作用
sodium-vanadium 钠－钒
molten ['məultən] a. 熔化的,熔铸的
chloride ['klɔːraid] n. 氯化物,漂白粉
acidic [ə'sidik] a. 酸性的
neutralize ['njuːtrəlaiz] v. 使中立,中和,取消
govern ['gʌvən] v. 治理,统治,支配
desulfurization [diːˌsʌlfərai'zeiʃən] n. 脱硫,去硫
slurry ['sləːri] n. 泥浆,水泥浆
kaolin ['keiəlin] n. 瓷土,高岭土
dense [dens] a. 密的,稠密的,浓厚的
fluctuate ['flʌktjueit] vi. 波动 vt. 使波动,变动

7.3 Control of Pollutant Gases

Air pollution control

The control of atmospheric pollution is one part of a prime present-day problem-environmental control. The by-products from boiler furnaces are by no means the major factor in producing air pollution. In the larger cities, other factors, particularly the automobile and industrial or manufacturing processes, produce the larger share of air pollution. Generally power plant stacks contribute only about 15% of the total weight of atmospheric contaminants emitted from all sources.

While air pollution has been increasingly present since the beginning of the industrial revolution, it is particularly in the last 25 years that the total release of pollutants from all sources has signaled a national air pollution problem of increasing proportions, indicating the necessity for remedial measures. Even though the combustion products from boiler furnaces constitute a small part of total air pollutants, the growth of industry indicates an increasing need for remedial measures. Some of these measures are currently available and in general use. Others are in the development stage and are expected to become available within the next few years. These developments are being spurred by an aroused public interest and an increasing amount of legislation.

It is important to note that there are substantial costs associated with equipment to remove particulates and gaseous pollutants from stack gases, and these costs must ultimately be borne by the consumer. In the case of the electric power industry, the costs of equipment to reduce air pollution necessarily increase power generation costs, and hence the kilowatt-hour cost to the consumer. The costs of this equipment can vary from $ 6 to $ 35 per kW of installed capacity, depending on the type and scope of equipment, and must be recognized as part of the price for maintaining a good atmospheric environment. Gaseous pollutants are more difficult to remove than particulate matter. Even though all forms of gaseous pollutants have not been identified, oxides of sulfur and nitrogen are recognized as being harmful.

Sulfur oxides

Sulfur oxides are produced in significant quantity by the combustion of most coals and fuel oils. The amount of sulfur oxides produced in gas-fired units is insignificant. However the demand for natural gas for domestic fuel makes it less available for steam generation

Sulfur oxides can be controlled by removing sulfur from the fuel prior to its use, or by removing the sulfur oxides from the combustion gases before they are released to the stack. Several systems to reduce the emission of gaseous sulfur compounds are under development or in pilot-plant operation. Meanwhile several governmental agencies have promulgated regulations limiting the fuels burned in congested areas to those containing a certain maximum sulfur content, typically 1% or less.

Some plants which have been burning fuel oil are meeting these requirements by using low-sulfur oil at a premium price. In some cases the sulfur-content limit is met by blending low-sulfur oils with less expensive higher-sulfur oils. Also a number of coal-burning plants are being converted to oil, or to oil and gas firing.

In the case of coal, transportation costs are such an important factor that the coals which can be burned in a particular locality are generally limited to those that are mined within a distance of 150 to 200 miles or those that can be transported by water. The economics of removing sulfur from the higher sulfur coals appears less encouraging than removing sulfur oxides from the gaseous products of combustion. Hence there is an increasing incentive to develop methods for the removal of sulfur oxides from flue gases.

Since sulfur dioxide (SO_2) represents 98% of sulfur oxide pollutants, the principal interest attaches to the removal of sulfur dioxide. As of 1970, four principal approaches are being investigated:

1. Addition of materials such as limestone or dolomite in the combustion furnace.

2. Wet scrubbing of flue gases without sulfur recovery.

3. Wet scrubbing of flue gases with sulfur recovery.

4. Dry Sorbent systems.

Limestone addition

In this system an additive, such as limestone, is injected into the furnace of the steam generator. Once in the furnace the carbonate is calcined by hot combustion gases to form calcium oxide, which combines with the sulfur dioxide and oxygen to form calcium sulfate. The calcium sulfate can be removed subsequently in a dry state by more conventional particulate-removal systems. However, SO_2 removal efficiencies are low with this method, commonly ranging from 20% to 35%.

When limestone is used as the additive, successful results are obtained when the additive system is combined with aqueous scrubbing, but equally good results can be obtained with aqueous scrubbing alone.

Wet scrubbing system without sulfur recovery

A wet scrubbing system without sulfur recovery is shown diagrammatically in Fig. 7.2. A limestone slurry is used as the scrubbing fluid to remove up to 85% of the sulfur oxides and about 99% of the particulates from the flue gas. This system requires a minimum capital expenditure;

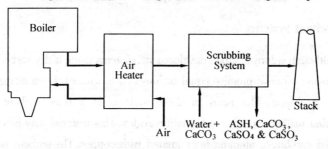

Fig.7.2 Wet-scrubbing system without sulfur recovery

however, large quantities of refuse must be disposed of and operating costs are high.

Magnesium-oxide system with sulfur recovery

A magnesium-oxide wet-scrubbing system with sulfur recovery is shown in Fig. 7.3. Magnesia solutions or slurries are used to remove up to 95% of the sulfur oxides and 99% of the particulates from the flue gas. The scrubbing effluent is regenerated to recover MgO for reuse. A salable sulfur product is produced.

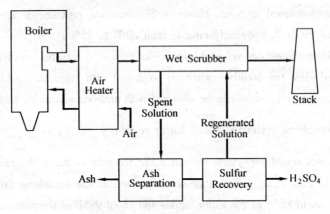

Fig. 7.3 Wet-scrubbing system with sulfur recovery

Dry sorbent systems

Although a longer range development, systems using a dry sorbent for sulfur-oxide removal promise equal or lower costs without the disadvantage of wet scrubbing. The heart of these systems is a fixed sorbent bed containing material to adsorb the sulfur oxides. This material may be char, activated carbon, or alumina impregnated with copper. The sorbent bed is located ahead or after the air heater, depending on the gas temperature which is most suitable for the sorbent material used. The sorbent material is regenerated, and sulfur, usually as acid, is reclaimed as a byproduct. Efficiencies of 90% and perhaps higher appear to be practicable. Although a precipitator is required for particulate removal, capital requirements are projected as equal to those of the magnesium-oxide wet-scrubbing system.

Oxides of nitrogen

The oxides of nitrogen also contribute to air pollution and much effort is being directed toward their control, particularly in large urban areas. The reaction leading to the formation of oxides of nitrogen proceeds rapidly at combustion temperatures in excess of 3 000 °F. To help reduce this type emission, flame temperatures are moderated by two-stage combustion or recirculation of flue gas through the burners.

Words and Expressions

contaminant [kən'tæmənənt] n. 污染物,沾染物
emit [i'mit] v. 放射,发出,发行
remedial [ri'mi:diəl] v. 补救的,改正的
legislation [ˌledʒis'leiʃən] n. 法规,立法
scrub [skrʌb] v. 用力擦洗
limestone ['laimstəun] n. 石灰石
reuse ['ri:'ju:z] v. n. 再使用
sorbent ['sɔ:bənt] n. 吸收剂,吸着剂
alumina [ə'lju:minə] n. 氯化铝,矾土
impregnate ['impregneit] v. 使充满
urban ['ə:bən] a. 都市的,城市居民

7.4 Fans

A fan moves a quantity of air or gas by adding sufficient energy to the stream to initiate motion and overcome all resistance to flow. The fan consists of a bladed rotor, or impeller, which does the actual work, and usually a housing to collect and direct the air or gas discharged by the impeller. The power required depends upon the volume of air or gas moved in unit time, the pressure difference across the fan and the efficiency of the fan and its drives.

Power may be expressed as shaft horsepower, input horsepower to motor terminals, if motor driven, or theoretical horsepower computed by thermodynamic methods. Each has its own significance. As far as the fan is concerned, the important factors are the power input to the shaft and the power dictated by thermodynamic calculations.

Stacks seldom provide sufficient natural draft to cover the requirements of modern boiler units. The 200 foot high stack of the previous example with a 490 °F average gas temperature will develop a theoretical natural draft of approximately 1.15 in. of water, whereas resistances to gas and air flow may be as high as 50 inches. These higher draft loss systems require the use of mechanical draft equipment and a wide variety of fan designs and types is available to meet this need.

The forced draft fan

Bolers operating with both forced and induced draft use the forced draft fan to push air through the combustion air supply system into the furnace. The fan must have a discharge pressure high enough to equal the total resistance of air ducts, air heater, burners or fuel bed and any other resistance between the fan discharge and the furnace. This makes the furnace the point of balanced draft or zero pressure. Volume output of the forced draft fan must equal the total quantity of air required for combustion plus air heater leakage. In many boiler installations, greater reliability is obtained by division of the total fan capacity between two fans operating in parallel. If one fan is out of service, the other usually can carry 60 percent or more of full boiler load, depending on how the fans are sized.

To establish the required characteristics of the forced draft fan, the system resistance from fan to furnace is calculated for the actual weight of air required for combustion plus the expected leakage from the air side of the air heater. It is usual boiler design practice to base all calculations on 80 °F air temperature entering the fan. The results are the net requirements which are then adjusted to test block specifications by the safety factors previously discussed.

For pressurized units without an induced draft fan, the forced draft fan is sized for the entire system to the stack entrance.

A forced draft fan for boiler service operates under far more stringent conditions than the ordinary ventilating fan and selection should consider the following general requirements:

Reliability. Modern boilers must operate continuously for long periods (up to 18 months in some instances) without shutdown for repairs or maintenance. Thus the fan must have a rugged rotor and housing and conservatively loaded bearings. The fan must also be well balanced, and the blades so shaped that they will not collect dirt and disturb this balance.

Efficiency. High efficiency over a wide range of output is necessary because boilers operate under varying load conditions.

Pressure. Fan pressure should vary uniformly with output over the capacity range. This facilitates damper control and assures minimum disturbance of air flow when minor adjustments to the fuel-burning equipment change the system resistance.

Capacity. When two or more fans operate in parallel, the pressure-output curves should have characteristics similar to the straight blade or backward-curved blade fans in order to share the load equally near the shutoff point.

Horsepower. Motor driven fans require self-limiting horsepower characteristics, so that the driving motor can not overload. This means that the horsepower should reach a peak and then drop off near the fullload fan output.

In general, backward-curved centrifugal designs meet most forced draft fan requirements. Small boiler units, however, may use a single propeller-type fan mounted directly on the burner windbox. This fan saves space and the cost is low.

The induced draft fan

Units designed to operate with balanced furnace draft or without a forced draft fan require induced draft to move the gaseous products of combustion over convection heating surfaces and through the gas passages between the furnace and stack. Where it is not practical or economical to design for natural draft, induced draft fans discharging essentially at atmospheric pressure are used to provide the necessary negative static pressure.

The gas weight used to calculate net induced draft requirements is the weight of combustion product gas at maximum boiler load plus any air leakage into the boiler setting from the surroundings and from the air side to the gas side of the air heater. Net gas temperatures are based on the calculated unit performance at maximum load. Induced draft fan test block specifications of gas weight, negative static pressure and gas temperature are obtained by adjusting from net values by margins similar to those used for forced draft fans.

An induced draft fan has the same basic requirements as a forced draft fan except that it handles higher temperature gas which may contain erosive ash. Flat, forward-curved and occasionally backward-curved blades are used. If backward-curved blades are used curvature is usually less than found in forced draft fans. Using a lesser curvature results in a lower tip speed for the same head, which diminishes the erosive effect of ash particles, and, because of its shape, less dirt clings to the back of the blades. A flat-bladed centrifugal fan of lower speed may be selected to handle particularly dirty or erosive gases. Excessive maintenance from erosion is sometimes avoided by protecting casing and blades with replaceable wear strips. Bearings, usually water-cooled, have radiation shields on the shaft between rotor and bearings, to avoid overheating.

Gas recirculating fans used variously for controlling steam temperature, furnace heat absorption and slagging of heating surfaces, are generally located to extract gas at the economizer outlet and inject it into the furnace at locations depending on the intended function. This multiple purpose is also an important consideration in properly sizing and specifying gas recirculating fans. This selection may be dictated by the high static pressure required for tempering furnace temperatures at full load on the boiler unit, or by high volume requirement at partial loads for steam temperature control.

Even though gas recirculating fans have the same basic requirements as induced draft fans, the designer or engineer must consider additional factors. Since the gas recirculating fan operates at higher gas temperatures, intermittent service may cause thermal shock or unbalance. When the fan is not in service, suitable protection in the form of tight shut-off dampers and sealing air must be provided to prevent the backflow of hot furnace gas and a turning gear is often used on large fans to rotate the rotor slowly to avoid distortion.

Words and Expressions

fan [fæn] n. 风机,扇子
impeller [im'pelə] n. 推进器,叶轮,叶轮激动器
leakage ['li:kidʒ] n. 漏出,泄漏,漏风
entrance ['entrəns] n. 入口,进入
ventilate ['ventileit] v. 使通风,安装通风设备
damper ['dæmpə] n. 节气闸
negative ['negətiv] a. 负的
margin ['ma:dʒin] n. 系度,亲裕
erosive [i'rəusiv] v. 腐蚀性的,侵蚀的
cling [kliŋ] vi. 粘住,依附,坚持
inject [in'dʒekt] n. 引入,注入
distortion [dis'tɔ:ʃən] n. 扭曲,变形

7.5 Stokers

Mechanical stokers, as an improvement over hand firing, were developed early in the history of the steam boiler. Today many small and medium size boilers are fired with stokers, and several types of stokers are available. All are designed to feed fuel onto a grate within the furnace and to remove the ash residue. Higher rates of combustion are possible than with hand firing, and the continuous process of stoker firing permits good control and high efficiency.

A successful stoker installation requires the selection of the correct type and size for the fuel to be used and the desired capacity. Also, the associated boiler unit should have the necessary instruments for the proper control of the stoker. The grate area required for a given stoker type and capacity is determined from allowable rates established by experience. Table 7.1 lists allowable fuel burning rates (Btu/sq ft, hr) for various types of stokers, based on using coals suited to the stoker type in each case.

Table 7.1 Maximum allowable fuel burning rates

Type of Stoker	Btu/sq ft, hr
Spreader – stationary and dumping grate	450 000
Spreader – traveling grate	750 000
Spreader – vibrating grate	400 000
Underfeed – single or double retort	425 000
Underfeed – multiple retort	600 000
Water – cooled vibrating grate	400 000
Chain grate and traveling grate	500 000

For a boiler of a given steam capacity, these maximum fuel burning rates determine the plan area for a stokerfired furnace. As boiler unit size is increased, practical considerations limit stoker size and, consequently, the maximum rate of steam generation with this method of firing. Because of the greater flexibility in furnace design with pulverized-coal and Cyclone-Furnace firing and the trend toward larger boiler units, the present market for stokers is less than in former years. The practical steamoutput limit of boilers equipped with mechanical stokers is about 400 000 lb/hr, although many engineers limit the application of stokers to lower steam capacities. However, within their capacity range, mechanical stokers are an important and valued element of modern equipment for the production of steam or hot water. When applicable, stokers are often preferred over pulverizers because of their greater operating range, capability of burning a wide range of solid fuels, and lower power requirements.

Almost any coal can be burned successfully on some type of stoker. In addition, many by-products and waste fuels, such as coke breeze, wood wastes, pulpwood bark and bagasse can be used either as a base or auxiliary fuel.

Mechanical stokers can be classified in four main groups, based on the method of introducing fuel to the furnace:

1. Spreader stokers.
2. Underfeed stokers.
3. Water-cooled vibrating-grate stokers.
4. Chain-grate and traveling-grate stokers.

Among these several types, the spreader stoker is the most generally used in the capacity range from 75 000 to 400 000 lb of steam per hr, because it responds rapidly to load swings and can burn a wide range of fuels.

Underfeed stokers of the single-retort, ram-feed, side-ash-discharge type are used principally for heating and for small industrial units of less than 30 000 lb of steam per hr capacity. Larger size underfeed stokers of multiple-retort, rear-ash-discharge type have been largely displaced by spreader stokers and by the water-cooled vibrating-grate stokers in the intermediate range. Chain and traveling-grate stokers, while still used in some areas, are gradually being displaced by the spreader and vibrating-grate types.

Spreader stokers

The spreader stoker is capable of burning a wide range of coals, from high-rank . Eastern bituminous to lignite or brown coal and a variety of by-product waste fuels.

As the name implies, the spreader stoker projects fuel into the furnace over the fire with a uniform spreading action, permitting suspension burning of the fine fuel particles. (Fig. 7.4). The heavier pieces, that cannot be supported in the gas flow, fall to the grate for combustion in a thin fast-burning bed. This method of firing provides extreme sensitivity to load fluctuations as ignition is almost instantaneous on increase of firing rate and the thin fuel bed can be burned out rapidly

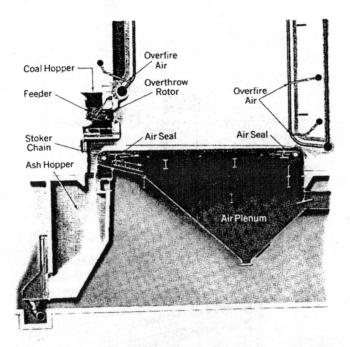

Fig. 7.4 Traveling-grate spreader stoker with front ash discharge

when desired.

The modern spreader stoker installation consists of feeder-distributor units in widths and numbers as required to distribute the fuel uniformly over the width of the grate, specifically designed air-metering grates, forced draft fans for both undergrate and overfire air, dust collecting and reinjecting equipment, and combustion controls to coordinate fuel and air supply with load demand.

Spreader mechanism

Fig. 7.5 illustrates a fuel feeder-distributor unit of the variable stroke, reciprocating-feed-plate type. The reciprocating-feed plate moves coal from the supply hopper over an adjustable spill plate to fall onto an overthrow rotor. This rotor is equipped with curved blades for uniform coal

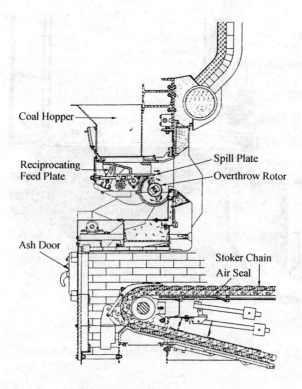

Fig. 7.5 Reciprocating-feeder distributor and overthrow rotor for spreader stokers

distribution over the furnace area.

While the details of the several means used to feed and distribute the coal may vary with different manufacturers, the overthrow rotor design illustrated has the widest usage. The object in all cases is to provide a continuous well-distributed supply of fuel at a variable rate as required by the load demand.

Words and Expressions

stoker ['stəukə] n. 加煤机,抛煤机
flexibility [ˌfleksə'biliti] n. 适应性,易曲性

vibrating-grate 振动炉排
permit [pə'mit] v. 许可,容许 n. 许可证
uniformly ['juːnifɔːmli] adv. 一律地,一样地
illustrate ['iləstreit] v. 显示,加插图,说明

7.6 Flue Gas Desulfunzation

Background

The first commercial application of flue gas desulfurization(FGD) to power plant sulfur oxide control was in the United Kingdom in the early 1930s. The Battersea A Power Plant(228 MW) of the London Power Company, London, UK, began flue-gas washing in 1933. The process utilized wet scrubbing with Thames River water providing most of the alkaline absorbent. The spent absorbent was discharged back into the Thames after settling and oxidation. The FGD system operated successfully at up to 95% SO_2 removal efficiency until the Battersea A Power Plant closed down in 1975. A similar FGD system operated on the Battersea B Power Plant(245 MW) between 1949 and 1969, when FGD operation was temporarily suspended because of adverse effects on the Thames water quality.

The ICI Howden process, also developed in England, was developed to avoid discharged scrubber effluent into the Thames. A solid sludge was produced and barged to sea for dumping. This process was applied to the Swansea Power Plant in 1935 and the Fulham Power Plant in 1937. These systems operated successfully until early World War II when they were shut down.

The next FGD unit was installed at the Electrolytic Zinc company in Tasmania in 1949. Tidal water was used there as the absorbent for SO_2 from smelter gas.

In 1952 the first unit of the new oil-fired Bankside Power Station in London, UK, was commissioned. This FGD system is an improved version of the Battersea system, using water from the Thames. This system is still operating at up to 98% removal efficiency and with a present capacity of 240 MW.

The 1950s and 1960s were a time of laboratory and pilot plant investigations of new processes. During the 1950s the Tennessee Valley Authority (USA) investigated lime/limestone systems, both dry and wet, and dilute acid processes; in Germany the first major carbon adsorption processes were developed. During the 1960s the magnesium oxide, copper oxide, and sulfite scrubbing processes were investigated among others.

Lime/limestone processes were installed in 1964 on an iron ore sintering plant in Russia and on a large sulfuric acid plant in Japan in 1966.

In 1966 Combustion Engineering developed a dry limestone injection process, which was installed at five boilers in the United States by 1972. Because of major problems associated with dry limestone injection including plugging (especially of the boiler tubes), low sulfur dioxide removal, and reduced particulate collection in the electrostatic precipitators, these systems proved inadequate. The five installations are now either closed down or converted to other control systems.

Japan has at present the largest installed capacity of FGD systems. Most of these systems were built between 1975 and 1977. Systems based on lime/limestone predominate. As of December 1977, the United States had 27 operating utility units treating about 35×10^6 Nm^3/h (normal conditions are 0℃ and 1 bar), 34 units under construction to treat 50×10^6 Nm^3/h, and 20 units are planned to treat 34×10^6 Nm^3/h; in addition 25 industrial boilers were operational or under construction with a capacity of about 5×10^6 Nm^3/h. In the Federal Republic of Germany, approximately 775 000 Nm^3/h of flue gas are being treated by lime and carbon adsorption processes, and in Norway 155 000 Nm^3/h are treated by seawater scrubbers on oil-fired boiler.

Process Categories

FGD process can most conveniently and usefully be categorized by the manner in which the sulfur compounds removed from the flue gases are eventually produced for disposal. In this way three main categories result:

(1) Throwaway processes, in which the eventual product is disposed of entirely as waste. Disposal can include landfill, ponding, discharge to water course or ocean, or discharge to a worked-out mine.

The processes in this category involve wet scrubbing of the flue gases for absorption, followed by various methods for neutralizing the acidity, separating the sulfur compounds from the scrubbing liquor, and usually recycling at least part of the scrubbing liquor.

(2) Gypsum processes, which are designed to produce gypsum of sufficient quality either for use as an alternative to natural gypsum or as well-defined waste product with good disposal characteristics.

As with the throwaway processes, this category involves wet scrubbing for absorption followed by various methods of neutralizing lime or limestone and recovering the sulfur compound. An oxidation step is included to insure recovery of the sulfur compounds in the form of gypsum.

(3) Regenerative processes, which are designed specifically to regenerate the primary reactants and concentrate the sulfur dioxide that has been removed from the flue gases. Further chemical processing can then convert the concentrated SO_2, into sulfuric acid or elemental sulfur, or physical processing into liquefied sulfur dioxide. The surveyed

processes in this category contain both wet scrubbing and dry adsorption processes.

Status of Operating FGD Systems

There are now 144 known FGD systems operating on fossil-fueled combustion sources. Of these, 74 are operating on power utility boilers, representing about 70×10^5 m^3/h of flue gas capacity from about 20 GW generation. The remainder is operating on industrial combustion sources, principally boiler plants, but also on iron- ore sinter plants and petroleum refinery plants.

In the NATO-CCMS Process Status Reports, 35 FGD systems were surveyed. Although it was originally desired to include only the large, commercially available installations with adequate operating experience, it was necessary to include data on some smaller scale operation and some that had been installed originally for demonstration purposes in order to provide sufficient comparability between the various processes.

Throwaway Processes: This category includes the three processes that produce a calcium sulfite/sulfate sludge and also the seawater scrubbing process. The sludge processes are becoming the most widely used FGD systems; 30 systems are in operation and 53 are planned or under construction. They have been used successfully on both coal and oil-fired plants with a wide range of fuel sulfur contents and are reported to have high SO_2 removal efficiencies, whereas plant availabilities are variable.

. Double Alkali Process: It is a further development designed to overcome the scaling, plugging, arid erosion problems that have been generally associated with lime or limestone systems. Double alkali systems are presently used mainly with small to medium-sized boilers where the extra process equipment can be offset by lower maintenance coasts.

Gypsum Processes: These processes are designed to produce a

quality of gypsum that may be used in place of natural gypsum in such markets as plaster or plaster wallboard, or as a setting retarder in cement manufacture. It is expected that if sufficient markets are not available for gypsum, it will be disposed of as a solid waste. Gypsum has better setting characteristics than sludges containing calcium sulfite from the throwaway processes.

Words and Expressions

scrub [skrʌb] vt. 擦洗,洗涤
alkaline absorbent 碱性吸收剂
SO_2 removal efficiency 脱硫效率
ICI 帝国化学公司
solid sludge 污泥,泥渣
lime/limestone 石灰/石灰石
magnesium oxide 氧化镁
copper oxide 氧化铜
sulfite ['sʌlfait] n. 亚硫酸
electrostatic precipitators 静电除尘器
predominate [pri'dɔmineit] vi. 支配,统治
worked-out 用过的,废弃的
neutralizing the acidity 中和酸
gypsum ['dʒipsəm] n. 石膏
recover [ri'kʌvə] vt. 回收
concentrate ['kɔnsentreit] vt. 浓缩,冷凝
sulfur dioxide 二氧化硫
NATO 北大西洋公约组织(即北约)
calcium sulfite 亚硫酸钙
calcium sulfate 硫酸钙
under construction 正在建设中

sulfur contents 含硫量
plaster ['plɑ:stə] n. 熟石膏,烧石膏
retarder [ri'tɑ:də] n. 抑制剂,控制剂,阻滞剂

7.7 Steam Separation

Separation and solids removal

In a modern drum boiler, the separation of steam from the mixture delivered by the steam-water risers (Fig.7.6) usually takes place in two steps. The primary separation removes nearly all the water from the

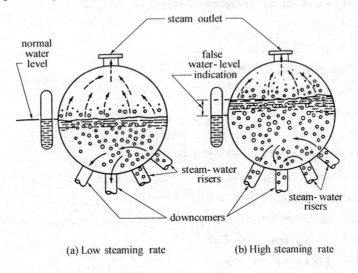

Fig.7.6 Effect of rate of steam generation on steam separation in a boiler drum without separation devices

mixture, so that, in effect, no steam is recirculated to the heating tubes. However, the steam may still contain solid contaminants which must be removed or reduced in amount before the steam is sufficiently pure for use in high-pressure turbines. This step is called secondary separation or "steam scrubbing". Both steps are usually accomplished in one steam drum.

Part of the contamination of the steam is caused by dissolved solids contained in tiny water droplets that may remain after primary separation. The rest of the contamination appears to be silica, either in solution in steam or in vaporized form. This type of contaminant cannot be mechanically removed by primary separation. Washing or scrubbing is necessary for its dilution or removal.

Gross impurities in the steam may be caused by periods of abnormally high water level from operational upsets, during which the separating equipment is submerged, allowing the water to be carried over in gulps. This action is called "priming". Another type of gross carry-over can occur if the boiler water produces excessive foam in the drum. With high concentration of solids in the boiler water, this "foaming" may be severe enough to render the separating devices ineffective. Foaming and priming are comparatively rare occurrences in the modern boiler with proper water-level regulation and control of boiler-water quality by chemical methods.

Factors affecting steam separation

Separation of steam form the mixture discharged into the drum from steam-water risers is related to both design and operating factors, which may be listed as follows

Design factors

1. Design pressure
2. Drum size, length and diameter
3. Rate of steam generation
4. Circulation radio-water circulated to heated tubes divided by steam generated

5. Type and arrangement of mechanical separators

6. Feedwater supply and steam discharge equipment and arrangement

7. Arrangement of downcomer and riser circuits in the steam drum

Operating factors

1. Operating pressure
2. Boiler load (steam flow)
3. Type of steam load
4. Chemical analysis of boiler water
5. Water level carried

In steam drums without separation devices, where separation is by gravity only, the manner in which some of the above items affect separation is indicated in simplified form in Fig.7.6 and Fig.7.7.

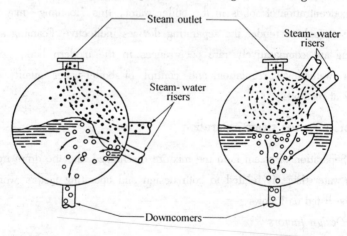

(a) Discharge tubes near drum center line

(b) Discharge tubes above drum center line

Fig.7.7 Effect of location of discharge from risers on steam separation in a boiler drum without separation devices

For a low rate of steam generation (up to about 3 ft/sec velocity of steam leaving the water surface) there is sufficient time for the steam bubbles to separate from the mixture by gravity without being drawn into the downcomers and without carrying entrained water droplets into the steam outlet (see Fig.7.6(a)). However, for this same arrangement at a higher rate of steam generation (Fig. 7.6(b)) the time is insufficient to attain either of these desirable results. Moreover, the dense upward traffic of steam bubbles in the mixture may cause a false water level, as indicated.

The effect of the location of the riser circuits in relation to the water level is illustrated in diagrams (a) and (b), Fig. 7. 7. Neither arrangement is likely to yield desirable results in a drum where gravity alone is used for separation.

Separation by the action of gravity alone is possible if the velocity of either the mixture or the steam bubbles within the mixture is sufficiently low, but the arrangement will probably be uneconomical. For gravity separation in a single drum, the steam generated per sq. ft of disengaging surface must be kept extremely low. A single drum under these conditions is generally uneconomical except for small low-duty boilers. By using multiple drums of reasonable size in series, some what higher steam outputs per ft length of drum are possible with gravity separation.

Operating pressure has an effect on the natural tendency of steam and water to separate. The relationship between pressure and the differential in the densities of water and steam is indicative of this effect. In the separation of steam from water, the limiting velocity of a water particle conveyed in steam and the force of gravity both vary directly with the differential in the densities of the water and the steam. Hence, as the density differential diminishes with increase in operating pressure, so does the force of gravity available for separation. The effect of increasing operating pressure (above 300 psi for comparison) on steam flow per unit of flow area, on steam velocity above the drum water level, and on the force of gravity for separation is shown in Fig.7.8. It will be noted that

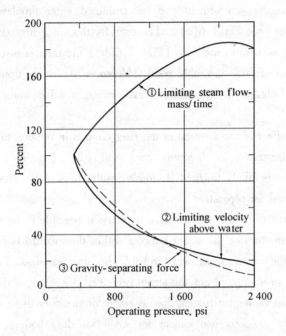

Fig.7.8 Effect of increase in operating pressure (above 300 psi for comparison on ① limiting steam flow per unit of flow area, ② limiting velocity above water, and ③ gravity-separating force-steam and water

the percentage drop in gravity-separating force closely follows the drop in limiting velocity.

As steam pressure increases, the density of steam increases, and the size of steam bubbles in the mixture decreases. Consequently, the velocity of the mixture leaving the riser circuits is reduced. This permits a higher capacity per ft length of a given diameter drum, or the use of a small drum.

Words and Expressions

silica ['silikə] n. 硅土,氧化硅
dilution [dai'lu:ʃən] n. 冲淡,稀释物
foam [fəum] vi. 起泡沫,充满 vt. 使起泡沫
discharge [dis'tʃa:dʒ] v. 排出,发射 n. 发射,放电量
list [list] n. 目录 v. 列表
indicate ['indikeit] v. 指示,表示,说明
bubble ['bʌbl] n. 气泡,泡沫 v. vi. 起泡,沸腾
tendency ['tendənsi] n. 趋势,倾向

7.8 Pulverizers

Design fundamentals

1. **Feeding** In direct-firing systems the fuel rate must be capable of automatic control by the boiler load demand. Pulverizer air flow must be proportioned to fuel rate to provide the air required for drying, the correct primary-air-coal ratio, and the velocity required for transporting the fuel to the burners.

B & W uses a control that maintains a predeter mined variable air-fuel ratio over the entire operating range of the pulverizer. Air flow is measured by an orifice or a pitot tube in the duct supplying air to the pulverizer and fuel flow is measured by feeder speed, a gravimetric feeder, or by the static pressure differential across the pulverizer grinding zone.

2. **Drying** In order to pulverize and circulate fuel pneumatically within a pulverizer, enough of the moisture must be removed to leave the fuel dry and dusty. For most commercially available coal, preheated air to the pulverizer is required. Drying is accomplished quickly as the coal is

being circulated and ground. The use of preheated air permits control of the temperature of the fuel-air mixture to the burners for the most stable ignition.

3. **Grinding**　The pulverizer must do adequate work on each passage of the material through the grinding zone and without the production of excessive superfines. This is best accomplished by internal recirculation of coarse material. The pulverizer should maintain its grinding ability over the life cycle of the grinding elements and be able to reject foreign matter that enters with the feed. These objectives should be attained without excessive wear and power consumption.

The grinding elements of B & W pulverizers are spring loaded to provide the necessary grinding force throughout the life of the elements. Shallow cupped rings furnish adequate grinding surface, allow rapid material flow, and facilitate the discharge of foreign material.

4. **Circulating**　Circulation of coal within a pulverizer is required (1) to promote rapid drying by mixing the incoming feed with dry material in the pulverizer, (2) to keep the grinding elements loaded at all times, and (3) to remove pulverized material from the grinding elements.

Rapid circulation is maintained in B & W pulverizers by utilizing the pulverizer air in combination with centrifugal force and gravity to move the material as desired.

5. **Classifying**　It is not feasible to grind all the coal to the desired fineness in a single passage through the grinding elements. Therefore a device called a "classifier" is provided. Coal pulverized to the proper fineness leaves the pulverizer and goes to the burners. Oversize coal is separated out by the classifier and returned to the grinding zone.

If separation is not discriminative, oversize particles will go to the furnace and cause unburned combustible loss. Separation must be effective over the entire operating range, and the classifier must be adjustable for product size, since the required fineness is not the same for all applications.

The stationary, multiple-inlet-cyclone-type classifier used in the B & W pulverizer meets these requirements. The shrouded discharge prevents reentrainment of oversize particles. Fineness varies inversely with rating so that the highest fineness is obtained at the lowest load. The movable inlet vanes permit adjusting the classifier for the fineness desired.

6. *Transporting* The velocity in pulverizer discharge lines must be sufficiently high to prevent settling and drifting of coal. At the burners the air-coal mixture must be uniform and the velocity suitable.

The B & W system, by a variable controlled air-coal relationship, increases the air-coal ratio at lower loads and decreases it at higher loads to provide a maximum load range. The uniform discharge from the classifier and the symmetrical take-off of burner lines from the pulverizer assure equal distribution of coal to each burner.

Pulverizer requirements

1. Rapid response to load change and adaptability to automatic control.

2. Continuous service for long operating periods.

3. Maintenance of prescribed performance throughout the life of pulverizer grinding elements.

4. A wide variety of coals should be acceptable.

5. Ease of maintenance with the minimum number and variety of parts, and space adequate for access.

6. Minimum building volume required.

The rank of coal can its end use govern the fineness to which coal must be ground. The data of Table 7.2 are helpful in this specification.

Table 7.2 Required pulverized fuel fineness percent through 200 U.S. sieve*

Type of Furnace	ASTM Classification of coals by rank					
	Fixed carbon, %			Fixed carbon below 69%		
	97.9-86 (Petroleum coke)	85.9-78	77.9-69	Btu/lb above 13 000	Btu/lb 12 900- 11 000	Btu/lb below 11 000
Marine boiler	—	85	80	80	75	—
Water-cooled	80	75	70	70	65**	60**
Cement kiln	90	85	80	80	80	—
Metallurgical	(As determined by process, generally from 80% to 90%)					

* The 200-mesh screen (sieve) has 200 openings per linear inch or 40 000 openings per square inch. For U.S. and ASTM sieve series, the nominal aperture for 200 mesh is 0.0029 in. or 0.074 mm. The ASTM designation for 200 mesh is 74 microns.

** Extremely high ash content coals will require higher fineness than indicated.

Selecting pulverizer equipment

A number of factors must be considered when selecting pulverizer equipment. If selection anticipates the use of a variety of coals, the pulverizer should be sized for the coal that gives the highest "base capacity". Base capacity is the desired capacity divided by the capacity factor. The latter is a function of the grindability of the coal and the fineness required.

The extent of drying in a given pulverizer depends upon its design and the method used to introduce preheated air into the grinding zone. Raw coal with very high surface moisture, over 15%, can be efficiently dried when fed into the grinding zone of a pulverizer designed for a high internal circulating load, i.e., a high ratio of coal recirculated to coal feed. As the recirculated material is dry, the more of it there is, the less effect the wet feed has on the performance of the mill.

As a practical matter, temperature is the only variable for controlling the heat input for drying, since the weight of primary air is usually a fixed quantity at any given output.

The percentage of volatile matter in the fuel has a direct bearing on the probability of premature ignition of the primary-air-fuel mixture at the burners. The generally accepted safe values for exit fuel-air temperatures are given in Table 7.3.

Table 7.3 Prevalent pulverizer exit primary-air-fuel temperature

Fuel	Exit Temp, F
Lignite	120 – 140
High-volatile bituminous	150
Low-volatile bituminous	150 – 175
Anthracite	200
Petroleum coke	200 – 250

The temperature of the primary air entering the pulverizer may run 650°F or more, depending on the amount of surface moisture and the type of pulverizer.

Fine grinding of coal is necessary to assure complete combustion of the carbon for maximum efficiency and to minimize the deposit of ash and carbon on the heatabsorbing surfaces. This applies not only in the firing of steam boilers but also in other applications where close temperature control and the avoidance of carbon contamination are important. Chemical and metallurgical processes using pulverized coal as a source of thermal or chemical energy generally require very finely ground coal to assure the optimum reaction in a limited combustion zone and often under difficult firing conditions.

Fineness is expressed as the percentage of the product passing through various sizes of sieves, graded from. No. 16 to No. 325 in the

ASTM designation. Coal classification by rank and the end use of the product determine the fineness to which coal should be ground.

The range through which the equipment will operate must be considered in selecting pulverizing equipment for direct firing. The range through which a single pulverizer can operate is an inherent feature of the pulverizer. For B & W pulverizers it is about 3 to 1. However, the range for safe operation depends on the type and number of burners, type of fuel, and whether the furnace is "hot" or "cold".

When B & W pulverizers are operated at fractional loads, the fineness of the product increases automaticaly as the air flow is decreased. This is beneficial to low-load operation as it assists in ignition and flame stability.

Words and Expressions

orifice ['ɔrifis] n. 口,洞,孔
gravimetric [grəvi'metrik] a. 重量分析的,重量的
promote [prə'məut] v. 升级,促进,发起
drift ['drift] n. 吹积物 v. 吹积,漂流
symmetricical [si'metrikəl] v. a. 对称的,整齐的
prescribe [pri'kraib] v. 限定,限制
metallurgical [,metə'lə:dʒikəl] a. 冶金的 n. 冶金学者
index ['indeks] n. 索引,指针,路标 v. 指示

7.9 Prevention of Scaling in Boilers

The term scale describes a continuous, adherent layer of foreign material formed on the water side of a surface through which heat is exchanged. By adding certain chemicals the growth of scales can be inhibited and the insoluble particles can be dispersed in the recirculating water and removed by blowdown. Should the particles come out of suspension, however, they can accumulate as sludges in quiet sections of a boiler. Deposit is a rather general term applied to more-or-less loose accumulations often found in less turbulent sections of boilers and water-treating systems. Scales are objectionable because of their insulating effect. In a boiler tube, for instance, they cause overheating and eventual failure of the metal. Deposits often cause plugging in critical areas such as waterwalls, waterwall headers, in blowdown lines, and in gauge glasses.

Types of Scale

Many different mineral structures have been identified in boiler scales by the methods of x-ray diffraction, electron diffraction, and polarizing microscopy. Examples of silicate scales are: acmite, $Na_2O \cdot Fe_2O_3 \cdot 4SiO_2$; analcite, $Na_2O \cdot 3Al_2O_3 \cdot 4SiO_2 \cdot 2H_2O$; serpentine, $3MgO \cdot SiO_2 \cdot 2H_2O$; sodalite, $Na_2O \cdot 3Al_2O \cdot 6SiO_2 \cdot 2NaCl$; and xonotlite, $5CaO \cdot 5SiO_2 \cdot H_2O$. When phosphate is used for internal treatment, ferric phosphate, $FePO_4$, basicmagnesiumphosphate, $Mg_3(PO_4)_2 \cdot Mg(OH)_2$, and hydroxyapatite, $Ca_{10}(PO_4)_6(OH)_2$, may also be encountered, as well as the more common anhydrite, $CaSO_4$, and aragonite, $CaCO_3$. As noted before, the presence of these and other scales impedes the circulation of water and reduces heat transfer, both of which cause overheating and failure of tubes.

Mechanism of Scale Formation

Scales and deposits form because the compounds of which they are composed are insoluble under the conditions prevailing in the boiler. Two factors combine to make calcium salts especially troublesome: certain anhydrous calcium salts, notably the sulfate, decrease in solubility as temperature and pressure increase, whereas increasing temperature shifts the equilibrium of the following reaction to the right, causing $CaCO_3$ to precipitate:

$$Ca^{2+} + 2HCO_3^- \rightleftharpoons CaCO_3 + H_2CO_3 \quad (7.1)$$

In addition, hydrolysis of excess bicarbonate increases the concentration of hydroxyl ion, precipitating $Mg(OH)_2$, the solubility product of which is 5.5×10^{-12}. The solubility of $CaSO_4$ decreases rapidly with increasing temperature, producing an extremely hard, adherent coating on boiler tubes, especially in locations where heat flux is high. The compositions of several scales containing aluminum, magnesium, calcium, and silicate are given above. Analcite and acmite, which form at high temperature, are invariably found beneath sludges of hydroxyapatite or serpentine, or under porous deposits of iron oxides. Occasionally other extremely, insoluble iron or magnesium silicates are also encountered, and now and then aquartz, SiO_2 appear, usually originating from colloidal silica, finely divided silt, or sand in the feed water.

Accumulations in boiler drums are most often in the form of mud or sludge. When oil is present as a contamination in boiler water, loose scales may form, particularly in water-wall tubes. Oil serves as a nucleus and binder for scaling at hot spots, although these scales are often merely baked mud that is easily dislodged by hammering the tubes. The " oil balls " found in steam drums and water-wall headers are typical formations in turbulent sections; they are especially common in steam drums, where they are formed by the rolling motion of water.

Chemical Treatments

Obviously, the most effective method for preventing scaling is to eliminate scale-forming elements from the feed water, or to transform them by some means into, an innocuous form. The methods for doing this are conveniently classified as external and internal treatments.

Chemical Softening. The treatments of water that are accomplished outside of the boiler are referred to as preboiler, or external treatments. The processes for removing calcium and magnesium ions from water are called softening, and are signal importance in preventing scales. It is apparent from the equation:

$$Ca^{2+} + 2HCO_3^- \rightleftharpoons CaCO_3 + H_2CO_3 \qquad (7.2)$$

That calcium is precipitated if carbonic acid is neutralized by adding an alkaline reagent. If an excess of alkali is added, magnesium hydroxide also precipitates and the total hardness of the water is reduced. Lime is the alkaline reagent most often used because its cost is low and it is relatively easy to handle; the process is called lime softening.

Softening by Cation Exchange. The removal of calcium and magnesium ions by cation exchange is commonly called zeolite softening, from the reaction characteristic of the mineral zeolites. The latter are hydrous sodium aluminum silicates in which the sodium is labile and exchangeable for calcium and magnesium ions flowing over through the mineral. The exchange reaction is:

$$Na_2Z + Ca^{2+} \rightleftharpoons CaZ + 2Na^2 \qquad (7.3)$$

In this type of treatment the cation exchange resin is in the acid form, while the anion exchange resin, which removes negative ions, is in the hydroxide form.

Precipitants. The amount of hardness that can be tolerated in feed water decreases as the pressure of the boiler increase, but in any case calcium and magnesium are prevented by adding phosphate to the boiler water; this precipitated both calcium and magnesium in a soft dispersed form. The precipitate formed by calcium and orthophosphate is usually represented as the normal phosphate. $Ca_3(PO_4)_2$. Attempts to precipitate this salt in the laboratory, however invariably produce hydroxyapatite, the formula of which can be written in various ways including

$Ca_{10}(PO_4)_6(OH)_2$, $3Ca_3(PO_4)_2 \cdot Ca(OH)_2$, and $Ca_5(PO_4)_3OH$. A consideration of the solubility products $[Ca^{2+}][CO_3^{2+}] = 4.8 \times 10^{-9}$, $[Ca^{2+}]^3[PO_4]^2 = 1.3 \times 10^{-12}$, and $[Ca^{2+}]^2[PO_4][OH^-] = 3 \times 10^{-58}$ indicates that the basic salt forms in boiler water. Magnesium forms similar salts such as than $Mg(OH)_2$.

Magnesium salts are sometimes added to boilers operated at low pressure to precipitate magnesium silicate. This salt separates as a flocculent precipitate that can be removed by blowdown. Also, soda ash, Na_2CO_3, is used in low-pressure boilers fed with water containing 20 ~ 75 mg/L of hardness to precipitate $CaCO_3$ and $Mg(OH)_2$.

Words and Expressions

come out of   有……结果
diffraction   [di'frækʃən]   n. 衍射
polarize   ['pəuləraiz]   v. 偏振,极化
acmite   ['ækmait]   n. 锥辉石
analcite   [ə'nælsait]   n. 方沸石
serpentine   ['sə:pəntain]   adj. 蛇纹石
sodalite   ['səudəlait]   n. 方钠石
xonotlite   ['zəunətˌlait]   n. 硬硅钙石
hydroxyapatite   [haiˌdrɔksi'æpətait]   n. 含氧酸磷灰石
anhydrite   [æn'haidrait]   n. 酸酶
aragonite   [ə'rægənait]   n. 散文石
anhydrous   [æn'haidrəs]   adj. 无水的
hydrolysis   [hai'drɔlisis]   n. 水解
hydroxyl   [hai'drɔksil]   n. 氢氧
binder   ['baində]   n. 黏合
innocuous   [i'nɔkjuəs]   adj. 无害(毒的)
zeolite   ['zi:əlait]   n. 沸石

orthophosphate [ˌɔːθəu'fɔsfeit] n. 亚磷酸盐

7.10 Air Pollution

A great deal of energy is needed to run the factories of modern industrial nations. Automobiles, trains, planes, and buses need energy, too. Nearly all of this energy is produced in the same way—by burning fuels. The burning produces wastes. Some of the wastes get into the air, causing air pollution.

Government officials in the United states estimate that 200 000 000 tons of these wastes enter the air each year—1 ton for each person in the country!

A curtain of smog often hangs over big cities. It irritates the eyes and chests. The word "smog" is a combination of the words "smoke" and "fog", but "smog" itself is a mixture of many more ingredients. It begins with some of the pollution from burning: carbon monoxide, and oxides of nitrogen and sulfur are among them. Some of the pollutants react with one another to form new irritating substances. Energy is needed for the reactions, and it is supplied by the light of the sun. The resulting mixture is photochemical smog. ("Photo" means light.) It can be deadly.

In London, Tokyo, New York and other cities, a weather condition called a temperature inversion allows smog to hang over the city for several days at a time. Many people become ill, and the death rate among elderly people and people with lung disorders climbs rapidly.

At least half of the pollutants in the air come from the engines of motor vehicles. As they burn fuel, they give off carbon monoxide as a waste. Carbon monoxide is a colorless, odorless gas, and a deadly poison. The amount of carbon monoxide that an engine gives off can be reduced by special devices designed to make the engine burn the fuel more efficiently.

Automobile manufacturers are working on experimental cars run by electricity or other means that will reduce pollution. City governments in various parts of the world have begun to close certain streets to automobile traffic, hoping to lower pollution levels. Many city planners believe that cities, or at least their central areas, should be kept free of automobiles.

Motor vehicles are not the only air polluters. Coal and oil, used to heat homes and factories and to generate electricity, contain small amounts of sulfur. When the fuels are burned, sulfur dioxide, a poisonous gas, is produced. It is irritating to the lungs. Some cities have passed laws that allow coal and oil to be burned only if their sulfur content is low.

Most electricity is generated by steam turbines. About half of the sulfur dioxide in the air comes from burning fuel to make steam. Nuclear power plants do not burn fuel, so there is no air pollution of the ordinary kind. But the radioactive materials in these plants could present a danger in an accident. Also, there is a problem in disposing of the radioactive wastes in a way that will not endanger the environment.

Another type of pollution, called thermal (heat) pollution, is caused by both the fuel-burning and nuclear plants. Both need huge amounts of cold water, which is warmed as it cools the steam. When it is returned to the river, the warm water may stimulate the growth of weeds. It may also kill fish and their eggs, or interfere with their growth.

Physicists are studying new ways of generating electricity that may be less damaging to the environment. In the meantime, many power plants are being modernized to give off less polluting material. Also, engineers try to design and locate new power plants to do minimum damage to the environment.

Words and Expressions

smog　[smɔg]　*n*. 烟雾

irritate　['iriteit]　*v*. 激怒,使急躁,使兴奋

ingredient [in'gri:diənt] n. 成分,组成部分,原料,要素
monoxide [mə'nɔksaid] n. 一氧化物
photochemical [ˌfəutəu'kemikəl] a. 光化学的
inversion [in'və:ʃən] n. 逆温,逆增
lung [lʌŋ] n. 肺
disorder [dis'ɔ:də] n. (身心,机能的)失调,轻病
odo(u)rless ['əudəlis] a. 没有香气(气味)的
poison ['pɔizn] n. 毒,毒物 v. 毒害,毒死
engine ['endʒin] n. 发动机
radioactive [ˌreidiəu'æktiv] a. 放射性的
fuel-burning a. 燃料燃烧的

7.11 Pressure Measurement

Instruments and methods for measuring pressure, temperature, flow and the quality and purity of steam are essential in the operation of a steam generating unit. Serving to assure safe, economical and reliable operation of the equipment, they range from the simplest manual devices to the measuring devices used to actuate the complete automatic control of boilers and all associated equipment.

Test instrumentation, often of a portable nature, is employed in the performance testing of equipment to determine flow, pressures and temperatures required to satisfy the user and the equipment supplier that the conditions of design and operation have been met. Requirements for these instruments are summarized in the *ASME Performance Test Codes*. These instruments require skilled technical operators, careful handling, and frequent calibration. They are generally not suitable for long-term continuous commercial operation.

Commercial instruments are those permanently installed and are expected to give satisfactory accuracy for extended periods. The emphasis is on dependability and repeatability. This often demands some compromise in absolute accuracy. However, the accuracy of commercial instruments is being improved, and they are being used increasingly for test purposes.

The pressure gage is probably the earliest instrument used in boiler operation. Today more than one hundred years after the first "water-tube-safety boiler", the use of a pressure gage for determining steam drum pressure is still a requirement, even though modern controls and interlocks make overpressuring of a boiler virtually impossible. The Bourdon tube gage (Fig. 7.9) illustrates a type of gage which has been used for many years for pressure indication. Although improvements have been made in construction and accuracy, the basic principle has not changed.

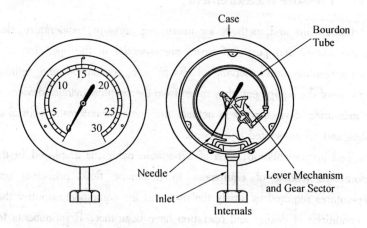

Fig. 7.9 Bourdon gage

Pressure-measuring instruments take various forms, depending on the magnitude of the pressure, the accuracy desired and other conditions.

Manometers, which may contain a wide variety of fluids, depending on the pressure, are capable of high accuracy with careful use. The fluids used vary from those lighter than water for low pressures to mercury for relatively high pressures. Fig. 7.10 illustrates an inclined manometer for reading small differentials at low pressure. Differential diaphragm gages using a magnetic linkage are now coming into use for low-pressure measurement. Fig. 7.11 shows a high-pressure mercury manometer. Manometers are considered an accurate means of pressure or pressure-differential measurement and are acceptable for *ASME Performance Test Code* purposes. For greater precision in measuring small pressure differentials, such as the accurate reading of flow orifice differentials, hook gages or micro-manometers may be used. A hook gage is illustrated in Fig. 7.12.

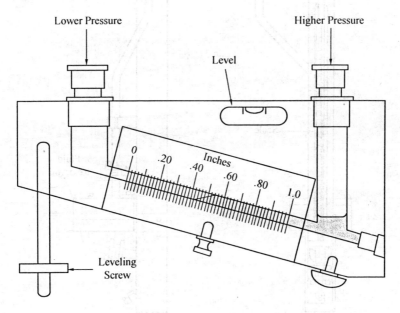

Fig. 7.10 Inclined differential manometer (*Dwyer Instruments, Inc*).

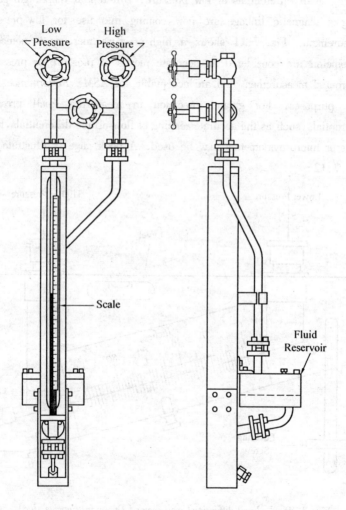

Fig. 7.11 High-pressure mercury manometer (*Meriam Instrument Company*).

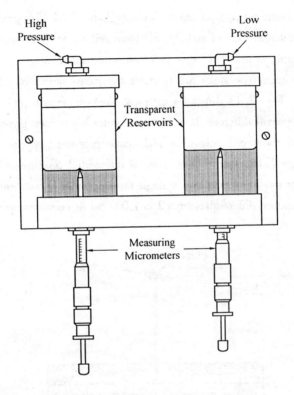

Fig. 7.12   Hook gage (*Dwyer Instruments, Inc.*).

Bourdon tube gages are available for the measurement of a wide range of static pressures in varying degrees of precision and accuracy. The precision and accuracy necessary are determined by the requirements of the application. Pressure gages used as operating guides need not be of high precision and normally have scale subdivisions about 1% of full-scale range. For certain test procedures, such as hydrostatic testing of pressure parts and boiler efficiency tests, a higher degree of precision is required. Gages with scale subdivisions of 0.1% of full-scale range are available and should be used for these purposes. For efficiency testing, where temperatures and pressures should be known with high precision for accurate determination of enthalpy of steam and water, dead-weight gages are preferable to Bourdon gages for pressure measurement.

Diaphragm-type gages are used for the measurement of differential pressures. Fig. 7.13 illustrates a typical slack-diaphragm pressure gage for reading small differentials in inches of water where total pressure does not exceed about one psig. For high static pressures, opposed bellows gages (Fig. 7.14) read a wide range of differential pressures. They are suitable for reading fluid pressure drops through boiler circuits and can be used to measure differentials from 2 to 1 000 psi at pressures up to 6 000 psi.

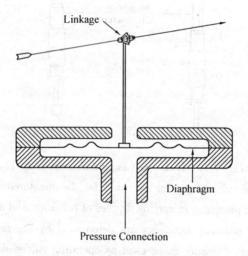

Fig. 7.13 Slack-diaphragm pressure gage.

More sophisticated devices for the measurement of pressures and differential pressures are now on the market. These are generally described as transducers and are based on a variety of principles. Some examples are transducers using a strain gage mounted on a diaphragm, or

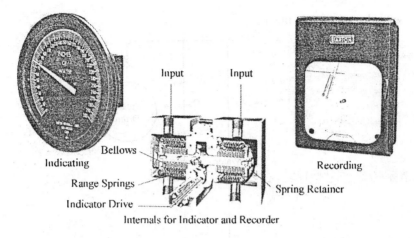

Fig. 7.14 Opposed bellows gage (*ITT BARTON*, a unit of *International Telephone and Telegraph Corporation*).

those using a crystal which undergoes a change in electrical resistance as the element is deformed. Since such elements necessitate elaborate and frequent calibration they are not normally used as basic instruments for operating guides or test equipment. However, with their rapidly increasing reliability and ease of application, pressure transducers are finding wider application.

Pressure readings

In recording and reporting pressure readings, suitable correction to gage readings must be made for water leg, where it exists, and for converting to absolute pressure by the addition of atmospheric pressure, if required. Water leg is merely the added pressure imposed on the gage not contributed by the actual pressure, but by an effective leg of condensate or water standing above the gage. Fig. 7.15 illustrates the application of water-leg correction to a pressure-gage reading. For practical usage it is sufficient to reset the gage to zero with pressure off the system and the water leg completely filled.

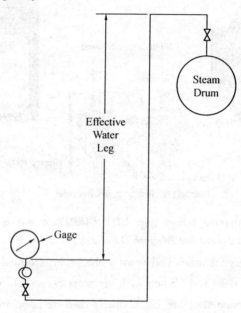

Fig. 7.15 Application of water-leg correction to pressure-gage reading.

Pressure drops across various types of devices such as orifices, nozzles, or pitot tubes provide a means of measuring flow and are described in a later section of this chapter.

Instrument connections for pressure measurement

The guiding principles governing the location of connections to the pressure source for measuring devices are in general the same regardless of the magnitude of the pressure, the type of measuring device, or the fluid being measured.

Pressure connections, or taps, in piping, flues or ducts, should be located in a position which avoids errors due to impact or eddies, thus assuring that a true static pressure is being measured. The connecting lines should be as short and direct as possible and free of leaks. For differential-pressure readings it is preferable to use a differential-pressure-measuring device rather than to take the difference between the readings on two instruments.

Words and Expressions

measurement　['meʒəmənt]　n. 量度,测量
instrument　['instrumənt]　n. 仪器,器具
associate　[ə'səuʃit]　vt & vi. (使)发生联系,(使)联合　n. 伙伴,同事
intertocks　[ˌintə'lɔks]　n. 联动装置
manometer　[mə'nɔmitə]　n. 压力计
diaphragm　['daiəfræm]　n. 膈,隔膜,光圈
precision　[pri'siʒən]　n. 精确度,准确(性)
sophisticated　[sə'fistikeitid]　adj. 精密的,尖端的

7.12　Clean Coal Technologies

Coal is well known to be a dirty fuel, so it is necessary to develop "clean coal" techniques in order to comply with more and more stringent environmental legislation.

The first approach consists in reducing emissions from existing Pulverized Coal(PC) installations by developing depolluting devices that act on combustion in the furnace (primary process) and/or that treat flue gas leaving the furnace (secondary process).

The second approach consists in designing entirely new technologies, all based on fluidized bed combustion, which enables to set coal combustion conditions favorable to simultaneous NO_x and SO_x depollution in the furnace. In addition, coal gasification is considered.

So, the Clean Coal Technologies to be considered in this study are the following:

1. Primary and Secondary Depolluting Systems for Existing Units;
2. Pulverized Coal with Flue Gas Treatment (PC + FGT);

3. Atmospheric Circulating Fluidized Bed Combustion (ACFBC);

4. Pressurized Bubbling Fluidized Bed Combustion (PBFBC);

5. Pressurized Circulating Fluidized Bed Combustion (PCFBC);

6. Integrated Gasification Combined Cycle (IGCC);

7. Hybrid Cycle Applied to Circulating Fluidized Beds (HC: HC-ACFBC and HC-PCFBC).

Clean Coal, Technologies for Existing Units

•Primary Processes

Denitrification Devices. Burners are more and more designed to limit nitrogen oxide formation during combustion. These burners, known as "low-NO_x", rely on the concept of air injection staging and of fuel distribution modification. The principle is to avoid too high flame temperatures and to reduce oxygen excess in the furnace, which favors nitrogen oxide formation. Another primary process consists in staging the combustion air in the furnace and is known as Over Fire Air (OFA). An additional process consists in staging the fuel injection into the furnace and is known as "reburning".

Desulphurization Devices. The primary desulphurization processes consist in injecting lime or limestone as a fine powder into the furnace in order to absorb the generated sulphur dioxide. If necessary, slaked lime and water are injected into the flue gas in order to improve the desulphurization efficiency. These processes can be used because of their low cost even if their efficiency is moderate: about 40% to 70%.

•Secondary Processes

Denitrification Devices. The reduction of NO_x emissions can be also achieved by means of catalytic or non-catalytic chemical processes. The most used secondary process (95% of installed systems) is the Selective Catalytic Reduction. Gaseous ammonia is mixed with combustion gas at the boiler outlet before the air-heater. The mixture gets then across a reactor containing catalysts to give N_2 and water. The temperature range of operation is 350 ~ 430℃.

Desulphurization Devices. For the recent installations, the SO_2 emissions are generally reduced by wet limestone/gypsum Flue Gas Desulphurization (FGD) systems. Sulphur dioxide is removed from combustion gas in the form of gypsum ($CaSO_4$), essentially through a wet process using a solution of carbonate, sulphite and sulphate of calcium in-suspension.

Atmospheric Circulating Fluidized Bed Combustion

The principle of Atmospheric Circulating Fluidized Bed Combustion (ACFBC) power plant consists in producing steam at high temperature and pressure from the heat generated by the complete coal combustion in a fluidized bed furnace. Pressure in the furnace is about atmospheric pressure and fluidizing velocity is high. Solid particles leaving therefore the furnace are collected and recirculated into the furnace. This recirculating of solid matters in the furnace enables an efficient coal combustion kept at about 850℃ (in order to favour sulphur dioxide retention by limestone and to minimize nitrogen oxide formation). Electricity is delivered by an alternator associated with a steam turbine where the steam generated by the process is expanded.

Pressurized Bubbling Fluidized Bed Combustion

In a Pressurized Bubbling Fluidized Bed Combustion (PBFBC) power plant, the boiler is operating under pressure; between 1.0×10^6 Pa and 1.6×10^6 Pa, and the bed fluidizing velocity is low. So the fluidized bed presents a free solid surface distinct from the gaseous phase above. At this fluidizing velocity, gas bubbles are getting through the bed to its surface, and it is called as "Bubbling Bed". Electricity is delivered by two generators, the first one associated with a steam turbine where the steam generated by the process is expanded, the second one with a gas turbine where flue gas is expanded. The PBFBC technology involves a combined cycle.

Pressurized Circulating Fluidized Bed Combustion

In a Pressurized Circulating Fluidized Bed Combustion (PCFBC) power plant, the boiler is operating under pressure, between 1.0×10^6 Pa, and 1.6×10^6 Pa, and the bed fluidizing velocity is high, similar to ACFBC. The PCFBC properties due to the Circulating Fluidized Bed are the same as those of ACFBC. The only difference is that the PCFBC furnace operates under pressure.

Integrated Gasification in a Combined Cycle

In IGCC, gas obtained from coal gasification is cleaned up in order to eliminate in particular dust and sulphur compounds, prior to being burnt, generally in a gas turbine, to generate electricity. A heat recovery boiler allows to recover part of the sensible heat of flue gas by producing steam. This steam is also used to drive a steam turbine to generate electricity also.

The new techniques of coal or oil residue gasification offer today the possibility to generate electricity in combined cycle with high efficiency. The IGCC technology presents many variants. They can be notably distinguished not only by the gasified type (fixed bed, fluidized bed), but also by the oxidizer used (air or oxygen) and by the gas cleaning system.

Words and Expressions

Clean Coal Technology(CCT) 洁净煤技术
emission [i'miʃən] n. 发出,排出物
Pulverized Coal(PC) 煤粉
flue gas 烟道内烟气

fluidized bed combustion 流化床燃烧
coal gasification 煤气化
Circulating Fluidized Bed(CFB) 循环流化床
Bubbling Fluidized Bed(BFB) 鼓泡流化床
Integrated Gasification Combined Cycle(IGCC) 整体煤气化(蒸汽一燃气)联合循环
Hybrid cycle 混合循环
denitrification device 除氮装置
burner ['bə:nə] n. 燃烧器
air injection staging 空气分段送人
nitrogen oxide 氮氧化物
Over Fire Air(OFA) 过燃风
desulphurization devices 除硫装置
lime [laim] n. 石灰
limestone ['laimstəun] n. 石灰石
sulphur dioxide 二氧化硫
slaked lime 熟石灰
Selective Catalytic Reduction(SCR) 选择性催化剂脱氮装置
gaseous ammonia 氨气
catalyst ['kætəlist] n. 催化剂
carbonate ['ka:bəneit] vt. 碳酸盐
sulphite ['sʌlfait] n. 亚硫酸盐
sulphate ['sʌlfeit] n. 硫酸盐
calcium ['kælsiəm] n. 钙
suspension [səs'penʃən] n. 悬浮
alternator ['ɔ:ltə(:)neitə] n. 交流发电机
deliver [di'livə] vt. 释放,发出
sensible heat 显热
gasifier ['gæsifaiə] n. 气化床
oxidizer ['ɔksidaizə(r)] n. 氧化剂

参考译文

流体的定义和流体流动的分类(1.1)

凡受到再小的切应力都会发生连续不停变形的物质，叫做流体。切力是作用力沿表面相切的方向上的分力，该力除以面积，便可得到此面积上的平均切应力。当面积缩成一点时，切力对面积比值的极限值，即为该点上的切应力。

如图1.1(见原文)所示，彼此靠得很近的平行放置着的两块平板间充以某物质，平板很大，从而可以不考虑板四周边缘处的情况。固定下板，对上板施加一个作用力 F，处在板间的物质便会受到切力 F/A 的作用，A 代表上板面积，只要力 F 能使上板以恒定(不等于零)的速度运动，而不论力 F 的量值多么小，你就可以断定板间的物质是一种流体。

紧贴固体边壁处的流体有同边壁相同的速度，也就是说，交界处并无滑移。这一事实已为不同流体和不同边壁材料进行的千万次实验证实。面积 $abcd$ 里的流体流到新的位置 $ab'c'd$ 处，每一流体质点均平行于平板运动，其速度 u 自固定平板上的零值均匀地变化到上板处的 U。实验表明，保持其它诸参量不变时，则 F 同 A 和 U 成正比，且同厚度 t 成反比。用公式表示即为

$$F = \mu \frac{AU}{t}$$

式中，μ 是依所选用的流体而定的比例系数。令 $\tau = F/A$ 代表切应力，则有

$$\tau = \mu \frac{U}{t}$$

比值 U/t 即为线段 ab 的角速度，或者说是流体的角变形速度，即 bad 角减小的速度。角速度还可以 du/dy 表示，因为 U/t 以及 du/dy 两者都表示了速度变化量所需的那段距离。不过 du/dy 更具普遍性，因为它适用于角速度和切应力随 y 变化的情况。速度梯度 du/dy 还可以形象地看作某层相对于

其邻层流体间的速度。表示成微分形式便有

$$\tau = \mu \frac{du}{dy} \quad (1.1)$$

上式即为流体的一元流动中切应力同角变形率间的关系。比例系数 μ 称为流体的粘度。方程(1.1)就称为牛顿粘性定律。

非流体材料就不能满足流体的定义。塑性物质会随着所施加作用力的大小而发生一定的变形,但当作用其上的应力小于屈服的切应力时,变形即告中止。两平板间若是完全真空,变形速率将渐次增大不已,要是把沙粒填进二块平板间,那么库伦摩擦要求作用力必须超过某值时才会引起连续的运动。因而,塑料和固体均无法归入流体的分类里。

流体可分成牛顿型流体与非牛顿型流体。牛顿型流体里施加的切应力的大小同其所引起的角变形速率有着线性的关系(方程(1.1)中的 μ 为常数)。非牛顿型流体中,施加的切应力的大小同其所引起的角变形速率间有非线性的关系。理想塑性体有一确定的屈服应力,同时其中的 τ 与 du/dy 间有着一定的线性关系。触变性物质,如油墨之类,其黏度依该物质当时经历的角变形而定,且在静止不动时趋于凝聚态。各种气体和稀薄液体近乎牛顿型流体,而稠厚的长链碳氢化合物则常为非牛顿型流体。

为了分析问题起见,通常假定流体是无黏性的。黏度为零时,不管流体是否流动,切应力总等于零。若把流体看成是无黏性的,那么这就称为理想流体。

流体的流动可用多种方式加以分类,如恒定流或非恒定流,有旋流或无旋流,可压缩流或不可压缩流,以及黏性流或无黏性流等。

流体的流动可以是恒定的或者非恒定的。如果在任一给定点处流体的速度不随时间而变化,这种流体的流动就称为恒定流。也就是说,流经恒定流中任一给定点的每一流体质点的速度总是相同。在另一点上某质点的流动速度可能不同,但任一通过该第二点上的其它质点恰好同该质点经过此点时的速度相同。在低的流动速度下就可能出现这种情形,徐缓的溪流便是其中一例。非恒定流方面,可以举出涨潮时的激浪为例,其速度是时间的函数。诸如急流或瀑布——紊流情形里,各点间以及不同时刻下的速度均变化不定。

流体流动可以是有旋的或者无旋的。如果每个点上的流体微团绕该点均无净角速度,这时的流体流动便是无旋的。我们不妨设想在运动流体中有个小的自行车蹬,只要车蹬运动时不发生旋转,这种运动便是无旋的;否则就是有旋的。有旋流动包含像一些涡漩那样的旋涡运动。

流体流动可以是可压缩的或者不可压缩的。各种液体通常可作为不可压缩流动看待,不过即使某种有高度压缩性的气体,有时它的密度并未表现出多大的变化,这样的流动实际上仍是不可压缩的。飞行速度远小于空气中的声速时(在亚声速空气动力学中述及),空气相对于飞机机翼的运动便是一种不可压缩流动。

流体流动还可以是黏性的或者无黏性的。流体流动中的黏性可以比作固体运动中的摩擦。许多情形里,比如在润滑问题中,这是极其重要的,但有时又可予以忽略。黏性引起流体相对运动各层间的切向力,从而导致了机械能的损耗。

流体力学发展史(1.2)

流体力学这门科学起源于古代中国、埃及、美索不达美亚和印度,它是随着水利灌溉和舟船航行的需要对水进行治理而出现的。虽然这些文明之邦都黯熟河道水流的本质,但尚无根据说明他们曾经提出过什么定量规律以指导其工作。直到公元前250年,阿基米德才发现并记载了有关水静力学及浮力方向的一些定理。尽管水动力学方面的实际知识始终不断地促使人们改进并推动流体机械的发展,造出更好的帆船,建成日益错综复杂的运河水系,然而作为经典水动力学方面的一些基本定理,还是要等到十七八世纪时开始建立起来。牛顿、丹尼尔·伯努利、列昂纳德·欧拉都曾为建立这些定理作出过最大的贡献。

在19世纪,流体力学领域里形成了两种想法不同的学派,一派从理论角度处理流体流动,另一派则从实际流动情况出发。经典水动力学虽然作为一门吃香的学科吸引了一批数学家,但因其理论均从无黏性流体出发,所以无法用到许多实际问题里去。当时潜心于实际工作的工程师们正需要一些设计方法以对付有粘性的流体,因而他们提出了各种有用的、但使用范围有限的经验公式。于是就出现了这样的局面,一方面数学家和物理学家提出了一些工程师在许多场合下无法应用的理论,另一方面,工程师所使用的经验公式又只能在其导出范围以内应用。从某种意义上说来,这两派不同想法一直绵延至今,形成了数学领域里的水动力学以及实用科学中的水力学。

然而,在接近20世纪之初,人们为了求得在认清流动过程方面能有重大进展,数学家与物理学家的一般不够严密的方法同工程师的实验方法异途同归,融在一起,便成为势所必然。1883年,奥斯本·雷诺的一篇关于紊流的文章,以及随后几篇有关液体运动基本方程的论文,无可估量地促进了流体力学的发展。进入20世纪之始,1904年,路德维希·普朗特提出了边界层的概念。普朗特在他这篇短小而有说服力的文章里,对各种黏性不大的流体,一下子就提出了理想流体与实际流体两种运动间的本质联系,由此在很大程度上奠定了这代流体力学的基础。

流体力学在20世纪里的发展可分为四个时期:

1. 低速空气动力学,1900~1935年

流体力学开头的发展是同航空科学密切相关的。由于载重方面的严格要求,人们需要有对实际问题进行可靠的理论上的预先估计。随之而出现了把古老的水动力学与水力学中的基本要点结合起来构成一门理论流体力学学科。这个时期的重要发展有:(甲)普朗特的边界层理论;(乙)库塔和儒可夫斯基的翼展理论,它可以解释空气升力现象;(丙)冯·卡门等人的紊流理论。在此时期内,流体的流动速度不大,而且流动中的温差也小,从而我们可以把流体的压缩性忽略不计。气体与液体均可按同一分析方法处理。实际上水动力学与空气动力学并无区别。

2. 空气热力学,1935~1950年

气体流动的速度渐次地由亚声速增大为超声速。气体的压缩性效应不再能予忽视。气体与液体就必须加以区别对待。在气体动力学里,我们必须同时考虑到流动的力学与气体热力学,因而空气热力学这个术语便应运而生,以反映流体力学这个新的分支。这方面最重要的参数是马赫数。但气体或空气的温度范围仍在2 000 K以下,空气仍可看成是比热容为不变的理想气体。分子结构对气体流动几乎没有影响,不管是单原子还是多原子气体,仍都适用同样的方程。但是像激波、超声速流动等许多新现象已在此时期内被加以分析。

3. 流体物理学,1950~1960年

这是空间时代之始。流体速度与流体温度之高足以使我们必须考虑到流体力学同物理学中其它分支学科间的相互影响,即气体分子结构对流体的流动大有影响。我们必须计及离解、电离和热辐射的影响。像空气热化学、

磁性气体动力学、等离子体动力学以及辐射气体动力学等新学科把研究延伸开去,使我们不得不面对整门流体物理学。

4.流体力学的新纪元,1960年至今

以上三个时期内,我们主要关心的还是只有一种液体、气体或者等离子体的流体流动。近来,许多技术部门发展之广,促使我们必须涉及不仅单独一种流体的流动,例如同固体与液体的混合物打交道,这就是所谓的两相流动。在许多流变学问题中,一些流体的性质既有点像普通流体,又有点像固体那样。以上三个时期里,我们主要根据经典物理学原理处理流体流动问题。在许多流体流动的新问题中,我们必须考虑经典物理学之外的一些原理,如超流体,即使就其宏观性质而论,量子效应也有举足轻重的作用(量子流体力学);又如相对论流体力学,因其流速同光速相比已不能忽略而必须用到相对论力学;我们还醉心于生物流体力学,其中要研究到流体流动的物理学学科同生物学学科之间的相互影响。同各行各业一样,流体力学的现代发展也离不开使用高速计算机来解题。这方面已有重大进展,流体动力设计方面正愈来愈多地用到计算机。

应当指出,尽管我们把现代流体力学划分成以上四个时期,但就各门学科所涉及的研究而言,在这些时期内还互相交叉重叠。例如,低速流动的紊流研究作为第一时期中的主要学科,而它至今仍然是十分热门的研究题目,其中许多基本课题远未获得解决。

热力学的基本概念(2.1)

热力学的应用大部分都要求对系统及它的环境定义。热力系统定义为空间的某一区域或某一封闭面包围的物质质量,环境包括系统外面的一切物体,系统和环境由系统分界面分隔。这些分界面可以是运动的或固定不变的,可以是真实的也可以是假想的。

两个主要概念在任何热力系统中都适用,即能量和熵。熵计量某一给定系统分子的无序(程度),系统越混乱,它的熵就越大。相反,有序或不混乱的结构是一个低熵系统。

能量是产生某一效果的能力,并且可以分成储存能和瞬时能两类。储存型能量包括:

热(内)能 u ——由于分子运动和/或分子之间的作用力,系统所具有的能量。

势能 $P.E.$ ——由于分子间存在的吸引力或系统的高度,系统所具有的能量

$$P.E. = mgz \tag{2.1}$$

式中　m ——质量;

g ——当地重力加速度;

z ——相对于水平参考面的高度。

动能 $K.E.$ ——由于分子速度,系统所具有的能量

$$K.E. = mw^2/2 \tag{2.2}$$

式中　m ——质量;

v ——穿过系统边界的流体速度。

化学能 E_c ——由于组成分子的原子的排列,系统所具有的能量。

核(原子)能 E_a ——由于使质子和中子构成原子核的内聚力作用,系统所具有的能量。

瞬时能包括:

热能 Q ——系统由于温度不同,穿过边界传递的能量总是朝着温度降低的方向。

功量——系统由于压力(或任何种类的力)不同,穿过边界传递的能量,它总是朝着压力降低的方向;如果该系统产生的总的效果能归纳成重物的升高,那么只有功量穿过边界。机械功或轴功 W,是由机械如透平、空气压缩机或内燃机传递或吸收的能量。

流动功是进入或跨越系统边界的能量,这是由于在系统外某处的泵送过程发生流体进入该系统而引起的。它作为系统外边界面处的流体为迫使或推动相邻流体进入系统而作的功更容易理解。当流体离开系统时也会产生流动功。

$$流动功(每单位质量) = pV \tag{2.3}$$

式中　p ——压力;

V ——比热容或单位质量排开的体积。

系统的参数是任何可观察到的系统特性。系统的状态通过列出它的参数来确定。最常见的热力学参数是:温度(T)、压力(p)、比热容(V)或密度(ρ)。另外,热力学参数还包括熵、储存能和焓。

热力学参数常常结合起来形成新的参数。焓(h)(参数结合得出的结果)定义为

$$h = u + pV \qquad (2.4)$$

式中　u——内能；

　　　p——压力；

　　　V——比热容。

给定状态的每一参数只有一个确定值,并且任一参数在给定状态下总保持同一值,不管物质是怎样到达这一状态的。

过程即状态的变化,定义为系统参数的任何变化。过程可以通过指定初、终平衡态,路径(如果是可辨认的)及过程中穿过系统边界发生的相互作用来描述。循环是一个过程,或更经常地是指一系列过程,在这些过程中系统的初、终态相同。因而,在循环结束时,所有参数都有与它们在初态时相同的数值。

纯物质具有均匀不变的化学成分。它能以多相存在,但所在的相中化学成分是相同的。

如果物质以饱和温度下的气态存在,则称为饱和蒸汽(有时用干饱和蒸汽这个术语来强调其干度为100%)。当蒸汽温度比其饱和温度高时,为过热蒸汽,过热蒸汽的压力和温度是独立参数,因为当压力保持不变时其温度可以增加。气体是高度过热的蒸汽。

导　热(2.4)

导热可以认为是通过物质分子间逐渐进行的能量交换而在物体(或物体联合体)内从高温区到低温区传递热量。在导热过程中,没有产生分子的具体的位移。然而,就金属来说,自由电子的运动大大有助于导热。

导热的基本定律归功于傅里叶。该定律可表示如下:考虑稳态的单向热流通过一固体,如图 2.2(见原文)所示,取一横截面积为 A 的固体的厚片,该厚片垂直于热流路径。设厚片的厚度为 dx,厚片两端间的温差为 dt。傅里叶从试验中得出了如下关系

$$Q = -kA\frac{dt}{dx} \qquad (2.5)$$

式中　Q——单位时间的热流量；

k ——比例系数,称为导热系数;

dt/dx ——热流方向上温度随距离的变化率。

在国际单位制中,导热系数表示为

$$W/m^2 \div K/m = W/(m \cdot K)$$

大量的试验研究已得出了许多物质的导热系数值和温度对这些导热系数的影响。注意,任何金属的导热系数与任何气体的导热系数相比都是非常高的。已发表的金属导热系数值仅对指定纯度的金属才是正确的。尤其对那些具有最高导热系数值的金属,掺入少量其他金属就会引起导热系数的明显变化。

最佳的绝热固体应将其绝热性能归功于材料小孔内所含的空气或其他气体。这些小孔使热量经过长而弯曲的路径流经固体。另外,固体材料可得到的横截面积比投影面积小得多。实验证据表明,在使物质具有绝热值(性能)方面,许多单个小气孔要比有相同总体积的连接起来的一串气孔有效得多。任何给定的绝热材料,其导热系数都可能有很大的变化,因为导热系数取决于材料的密度、体积、小气孔的数量和吸湿量。

通过实验确定固体的导热系数,有几种可以接受的方法。只要适当注意,对成分已知的给定固体就可以得到相当准确的导热系数值。然而,要确定气体、蒸气或液体的导热系数值却要困难得多,因为要从中去掉通过对流所传递的热量(与导热同时发生)几乎是不可能的,况且还没有包括准确测量其他因素的困难。因为这些原因,已发表的流体导热系数值都有大约10%~25%的误差。图2.3(见原文)表示了在简单墙体中的热传导。假设墙体的宽度和高度要比墙体的厚度大得多,从而可以认为热流是单向的。墙体的一面维持均匀温度 t_1,另一面保持在温度 t_2。通过墙体的热量可以通过方程(2.5)积分得到。

考察附录中给出的各种物质的导热系数表明,对许多物质,其导热系数在相当大的温度范围内可以认为是恒定值。而且,对大多数物质,在信息可以得到的温度范围内,其导热系数是温度的线性函数。这样可以用导热系数的算术平均值 k_m 作为真实的导热系数。对简单墙体,方程(2.5)可积分如下

$$Q = \frac{k_m A}{x}(t_1 - t_2) \tag{2.6}$$

根据方程(2.6),热流速率正比于热流面积、引起热流的温差和 k_m/x 项。该项称为导热率。

当导热系数不随温度线性变化时,平均导热系数 k_m 就不容易确定。在这种情况下,就需要在方程(2.5)中把导热系数表示为温度的函数,然后进行积分。

液体燃料和固体燃料的燃烧(3.5)

液体燃料(石油、重油)燃烧时的点火温度,特别是燃烧温度,要高于包含在液体燃料成分内的各单独组成的沸腾温度,所以首先靠加热使燃料表面进行蒸发,而后燃料蒸气同空气混合,加热到着火温度并燃烧,在离开液体表面一定距离处(0.5~1 mm 或更大)才形成火焰。

图 3.2(见原文)示出一滴液体燃料在不流动空气中燃烧时环绕着液滴形成向周围介质扩散的蒸气云。迎面有空气中氧的扩散,结果在离开液滴 r_{st} 处,可燃气体和氧之间达到了化学反应的配比。环绕液滴形成的球形燃料蒸气的燃烧前沿就在这里, $r_{st} = (4 \sim 10) r_d$(这里的 r_d 是液滴直径), r_{st} 和液滴尺寸与燃烧区的关系极大,在 $r < r_{st}$ 的区域内,主要是燃料蒸汽,而它的浓度随着与液体表面的距离增加而减小。在 $r > r_{st}$ 区域内,含有向燃烧区扩散的氧与燃烧产物形成的混合物。在反应区,燃烧温度达到最高值,然后它的两侧降低,而且越靠近液滴,温度降低得越剧烈,这是由于消耗热量来加热燃料蒸气的缘故。

因此,液体燃烧中液滴燃烧的速度取决于液滴从表面蒸发的速度、在燃烧区里化学反应的速度以及氧气向燃烧区扩散的速度。正如前面所述,在气态介质中的反应速度是很高的且不会限制总的燃烧速度。通过球形表面扩散的氧气量与其直径的平方成正比,所以燃烧区离开液滴表面不远处,氧气的供给量就显著增加(在氧气不足的情况下),因此,液体燃料的燃烧速度主要决定于它的蒸发情况。为了提高液体燃料的燃烧速度,必须保证在燃料燃烧前把它喷得很细,以增加其总的蒸发表面积。此外,随着液滴尺寸的减少,它从单位表面积蒸发的强度增加。悬浮在空气中的液体燃料油滴的特点是雷诺数很小, $Re \ll 4$,在这种情况下,通过球形表面的热流仅决定于通过边界层的导热系数 λ,而边界层的厚度又远大于液滴的直径,此时,放热系数 α 可用 Sokolsky 公式来表示

$$Nu = \alpha d / \lambda = 2 \tag{3.5}$$

因此，
$$\alpha = 2\lambda/d = \lambda/r \tag{3.6}$$
式中的 Nu 为努谢尔特数。

由式(3.6)可知，液滴同周围介质的热交换随着它的尺寸减少而增加，同时，液滴质量也在减少。结果是，液滴蒸发的时间正比于它的初始直径的平方。

固体燃料的燃烧 当煤粉在炉膛中与空气混合后，首先要经过燃烧预备阶段(图3.3，I，见原文)，这个过程包括剩余水分的蒸发和挥发分的分离。煤粉被加热到一定温度(400~600℃)时，挥发分在十分之几秒的时间内发生了巨大变化，然后挥发分被点着，因此，环绕煤粉粒处的温度迅速提高，煤粉加热变快。挥发分的强烈燃烧持续0.2~0.5 s，许多煤种(如褐煤、油页岩、泥煤)的挥发分燃烧后产生的热量足以将煤粉加热到着火点。当某些煤种所含挥发分较低时，煤粉必须通过外部因素另外加热，最后阶段是煤粉在800~1 000℃的温度下燃烧，这是一个不同种类组成的过程。它的反应速度决定于反应物表面氧的供给。煤粉燃烧的时间占总时间的大部分(1/2~1/3)，总时间约为1~2.5 s，它决定于煤种和颗粒的大小。

碳和氧的反应机理如下：氧从烟气中被吸收到煤粉表面，和碳发生化学反应生成复杂的碳-氧化合物 C_xO_y，然后它又分解成 CO 和 CO_2，在1 200℃左右的反应可表示为

$$4C + 3O_2 = 2CO + 2CO_2 \tag{3.7}$$

实验表明，主要产物的比率，即 CO/CO_2，随着煤粉温度的提高而迅速变大。例如，1 700℃左右时反应可表示为

$$3C + 2O_2 = 2CO + CO_2 \tag{3.8}$$

这里 CO/CO_2 的比率为2。

主要的反应产物不断地从煤粉表面向周围移动，在这个过程中，一氧化碳遇到反向扩散的氧，并与之反应生成二氧化碳，导致在近煤粉表面处供给氧的浓度大减，而 CO_2 的浓度提高。在较高的燃烧温度下，一氧化碳可能消耗所有的供给氧，结果，氧气不能到达煤粉表面(图3.4(b)，见原文)。在这种情况下，吸热反应将在煤粉表面发生，即 CO_2 将转变成 CO。

因此，碳粒表面的不同燃烧可以包括4个接连的反应，其中两个是主要的

$$C + O_2 = CO_2 + q_1$$

$$2C + O_2 = 2CO + 2q_2$$

另外两个反应是次要的

$$2CO + O_2 = 2CO_2 + 2q_3$$
$$C + CO_2 = CO - q_4$$

这里的 q 是反应的热，单位为 MJ/mol。

第一个反应的热效应 $q_1 = q_2 + q_3$, $q_4 = 0.57 q_3$。后面的等式表示即使吸热反应发生时，燃烧反应的温度仍能保持很高，这是由于容积中的反应放出更多的能量。

分析这些反应可知，碳表面的燃烧以部分气化的形式发生（形成的 CO 和容积中后期燃烧的气体），这个过程促进了碳粒的燃尽。

核燃料(3.6)

除了太阳能以外，传统的主要热能源是矿物燃料（例如木柴、煤、油和气）的燃烧。第二次世界大战期间，当美国曼哈顿工程(Manhatten Project)研制出原子弹时，惹人注目地出现了一种新能源，一般把它叫做"原子"能。从那以后，军舰推进和民用动力计划都成功地将原子核裂变作为一种实用的热能源加以利用。这种能源，严格地说来应该叫做"核"能，是通过裂变使原子核里的某些物质转换成能量的，可根据爱因斯坦的质能方程进行计算

$$E = mc^2 \tag{3.9}$$

式中　　E——能量；
　　　　m——质量；
　　　　c——光速。

用于生产蒸汽时，核能的各种实际应用都是利用裂变过程。一个重原子核分裂成两大块碎片，每块碎片都是一个轻原子核。分裂时，还释放出大量的能量。此外，还释放中子，这些中子可用于使别的原子裂变，从而形成"链式反应"。对链式反应加以控制，使它能保持连续不断地产生热能。

铀

铀是核动力工业的基本原料。它是稍带放射性的重化学元素，原子序数92，它是自然界里出现的非痕量的最重的元素。

在化学方面,铀是反应性强的金属,主要有 3 个化学价: +3, +4 和 +6。它有 3 个晶相,在 2 070 ℉时熔化。在 α 相中,它比较有延展性,并可用标准的金属加工技术制造。因为铀的小颗粒或碎片极易自燃,所以在加工和储存碎片时要求有特别的预防措施,例如使用冷却剂或惰性气体。

天然铀是三种同位素的混合物:铀$_{234}$(0.01%),铀$_{235}$(0.71%)和铀$_{238}$(99.28%)。铀$_{234}$量小,意义不大。铀$_{235}$是可裂变同位素,铀$_{238}$一般叫作增殖同位素。

铀的这三种天然同位素都具有放射性,放出 α 粒子。然而,它们的半衰期足够长,因此在处理天然铀时,需采取的预防措施很少。铀是化学毒物,人不得摄入。在处理铀的区域,空气中的铀含量必须保持在规定的容许值以下。

铀$_{235}$裂变是它的原子核吸收了中子的结果。1 g 铀$_{235}$裂变时,释放的热量大约相当于 1 兆瓦日(24 000 kW·h 或 82 000 000 Btu)。当 1 短吨铀$_{235}$裂变时,释放的热量相当于 220 亿 kW·h 或 750 000 亿 Btu,这相当于储藏在大约 300 万 t 煤里的热量。

各种能级的中子都能使铀$_{235}$裂变,并能维持链式反应。铀$_{235}$是一种可裂变物质,意即可被"慢"(低能量或热)中子裂变。

铀$_{238}$不能维持链式核反应,但高能中子可使其裂变到一定程度。当暴露给中子时(就像在核反应堆里那样),铀$_{238}$原子核在俘获中子以后,最终将转换成钚$_{239}$——一种新元素的可裂变同位素。钚$_{239}$能维持链式反应,裂变时,每克钚$_{239}$释放的热量约等于每克铀$_{235}$裂变时释放的热量。由于具有这种能够嬗变成裂变物质的能力,因此铀$_{238}$叫增殖物质。

铀因其两种主要的同位素铀$_{235}$和铀$_{238}$而成为核动力工业的基本原料。前者是在自然界发现的唯一的一种大量存在的裂变物质;后者是能产生可裂变钚的增殖物质。因为铀$_{238}$的储量是铀$_{235}$的 140 倍,因此作为能源来说,它的最终潜力是很大的。

另一种可转换元素钍,可用来生产动力,但需要用铀来将钍转换成裂变物质。

铀的利用

产生蒸汽用的矿物燃料需要连续不断地给料才能很好地燃烧。与矿物燃料不同,核燃料的使用是成批地进行的。它以名叫"燃料组件"的预制组件形式装入原子炉(或称反应堆)。这些燃料棒组件由装在合金包壳管里的氧化铀芯块组成。"包壳"一词并不是说一种金属覆盖于另一种金属之外,而是简单地指核燃料外罩,它用于防止腐蚀和防止裂变产物释放到冷却剂中去。对于使用这种燃料组件的大型动力堆,它的每个燃料组件可长达14 ft或更长一些,横截面可达8 in²或更大。在压水反应堆里,燃料棒必须设计成能承受高达2 500 psi的差压,那是在燃料组件使用初期由包壳管外的系统压力引起的。燃料管还必须承受燃料寿命期间累积的气体裂变产物所造成的内部压力。

下面是对产生蒸汽时使用的燃料(无论是核燃料或矿物燃料)的基本要求:

1. 控制反应堆或锅炉里的释热率;
2. 将燃料产生的热量传到水中去用以产生蒸汽;
3. 运行人员的防护,控制反应副产品;
4. 经济地使用燃料的设计。

液态副产品燃料(3.7)

沥青和焦油

石油和煤炭干馏出来的液体和半液体残余物质叫做沥青和焦油。这些残余物质的大部分都适合用作锅炉燃料。有些残余物质如同煤油一样便于处理和容易燃烧,而其它一些残余物质则会带来许多麻烦。为了证实某些沥青和焦油是否适合作为一给定设备的燃料,下列各项内容即是重要的:

水分 如果燃料中含有水分,就必须进行良好的乳化,防止燃料进入燃烧器时成为未蒸发的液滴。假如供给燃烧器的连续进料流程呈现瞬间中断,火焰即会熄灭。在重新供给燃料的同时,如果重新点燃燃烧器的时间延迟,炉膛就有可能发生爆炸。因此,如果未被蒸发的水滴将火焰瞬间熄灭的话,那末燃料供应中未被蒸发的水滴将是一场灾难。含水量高达35%的沥青和焦油亦可以在设计合适的设备中燃烧。

闪点和着火点 闪点的定义是,在一给定的条件下,液体燃料被充分地蒸发到一经点火就闪现瞬间火焰的最低温度。着火点的定义是,在给定的条件下,液体燃料被充分蒸发到一经点火就能连续燃烧的最低温度。许多液体燃料是由两种或两种以上不同液体组成的混合物。其中也许一种成分的闪点和着火点低,而另一种成分的闪点和着火点高。这样,低闪点的组成成分在燃烧器处燃烧掉了,而高闪点和高着火点的成分则在此燃烧,一般是有光亮的火焰,火焰呈暗黄色。实际上,如果燃烧器的紊流太小,或者燃烧产物从强燃烧区经过时因移动太快而熄灭,那末燃烧就会不完全,造成高的未燃尽可燃物质的损失。所以,正像闪点温度能用以确定燃料的贮存中是否包含着可能的危险一样,着火点则确定其是否适合在锅炉中燃烧。着火点高达600°F的燃料也可以在设计正确的锅炉中燃烧。

黏度 实际上,所有的沥青和焦油都可以按燃烧油的同样方法进行燃烧。沥青和焦油在燃烧器内的雾化器中变成雾状分散物,然后蒸发、燃烧。对于大部分雾化器来说,为了能产生细微的颗粒,燃烧油的黏度必须正确,不得超过180赛波特通用秒数(SUS),尽管燃烧器在炉膛内的布置合适,也可以使用粘度高达1 000赛波特通用秒数(SUS)的燃料。

悬浮物质 这些燃料中都含有悬浮物质。如果含有悬浮物质的燃料进入燃烧器,就会产生下列情况:

1. 雾化器会出现不正常的沾污,需要经常地清洗。
2. 燃烧器部件的磨损率过大。
3. 整个设备内会出现未燃碳的沉淀,或者烟囱中会有有害物质排出。

因此,这种燃料在送入燃烧器以前应用滤网过滤。

相容性 当一些燃料如果同一般性燃料油接触时,就会结合成硬块状物质。如果这种情况发生在管道里或容器内就会造成麻烦。这种燃料混合物不能从容器内泵出,而且如果管道堵塞,则经常需要将设备完全解体进行清洗,燃烧器的运行也会是不稳定和有问题的。因此,大量的沥青和焦油与燃料油混合之前,必须先在实验室进行这种燃料在贮存温度下和泵送温度下的实验,以确定这两种燃料的相容性。

理想的基本蒸气压缩制冷循环(4.1)

基本蒸气压缩循环的设备图如图4.1(见原文)所示。这种循环的组成部分至少包括压缩机、冷凝器、膨胀阀和蒸发器。理想循环考虑的是由管道连接的无压力损失冷凝器和蒸发器,可逆绝热(定熵)压缩机和绝热膨胀阀之间的热传递,连接用的管道既没有压力损失也没有与周围环境的热传递。制冷剂以低压、低温的饱和蒸气形式在点1离开蒸发器进入压缩机,在压缩机中被可逆绝热(定熵)压缩。在点2,制冷剂以高温高压的过热蒸气形式离开压缩机,进入冷凝器,在冷凝器中首先被降温,然后在定压下冷凝。在点3,制冷剂以高压、中间温度的饱和液体形式离开冷凝器进入膨胀阀,在膨胀阀中发生不可逆绝热膨胀(焓不变)。在点4,制冷剂以低压、低温、低干度蒸气形式离开膨胀阀,进入蒸发器,在蒸发器中可逆地定压蒸发到点1的饱和状态。对蒸发器和从冷凝器的热传递是在放热流体与吸热流体间不存在有限温差的情况下进行的。冷凝器降温过程中的情况除外。

从热力学第一定律可以得出能量平衡和某些性能参数。对基本蒸气压缩循环的每个组成部分应用第一定律的稳定流动(能量)方程,可导出下列关系式

1—2 压缩 $\dot{W}_2 = -(h_2 - h_1)\dot{m}$ (4.1)

2—3 冷凝 $_2\dot{Q}_3 = -(h_2 - h_3)\dot{m}$ (4.2)

3—4 膨胀阀 $h_3 = h_4$

4—1 蒸发器 $_4\dot{Q}_1 = (h_1 - h_4)\dot{m}$ (4.3)

在应用稳定流动方程中,略去动能和势能项,因为流速低以避免流体阻力和令人讨厌的压力损失,并且给定制冷系统内的高度变化通常很小,因此这些项在数值上是微不足道的。由于系统是循环的,在冷凝器中排出的热必须等于在蒸发器所吸收的热和压缩机功的总和。

性能系数(COP)被用来评价制冷系统的性能。COP = 制冷效果/输入的净功。

对基本蒸气压缩循环,从公式(4.1)和(4.3),COP是

$$COP = (h_1 - h_4)/(h_2 - h_1)$$

在评价压缩机对热力系统的贡献时,有必要考虑压缩机进口和出口的制冷剂参数,这两点间的状态变化是(1)理想压缩机的可逆绝热(定熵)变化,(2)绝热但不可逆变化(流体流经压缩机时伴随熵的增加),理想压缩机的变化用绝热压缩机效率来描述。

对容积式压缩机来说,一个热力学的重要考虑是余隙容积的影响,即留在压缩机内没有被运动部件排出的制冷剂体积。对活塞式压缩机来说,要考虑当活塞处于顶端中心位置时活塞和气缸头间的余隙容积。在气缸排出压缩气体后,随着压力降到进口压力,余隙内的气体再次膨胀到较大体积。因此,按进口压力和温度时的情况计量,压缩机排出的制冷剂质量比活塞扫过容积占有的质量要少,从数量上讲,这种结果可由容积效率 η_v 来表示

$$\eta_v = m_a / m_t \qquad (4.4)$$

式中　m_a——每冲程进入压缩机的新气的实际质量;

　　　m_t——由排气体积代表的并在压缩机进口压力和温度时所确定的气体理想质量。

容积效率度量了在使制冷剂蒸气在循环中移动时,压缩机活塞排量(体积)的有效度。由于制冷剂的比容大不相同,制冷剂的选择会影响压缩机排气量传送的质量流量。

多级压缩机的设计参数之一是级间压力的选择,在级间压力处制冷剂温度由中间冷却器降低。在最佳级间压力时,总功最小。对理想气体($Pv = RT$)的两级压缩来说,最佳级间压力是在吸气压力和排气压力的几何平均处,并导致两级功量相等。但是在制冷系统上使用多级压缩机不同于气体压缩机,因为级间压力处的冷却通常是由从循环某些其他部分转移来的制冷剂完成的。

吸收式热泵(4.4)

1. 吸收式热泵的功能

吸收式热泵从低温热源(如废热或地表水)取热,在较高的温度下输出热量用于冬天或其他场合供热,其效能系数大于1。

在日本和瑞典,吸收式热泵已经安装于利用工业废热来提供热水的供热工厂(代表性的温度是165°F),用于冬天供热或其他用途,其COP(效能系数)在1.4~1.7之间。

吸收式热泵单向用于冬天供热或双向用于夏天制冷、冬天供热。

对于吸收式热泵来说,可计算供冷的效能系数 COP_c,对于双级吸收式热

泵而言,供热的效能系数 COP_{hp} 计算如下

$$COP_{hp} = \frac{Q_{ab} + Q_{con}}{Q_{lg}} \tag{4.5}$$

式中　　Q_{ab}——从吸收器排出的热(Btu/h);

Q_{con}——从冷凝器排出的热(Btu/h);

Q_{lg}——输入到第一级发生器的热(Btu/h)。

除了溴化锂水溶液,还有几种吸收剂,即工作流体正在得以发展,例如,$LiBr/ZnCl_2$ 和 $LiBr/ZnBr_2/CH_3OH$,在吸收式热泵中,溴化锂水溶液($LiBr/H_2O$)仍然是最广泛使用的。

2. 吸收式热泵和蒸汽压缩式热泵的比较

尽管对离心式热泵来说,供热效能系数 COP_{hp} 值在 4~4.5 之间,而对吸收式热泵来说,供热效能系数 COP_{hp} 仅仅为 1.3~1.7,但是离心机使用的电能比吸收机使用的热能远远昂贵得多。

在选择过程中,应该对整个使用周期的成本进行分析。在考虑单位电价对天然气价比率时,特别应该考虑消耗费用和用电高峰时较高的电耗,在许多场合中,吸收式热泵可能是更经济的。

3. 串联吸收式热泵

串联吸收式热泵由两个单级吸收式热泵组成,每一级带有一个蒸发器、吸收器、发生器、冷凝器、热交换器和溶液泵。

液体水制冷剂在蒸发器内蒸发,水蒸气由吸收器内的浓溶液提出,传递到吸收器内热水中的吸收热用于区域供热。稀溶液通过热交换器从吸收器用泵打到发生器。在发生器中,来自工厂的蒸汽使稀溶液中的水汽化,汽化的水蒸气被排列冷凝器而冷凝成液体形式。冷凝潜热又传给区域供热的热水中。

来自发生器的浓溶液通过热交换器从发生器流到吸收器。冷凝液体水通过节流孔进入蒸发器,并且被喷射到管束上,在管束里,流入来自工厂的烟气冷却水。在吸收了来自烟气冷却水的汽化潜热之后,液体水在蒸发器内蒸发成水蒸气。

在这种串联吸收热泵中,第一级吸收式热泵在较高的温度下运行,而第

二级热泵在较低的温度下运行。

在运行期间,来自区域供热的热水回水在第二级吸收式热泵的吸收器和冷凝器中从 144 ℉被加热到 152 ℉,并且在第一级吸收式热泵的吸收器和冷凝器中,从 152 ℉被加热到 160.5 ℉在蒸发器内,热从低温热源,即烟气冷却水中释放出来,废气冷却水在 97.7 ℉的温度下进入吸收式热泵并且在 75.2 ℉的温度下离开。高温热源——蒸汽在 320 ℉下以 660 001 b/h 的流量从焚烧工厂送出,串联吸收式热泵的平均效能系数 COP_{hp}大约是 1.6。

4. 运行特性

吸收热传递装置在两个压力水平上运行:高压,包括蒸发器和吸收器;低压,包括发生器和冷凝器。

输入和输出流体有三个温度水平:
① 带有热输出的来自吸收器的流体在最高的温度水平。
② 热源(输入到蒸发器和发生器的废热)在中间的温度水平。
③ 冷凝器中的冷却水在最低的温度水平。

吸收热传递装置的用途是使输入废热流体的温度上升。吸收式热泵的功能是从较低的温度热源中获得一个较高的效能系数(COP)。

压缩机故障(4.6)

许多压缩机出现故障是由于一个或几个下列情况的原因:(1) 缓动;(2)液体满流;(3)润滑油损缺;(4)杂质;(5)不良配管;(6)不恰当的恒温膨胀阀过热定位;(7)满液启动。

缓动 缓动通常发生在压缩机启动时,只持续很短的时间。然而当压缩机运转时,在系统运行工况迅速改变期间,缓动有可能发生。这种缓动伴随格噻格噻的噪声产生,很像汽车发动机在重载下发出的声音。这种噪声是由液体制冷剂和/或油的压缩而产生的。按设计,压缩机只压缩蒸汽而不压缩液体,当液体通过压缩机被压缩时,在汽缸内会产生超过 1 000 psig(6 890 kPa)的液压。

缓动能够毁坏端盖和/或阀板密封垫,折断阀门弹簧片、活塞和损坏活塞销。如果这些情况中任何一项被发现,就应检查产生缓动的情况。一经发现就应纠正。

液体满流 液体满流是指制冷剂液滴连续不断地流到压缩机。液体制冷剂进入压缩机后,就进入曲轴箱,在曲轴箱里油被稀释。液体制冷剂是一种很好的清洗剂,会从压缩机表面洗去油。在多数情况下,油会起泡沫,从而降低了润滑价值和导致轴承表面过热。这种情况发生在空气冷却式压缩机上要比在制冷剂冷却式压缩机上更为可能。

在液体严重满流的情况下,活塞、气门和活塞环的损坏可能是由于缺少润滑。也有可能部件已损坏而外表却看不出什么磨损。通常,液体满流是通过离油泵最远的部件磨损较多而显示出来的。

润滑油损缺 润滑油损缺会导致压缩机损坏。磨损而将被卡死,发生过热,结果损坏。压缩机电机会过热,可能会被烧坏。随着曲轴箱油量的减少,剩油的温度就上升。压缩机油在 310~320 °F(136.66~142.22 ℃)时开始汽化,这就减少了对汽缸的润滑,造成活塞环和汽缸的过量磨损。油在 350 °F(158.89 ℃)时彻底分解,产生杂质,并完全失去润滑性能。

杂质 系统中的污染物包括空气、湿气、尘土和其他异物。这些杂质会引起系统的几种故障,如排气压力高、系统性能差、流量控制装置中水分结冰、油污染和酸。

不良配管 不良配管也能促使油离开压缩机。系统中如果允许有不必要的存油弯时,油就会在存油弯处沉积,从而使压缩机缺油运行。吸气管线的尺寸对合适的油回路极其重要。如果使用储液器,大小必须适合于该系统。储液器应当能够储备大约是较小系统制冷剂注入总量的1/2。一般来说,最理想的是要与储液器和设备生产厂家接洽征求他们的建议。此外,在非循环期间,储液器将不保护压缩机免使制冷剂回流。

不恰当的恒温膨胀阀过热定位 在检查和调整恒温膨胀阀过热定位时,程序应当是在蒸发器盘管处开始。如果膨胀阀多于一个,它们必须全部保持同样的过热定位,如果过热定位不一致,很可能会发生油阻塞,特别是在低温场合。

满液启动 一般说来,满液启动是在非循环期间制冷剂流到压缩机而引起的。当压缩机比系统其余部分温度低时,制冷剂就流入压缩机曲轴箱并与油混合。当压缩机启动时,液体制冷剂迅速蒸发,造成油起泡沫。

油所吸收的制冷剂量由油温和曲轴箱的压力所决定。温度越低、压力越高,油所吸收的制冷剂就越多。在一定的条件下,制冷剂和油的混合物将分离和分层,液体制冷剂沉降到曲轴箱底部,在那里被油泵首先吸入,压缩机启动时，油泵把液体制冷剂注入到轴承，那里的全部油会被洗掉。

锅炉水循环(5.3)

为了产生蒸汽和控制蒸汽发生设备中所有回路的管壁温度，需要充足的水和汽水混合物。在超临界压力下，流量是利用水泵机械地产生的。在低于临界压力时，水循环或者由重力作用自然地产生，或者由水泵来产生，或者既利用重力作用又利用水泵来产生。

在自然循环中，可用产生流量的重力，即来自回路中的下降管（下流）中的流体密度($1\ b/ft^3$)与上升管（上流）中的流体密度之差（图 5.3）。如果下降管中的流体是饱和温度的水，或是温度稍低于饱和温度的水，并且水中不含有气泡时，则有最大的泵水效果。在饱和温度下，吸收热量的上升管将密度比下降管中的水密度小的汽水混合物送到汽包中去。这个密度之差便产生了水循环可以利用的力。

为了在亚临界压力下进行强迫循环而设计的锅炉设备，其各个回路的流量都是用机械泵产生的。强迫循环系统有两种普遍采用的形式：直流系统和再循环系统。

在直流式强迫循环中，将给水设备供来的水，泵到受热面回路的进口。流体沿着回路的长度被加热，并产生蒸汽，一直到蒸发过程完成，然后再流过加热回路，使蒸汽过热。按照习惯，这种形式的强迫循环不需要用汽水包。直流的一种改进形式是将水蒸发到部分干度(90%的干度)，再在汽水分离器中除去多余的水。

再循环式强迫循环设备是用另外装置的循环泵将水送到受热面回路中去。由泵送进回路的水量大大超过产生蒸汽所用的水量，并且和自然循环锅炉一样，也需要有一个汽包作为汽水分离之用。分离出来的水与给水泵送来的水汇合后经下降管回路回到循环泵中去，作另一次"来回旅行"。

在强迫循环的再循环形式中，由于这另外装置的循环泵而造成了锅炉设备的净热损失。实际上，虽然所有需用于驱动泵的能量在水中以增加焓的形式再现，但是，这能量最初来自于转换为有用功系数小于 1.0 的燃料。如果用电动泵的话，按照一个热效率为 33% 的电厂所输入燃料的热量来计算，则其净能量的损失约为供给水泵电动机能量的 2 倍。

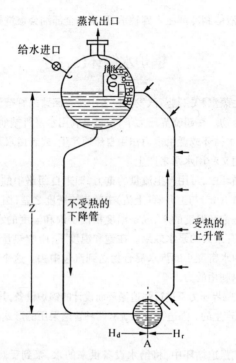

图5.3 简单的自然循环回路示意图(图中示出汽包中的一次汽水分离器)

自然循环

在自然循环系统中,循环量随着所供给热量的增加而增加(蒸汽出力也增加),并一直增加到最大的循环流体流量点才停止。超过这一点,吸热量的任何进一步增长,其结果都会使循环流量减少。在图5.4中所示的曲线形状是由两个相对的力形成的。由于吸热量的增加,下降管和上升管中的流体密度之差以及管内的流速也随之加大。与此同时,下降管和上升管中的摩擦损失和其他流动损失也增加了。当这些损失的增加率大于由于密度之差所得的力,则循环流量率开始下降,这些损失的增加主要是由于上升回路中比容的增加所造成的。因此,将所有的回路都设计在图5.4中曲线的上升部分才是适当的,也即设计在曲线顶点的左侧运行。

当设计条件限制在循环曲线的上升部分时,自然循环锅炉对于运行设备

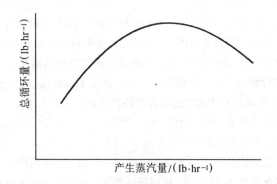

图 5.4 在既定压力下,锅炉回路中的循环量和产生蒸汽量的典型关系曲线(坐标尺度是任意选择的)

所遇到的各种吸热条件的变化都有自身补偿的趋势。这些变化包括突然过负荷、受热面表面清洁度的变化、不均匀的炉床或不均匀的喷燃器的条件,甚至在运行寿命期间所不能正确预料的实际条件。

在亚临界压力下,运行中的强迫循环锅炉不具备类似的补偿作用,因为上升回路总阻力中的一大部分是回路进口处所需要的流量分配设施造成的,这个阻力比自然循环的阻力大得多。在这种情况下,由于流量分配设施的不均衡阻力大,因此,个别回路内或一组回路内的吸热量的增加,仅仅使流速率稍有变化。

在锅炉回路中产生流动的方法,无论是自然方法,或是机械方法,实际上,只要管子的内表面始终被具有维持核态沸腾的合适干度的汽水混合物中的水所润湿,就不会对受热面的效率有所影响。只要符合于基本要求,水膜对热流的阻力是小得可以忽略不计的。并且,总热导取决于炉烟侧的管壁的热阻。在核态沸腾状况下,不管循环流量是由自然方式产生的,还是由水泵产生的,锅炉炉膛受热面上或者锅炉对流受热面上每平方英尺所吸收的热量基本上相等。无论采用两种循环方式中的哪一种,任何偏离核态沸腾方式都要求对强迫对流蒸汽膜的热传导系数和它对金属允许温度的关系予以特别考虑。

强迫循环或自然循环

在某些情况下,强迫循环用于产生蒸汽是有益的。为了在高于或近于临界压力(3 208.2 psia)下运行而设计的锅炉可采用机械方式使流体在回路中流动。在工艺过程和余热利用领域内也有这样的情况:由分散的各点进行温度控制或汇集热的采用都会由于泵的使用而使其经济性受到影响。

对自然循环能最有效利用的场合就是在由于吸热的结果而导致密度有足够变化的时候,所以,自然循环一般限于在低于临界压力的设计中使用。在这种情况下,蒸汽和水的密度有很大的差异。在压力高于 2 900 psi 时,自然循环系统不断增大,而且价格昂贵,采用泵可能较为经济。但是,强迫循环的原理在超临界和亚临界两个压力范围内同样适用。选用与"通用压力"这一名称相符合的锅炉,反映了直流强迫循环原理的广泛适用性。与在亚临界压力范围内保留自然循环相反,选用强迫循环主要决定于设备的经济性。

自然循环在接近于临界压力的很高压力下是有效的。自然循环仅仅依赖于下降管中流体(水)的平均密度与受热管中流体(蒸汽和水的混合物)的平均密度之差。下降管中的水是来自省煤器的欠热给水与汽包分离出来的饱和水的混合物,因此这水是欠热的。炉膛管子中的流体是汽和水的混合物,其密度比下降管中水的密度低。密度之差提供了泵水的压力,甚至在接近于临界压力的很高的压力下,自然循环仍然保持有高的有效的循环压头,如图 5.5 所示。只要在循环系统中有有效的汽水分离来维持这一差异的最大效果,如采用旋风分离器,则可不必借助于机械来循环。

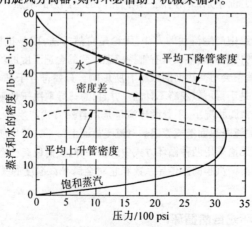

图 5.5　压力对下降管及上升管内的密度的影响

电力公用事业电站燃用矿物燃料的锅炉(5.4)

蒸汽发生设备的选择

美国使用的绝大部分电力是由燃用矿物燃料的蒸汽锅炉和高速汽轮机生产的。

每台锅炉必须以最经济的方式满足设备用户的特定要求。要达到这一点,就要求设计人员和设备用户的工程技术人员或顾问人员的密切合作。

在制订锅炉规范之前,设备用户或者电站的设计人员必须对整个电站进行成本评价。在矿物燃料费用高的地区,对核装置和矿物燃料装置进行评价并加以比较,可能是必要的,以便决定哪种装置能更好地满足设备用户的需要。

火电站的发电成本主要包括以下三种费用:

1. 设备的投资费用;
2. 燃料费用;
3. 其他运行、维修费用。

设备投资费用的调查必须包括锅炉、汽轮机和发电机、凝汽器、给水加热器和水泵、输煤装置、厂房和实际产业的费用。燃料费用的调查必须包括可能使用的各种燃料的费用,以及在电站的运行寿命期内,这些燃料价格可能发生的变化。电站效率和所使用的燃料之间有直接的关系,电站的效率和设备的费用之间也有重要的相互关系。

其他重要的项目是按燃料供应和电力用户所在地区来考虑发电站的厂址位置。在某些情况下,输送电力比运输燃料更为经济。一些大型火电站正在煤矿坑口进行建设,而其发出的电力却是用在几百英里以外的地方。如果电站设备的用户是电网系统的一个发电单位的话,那么电网系统中其他发电单位的要求也可能就是一个重要的因素了。当然在评价中还必须包括运行和维修费用预算。

对工程的各项因素进行全面考虑,需对将来的扩建或规划的变更作出判断,对明确的或不明确的事项做出估计等,来确立足够精确的基本资料是需要花费相当长的时间和精力的,以便使锅炉制造厂家和其他供货厂家的经验和工艺能够完全适合电站设计人员和电站主人的利益。设备用户应该在一开始就决定下来由谁来准备这些资料。如果设备用户缺乏具有必要资格的人员,那么就应该借助于顾问工程师的帮助。与锅炉制造厂家详细进行讨论,将能提供有助于设备用户做出正确决定的很多详细情况。

在选择设备之前,必须规划出运行的依据和整个锅炉设备的布置。最后,取得的资料必须编制成设备规范的形式,使各种部件的制造厂家能按设备用户的要求提供设备。在选择设备之后,必须准备基础、厂房、管道和通道的施工图纸。为了有效地经营和安装工作的完成,施工必须采用现代化的进行方式和管理技术进行配合。

对锅炉设计人员的要求

对锅炉设计人员来说,最重要的是所需要的蒸汽量和要使用的燃料,以及设备用户进行成本评价之后所规定的特定蒸汽条件。这些蒸汽条件包括主蒸汽和再热蒸汽的温度和压力。

锅炉的设计人员需要所有与蒸汽产生的有关资料,使他能够设计出最经济的蒸汽发生设备,以满足设备用户的需要。这就要求锅炉设计人员和设备用户、工程技术人员或顾问人员之间密切合作。

可作为设计人员选择设备的根据的要求和条件可以概括如下:

1. 燃料——目前可利用的资源,其成分的分析、价格和将来的趋势。

2. 蒸汽条件

(a)压力和温度——用汽地点和锅炉出口的压力和温度,允许的温度偏差。

(b)供热率(或蒸汽流量)——到终端用汽点的;到锅炉房辅助设备和给水加热器的;到排污点的;由锅炉出口的、最低、平均和最高的变化等的供热率,以及可预测的将来要求。

3. 锅炉给水——水源和水质分析,锅炉入口的给水温度。

4. 占用空间和地形的考虑——占地限制;新设备与现有老锅炉房设备之间的关系;环境要求和地方法律的限制;地震和风的要求;海拔高度;地基条件;气候以及运行和施工用的交通道路。

5. 辅助设备运转所消耗的能源种类和费用。

6. 运行人员——运行和维修人员的经验水平和人工费用。

7. 保证条件。

8. 评价基础——机组效率;所需厂用电量;厂房面积和各种固定费用。

有了这些资料,锅炉设计人员能够分析设备用户的特定要求,将设备投资与长期节省的费用进行平衡、协调组成整个锅炉的许多部件使之成为最经济的设计。

设计实践

锅炉设计人员一般按标准(即已设计好的)部件进行设计。这些部件的详细设计已经完成,因此加快了车间化生产的速度,而且操作经验证明是可靠的。这些标准设计的部件有燃烧器、磨煤机、炉膛组成部分、汽包和承压部件等。这些部件可以很容易地组成各种容量和尺寸的锅炉。这样使费用更低廉,交货期更迅速,而且也提高了设备运行的可利用率。

用于电力公用事业的整套设计几乎很少标准化。这主要是因为每个设备用户的条件特性不同。蒸汽容量、压力和温度的变化不像所燃用的燃料种类和设备用户在自己系统内采用什么蒸汽发生设备的方案变化那么大。这类方式的变化需要改变部件的设计和部件的总布置。这些因素连同不断变动的货币价值、燃料、材料和人工一起,使整个机组的标准化不可能实现。

燃油燃气锅炉炉膛设计(5.10)

燃气和油的燃烧条件普遍相同,所以两种燃料均可采用同一个炉膛设计。大多数情况下,这种炉膛设计以燃油为主,而以燃天然气为辅。油和天然气的燃烧特性有如下类似的几个方面。

1.两种燃料其本身均不含外在水分,而且燃烧后的燃烧产物的容积基本相等,因此,无论是燃油还是天然气,鼓风机都能有效地独立工作。

2.雾态燃烧的油或天然气,均遵循支链反应的规律。燃料燃烧的强烈程度均取决于内部混合工况,其允许的最大容积热负荷互相接近(燃油 300 kW/m³,燃气为 350 kW/m³)。因此,对燃用两种相通出力的锅炉,炉膛设计均可以采用相同的尺寸。

3.此两种燃料燃烧后几乎无灰分(油的燃烧产物中 A^d 小于 0.3%),这可避免炉膛内水冷壁的结焦,而且不必安装炉内清灰装置。基于此,燃油和燃气的锅炉炉膛可设计成底部水平,或稍微倾斜及供维修用的人孔。

4.因为燃油为气态(或雾状),所以它更易于与空气混合,这实际上可以保证燃料在低过量空气系数 $a_1'' = 1.02 - 1.05$ 下以高热释放率快速燃尽。对两种燃料来说,空气均可预热到同样的温度($t_{ha} = 250 \sim 300 \text{℃}$),这样,才有可能采用油气混合燃烧型燃烧器,而空气容积流量相同,且阻力基本相等。

在强烈燃烧下,两种燃料均在燃烧器附近形成短的火焰中心,在燃油中,火焰中心的温度更高,对水冷壁的热辐射最强,这会导致金属管壁过热,并且出现高温腐蚀,以至在火焰的行程中形成高浓度的氮氧化物。

在垂直截面内,燃油和燃气炉均可以采用开式或开式旋风炉膛。大多数工厂,在单一前置或双向(反向)前置燃烧器的常规菱形炉膛内安装油气混合燃烧器。在单一前置式炉膛内,燃烧器安装多层(3层或4层)。这种安装很经济,而且操作方便,但不能确保火焰充满炉膛及不能应用于浅式炉膛(小于6 m)。因为炉膛温度或水冷壁的吸热量会超负荷上升。

在燃烧器反向安装的炉膛内,炉膛水冷壁要工作在适当的环境内。火焰集中在炉膛空间的高温度区域内,反向火焰不利于形成旋流,而使燃料在烟气行程的尾部更好地燃尽。因为其导致了火焰中心区的热损失达20%~30%,收缩式炉膛可以促使火焰中心区及燃尽室的烟气混合流动。

在300 MW试验性锅炉中,新的建议是在主燃区内组织反菱形燃烧,以减少到达炉膛水冷壁的热流密度。菱形炉膛内形成的高旋流,可使燃料的85%~90%燃尽。菱形式炉室用具有金刚砂折射面的销钉管覆盖。然而,这种设计,会导致更高的火焰温度及过高的热流扩散到水冷壁,所以它并非是解决此类问题的最佳方案。

我们知道,气态燃料产生的火焰辐射能力,比油燃烧产生的要低,所以,当锅炉从燃油改为燃气时,炉膛吸热量要降低,而炉膛出口产物的温度会更高。在高负荷运行的开式炉膛,这样形成的温差达到100℃,这将不可避免地改变随后换热面(主要是过热器)的温度环境。在多层单前置式燃烧器布置的开式炉膛内,这种情况下产物的炉膛出口烟温的变化等同于改变火焰中心的位置,即当燃气时,仅用两到二层低层燃烧器,而改燃油时,运行高层燃烧器(在随后的设计中,烟气再循环到炉膛内,以达到同样的目的)。

最近,已经有人提议,在开式炉膛的底部安装燃烧器及通过控制二次风的旋流强度来降低炉膛水冷壁的局部热流强度。在燃油中降低二次风的旋流强度,以便火焰延伸到更高的高度,而显著减轻水冷壁的局部过热,使炉膛出口烟温大幅度上升。当燃气时,二次风的旋流强度增加,以便火焰范围更广,其行程更短。

过热器和再热器(5.12)

蒸汽机运行时,如果对蒸汽予以一定程度的过热,就会节约大量燃料,这一点早在 18 世纪就得到了证明。在 19 世纪后期,往复蒸汽机遇到了各种润滑问题,但一旦这些问题得到了解决,过热器又继续向前发展。

汽轮机的商业性发展加速了过热的普遍应用。到 1920 年,普遍同意蒸汽温度为 650°F,即相当于 250°F 的过热。在 20 世纪 20 年代初期,利用汽轮机抽汽加热给水的再生循环得到了发展,在没有进一步提高蒸汽温度的情况下改善了电站的经济性。同时,过热器的发展允许将蒸汽温度提高到 725°F。那时,进一步提高温度以使在经济上获得更多的收益,受到了过热器管金属容许温度的限制。这导致了再热的商业应用,即是从汽轮机高压级出来的蒸汽在另外的再热器里再热,待其温度和焓提高后再返回低压级。

用于电站的第一台再热机组于 1922 年提出,1924 年 9 月便投入运行。其设计压力为 650 psi。但运行时为 550 psi 和 725°F。汽轮机高压级的排汽在 135 psi 的压力下被再热至 725°F。

1924 年设计了压力更高的再热机组,主蒸汽压力为 1 200 psi,汽温为 700°F,再热蒸汽为 360 psi,700°F,于 1925 年 12 月投入运行。

过热和再热的优点

当饱和蒸汽用于汽轮机时,蒸汽在做功以后,即使压力有所下降,也有一部分蒸汽凝结成水造成一部分能量的损失。汽轮机能做的功量,受到汽轮机在其叶片不会过度磨损的情况下所能容许的水量的限制。正常情况下,水分在 10% ~ 15% 的范围之内,可以采用将汽轮机各级间的水分离出来的办法来增大做功量,但这只在特殊情况下才是经济的。即使进行水分离,与将水从给水温度提高到饱和温度然后再蒸发所需的热量相比,汽轮机里能转换成功的总能量还是少的。因此,在汽轮机设计中,水分是主要限制。

因为汽轮机通常将过热的热量转换为功,不会形成水分,因此在汽轮机里,基本上能将过热的热量全部回收。理想的郎肯循环温 - 熵图对此做了解释。从图中可以看出,加到饱和蒸汽线右边的热量 100% 能回收。尽管这并非总是完全正确的,但从郎肯循环图中可以看出,在实际循环中,这基本上是正确的。

前面的讨论并不是特别适用于临界点附近的蒸汽压力。在给处于或高于临界点的工作流体温度下定义时,"过热"一词并不真正合适。然而,当温度高于 705°F时,甚至压力超过 3 208 psia,所加入的热量基本上也能在汽轮机里全部得到回收。

图 5.7 用图表对过热的好处作了图解,从图中可以看出,当压力从 1 800 psi 增加到 3 500 psi 时,将蒸汽温度从 900 °F 提高到 1 100 °F,热循环的热耗就会降低。

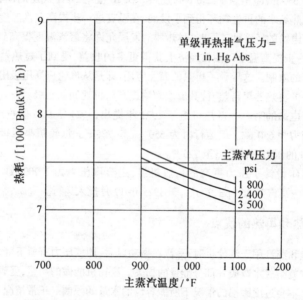

图 5.7 蒸汽温度和压力的变化对单级再热理想郎肯循环性能的影响

过热器的型式

过热器和再热器的原型是对流装置,这多少也是它们的基本型式。这种型式适用于辐射传热很小的各种炉烟温度。在这种型式的装置里,从过热器出来的蒸汽温度随锅炉出力的升高而升高。这是因为炉膛吸收的热输入比例减少,过热器能吸收的热量就增多。由于对流传热率差不多是出力的直接函数,过热器每磅蒸汽吸收的总热量随锅炉出力的增长而增长(见图5.8)。当过热器离炉膛较远,即进入过热器和炉烟温度较低,这一影响就更明显。

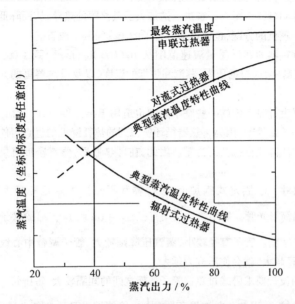

图5.8 将辐射式和对流式过热组件串联排列就能使整个出力范围内的最终蒸汽温度很均匀

另一方面,辐射式过热器从辐射热中接收热量,实际上,它没有从对流热中接受热量。因为炉膛中的受热面吸收的热量不是与锅炉出力成正比例增长,而是以慢得多的速度增长,所以作为负荷函数的辐射过热曲线随着锅炉出力的增长而向下倾斜。

在某些情况下,两条相对倾斜的曲线由于辐射式和对流式过热器组合的调整,使得过热曲线在广阔的负荷范围里都很平坦。图5.8所示就是典型曲线。布置在单独炉膛内的过热器的特点为,运行所得的过热曲线较平坦。

过热器的发展

最初的对流式过热器设置在深度大的锅炉管束的上面或后面,以便为过热器挡住火焰或高温炉烟。为了提高蒸汽温度,过热器需要吸收较多的热量,因此有必要将过热器移得靠近火焰一些。这一新位置给过热器带来了一些问题,这些问题在过热器位于原来的低温烟气区时并不明显。通过对过热器设计的改进,包括提高蒸汽质量流速,蒸汽和烟气分配的困难和管子金属普遍过热等问题终于得到了解决。这加大了蒸汽膜的热导,从而降低了管子金属温度。蒸汽的分配,也通过加大管子的压降得到了改善。

现代过热器的蒸汽质量流速范围从 100 000 lb/(ft²·h) 到 1 000 000 lb/(ft²·h)或更高些,这根据压力、蒸汽和炉烟的温度,以及过热器里的允许压降而定。

过热器设计时考虑的一些基本问题也适用于再热器设计,然而,再热器里的压降是关键性的,因为再热器循环所得到的热耗降低的优点可能被再热系统太大的压降完全抵消而为零。因此,在再热器里,蒸汽质量流量常常比较小。

管子尺寸 在固定式锅炉上,过热器和再热器主要是外径为 2 in 或 $2\frac{1}{2}$ in 的圆筒形光管。船用装置使用直径较小(1 in 或 $1\frac{1}{4}$ in)的管子是为了节省重量和空间。管子直径较小,蒸汽压降则较大,管子调整中心线也更困难,管子直径越大,就会使压应力越大。

最近的设计要求卧式过热器管子吊架之间的间隔较大,每排管子的管距较宽或根数较少,以避免灰渣堆积。$2\frac{1}{2}$ in 管能够满足这些新条件,牺牲的细管好处也最少。在某些情况下,使用 3 in 管也很好。当蒸汽温度升高时,由于容许应力的原因。可能迫使重新使用小直径薄壁管。

现代过热器装置几乎毫无例外地都用光管。过热器管采用鳍片、环或销钉等形式扩展受热面,这不仅使得炉烟侧的清洗变得困难,而且厚度增加会使金属温度和热应力增大超过允许限值。

过热器设计中的各种关系

有效的过热器设计要求解决几个因素。突出要考虑的是:
1. 要求的蒸汽温度;
2. 达到这一蒸汽温度所需的过热器受热面面积;
3. 要放置受热面的炉烟温度区;
4. 最适于制造受热面和支吊架的钢、合金钢或其它材料的种类;
5. 流过管子的蒸汽流速(质量流速),这受到允许蒸汽压降的限制,但反过来,它又是控制管金属温度的主要因素：

6. 受热面的布置要满足指望使用的燃料特性的要求,特别是关于管距,要避免积灰和结渣,或者采取措施将这样的形成物在其形成的最初阶段除去；

7. 过热器作为一种构架本身的设计和型式。

前 6 项中的任何一项发生变化,都会使其它各项随之而变化。

先进电站设计所要求的蒸汽温度是过热器设计人员和制造厂可以生产的经济结构的最高温度。在这种情况下,经济要求对下述相互有关的两个因素要作出决定。这两个因素是：初始费用,也就是初投资和以后的维修费用(为使运行故障,停机和更换都减少到最少的程度)。如果维修费用能大量减少,并在一段合理的时间内抵补超出的那部分初始费用,则较大的初投资是有根据的。因此,要求的蒸汽温度这一因素是根据对其它五项因素组合的最佳值的计算和特定工程需要的现有的全部配合认识而定的。最近几年的运行经验使得购买来安装在美国的几乎全部的大型机组都采用 1 000 °F 左右的蒸汽温度作为主过热和再热的蒸汽温度。

在要求的蒸汽温度具体确定或规定下来以后,下一步需要考虑的就是达到这一过热度所需要的受热面面积。需要的过热器受热面面积决定于余下的四项因素,由于相互关系不是单一的,所以受热面面积必须通过试布置的方法来确定,即将它放置在看来令人满意的炉烟温度区。在所谓的标准锅炉里,通过实际布置和通过先占据的过热器受热面空间就能很好地确定这一区域。

在确定了试布置的和试规定管距的受热面面积以后,就可以计算蒸汽质量流速 ,蒸汽压降和过热器管金属温度。然后为管子、联箱和其它部件选择合适的材料,还可能需要对几种布置进行比较,以便获得最佳组合。它们应考虑到如下几点：

1. 需要成本较低的合金。
2. 在不危及管子温度的情况下,得到一个较为合理的蒸汽压降。
3. 使蒸汽质量流速较高,以便降低管子温度。
4. 采用不同的管距,在燃料种类不定的情况下,那将更好地防止积灰。
5. 在知道了供给的燃料较为有利时,允许采用更小的管距,以便使布置更为经济。
6. 在通风阻力值很紧要的地方,管子将布置成能减少装置的通风阻力。

7. 允许过热器受热面位于炉烟温度较高的区域,从而节约一些受热面,与标准布置之差就可以得到补偿。

采用最佳的经济和运行特性,采用比较满意的各种准则,就可能完成实际的设计。但是,还需要大量的经验,并使用正确的实际原则,才能获得令人满意的结果。

再热器设计中的各种关系

总的说来,过热器和再热器需要考虑的问题差不多。但是,再热器的设计强度受到了允许蒸汽压降的限制。再热器管里的蒸汽质量流速应足以使汽膜温度降保持在150°F以下。一般情况下,再热器管里的压降小于5%就可以做到这一点。这允许再热器管路和阀门的压降再下降5%而不会超过通常允许的10%总值。

管子用金属

抗氧化性,最大允许应力和经济性决定了过热器和再热器管材料的选择。只要这些考虑可行,就应扩大碳钢的使用。在此限度以外,应使用经认真选择的合金钢。

汽轮机(6.1)

涡轮机是靠一股射向转子叶片的流体(液体或气体)来驱动的回转式发动机。在汽轮机中这股流体是蒸汽。蒸汽通过驱动涡轮叶轮旋转而将部分热能和压力能转换成机械能。涡轮机是靠蒸汽直接作用在叶轮或转子上而产生旋转运动的。在水轮机中,流体的流速是由水位降而产生的。在汽轮机中,流体的流速是由锅炉蒸汽的压力降而产生的。蒸汽在喷嘴中或叶片上,由高压侧向低压侧逐渐膨胀,靠着耗用热和压力使其速度逐渐增大。然后,由于对运动叶片作功,蒸汽的速度便减慢下来。

涡轮机最大优点是没有振动和噪音,转动力平稳而均匀,并能处理大量的流体——在汽轮机中就是蒸汽。汽轮机结构简单,运转可靠,使它成为一种适合于驱动泵、压轮机和其他设备的发动机。在这些情况下,汽轮机最有效的转速通常比它所驱动的机械的转速要高得多,因此通常必须利用减速箱,小型汽轮机的效率不是很高的。

大型汽轮机配上减速箱可用来驱动舰船。事实上,汽轮机是唯一适用于驱动舰船的发动机。在大型电站中,汽轮机得到了最大的发展,一些新电站正在安装每台功率超过 600 000 马力的汽轮机。

汽轮机由下列主要部件组成:

1.涡轮壳——通常沿平面中心线剖分为二,用螺栓固定在一起,以便于装配和拆卸,壳体上带有定叶系统。

2.转子——叶轮上装有动叶,转子两端装有轴颈。

3.轴承箱——安装在气缸上,用来支承转子的轴。

4.调速器和阀门系统——通过控制蒸汽流量来调节涡轮的速度和出力,同时还有轴承润滑系统以及一套安全装置。

5.某种类型的联轴器——用来连接从动机械。

6.管路接头——在进汽口接供汽管道,在涡轮壳出汽口接排汽系统。

图 6.1(见原文)所示为一种简单的冲动式汽轮机。在这种汽轮机里,蒸汽从一个固定的喷嘴(或若干喷嘴)中喷出,喷嘴的弯度正好使喷出的蒸汽能射向安装在转动叶轮或圆盘的一圈叶片上。这些叶片制造成一定的形状以便用来平稳地拦截从喷嘴喷出的蒸汽。叶片是弯曲的,以便改变蒸汽射流的方向,同时承受向前推进的冲力。

要是不使用固定的喷嘴和单独的叶轮而把喷嘴安装到轮子上,喷出的气流的反作用就会推动这个轮子朝向与冲击式叶轮相反的方向转动。最早期的汽轮机就是这种纯反力式涡轮机,但是由于种种原因现在已不采用了。

另外还有一种涡轮机,(见原文中图 6.2)它综合了冲力和反作用力的原理。但通常简称做"反力式"涡轮机,其喷嘴的基本特征是从进汽口起,通道逐渐变窄,因此流体进入通道时速度较低,离开喷嘴时速度必然要高得多。速度的增加是由于压力降而产生的,因为流体进入喷嘴时的压力比离开喷嘴时的压力要高。图 6.2 中的涡轮壳带有一整圈喷嘴,这些喷嘴和冲动式涡轮机里的一样,也是弯曲的,并以最有效的角度引导蒸汽喷向转动的叶片。这些转动叶片与固定喷嘴类似,也是喷嘴,但朝着另一个方向,除拦截从固定的喷嘴喷出的蒸汽并使之偏转之外,它们还能使蒸汽加速,其驱动力一半来自冲力,一半来自反作用力。这类汽轮机的气流速度是叶片转速相同的冲动式汽轮机的气流速度的一半。不论是冲动式的或是反力式的,离开动叶片时的蒸汽流的方向都大致与叶片运动的方向成直角。

最简单的汽轮机只有一个级，即定叶和动叶各一排。这种汽轮机通常用于最多几百马力的功率输出，具有中等的进汽温度和中等的进汽压力，排汽压力为一个大气压或高于一个大气压。在这些条件下，单级涡轮就能达到相当高的蒸汽利用效率。

为了从锅炉燃烧的每磅煤中获得尽可能多的动力，蒸汽在进入汽轮机时必须具有很高的温度和压力，而在排出时，压力要尽可能低。利用大量的冷却水把废汽在单独的冷凝器里冷凝，就能保持很低的排气压力，然后再用泵把冷凝蒸汽抽回到锅炉里作为纯净的给水。假如让蒸汽在一级里从锅炉压力膨胀到冷凝器压力，从喷嘴喷出的气流速度就会高到无法制造一个转速快到足以有效地利用这么高的气流速度的汽轮机；实际上单级式汽轮机的效率通常是很低的。为了使冲动式汽轮机或反力式汽轮机具有很高的热效率，就需要很大的功率输出，很高的进汽压力和很高的进气温度以及很低的排汽压力，这时单级式是不适用的。在这样的条件下，蒸汽可以得到的能量很高，为了有效利用能量，必须采用多级涡轮。此外，在这样的条件下，排汽流量增大，排汽级也必须不止一个，例如，大型汽轮机可以有三个平行的排汽级。在这些多级汽轮机中，安装在涡轮壳内的一排排定叶片和安装在转子上的一排排动叶片是交替排列的，这样的布置可使蒸汽以适当的角度进入每排定叶片和动叶片。定叶片总是喷嘴，对反力式汽轮机来说，转子上的叶片也是喷嘴，但是对冲动式汽轮机来说转子上的叶子只是导槽。

各级叶片通常是沿着水平轴一套一套地并列安排的，从而构成了所谓的"轴流式"汽轮机。蒸汽从一头进入而从另一头排出；如果流量非常大，蒸汽也可以从中间进入，而从两头排出，这种装置就称为"双流式"。机壳是由上下两半组成，下半部通常安装有轴承以支承转子，当转子安装就位以后，再把上半部沿水平配合面用螺栓连接在下半部上。

当级数很多时，业已证明用两个或两个以上的汽轮机壳或气缸是最切实可行的，这些气缸通常排成一直线，所有的轴都连接在一起。

现代的汽轮机是用锅炉来提供高度过热蒸汽的。当蒸汽通过汽轮机时，压力和温度逐渐下降，直到在某一级过热已全部消失，此后，有些蒸汽就会冷凝成水滴。这些水滴会损害叶片并降低汽轮机的效率，这就是蒸汽在通过高压涡轮之后，和进入中压涡轮之前，有时要予以再过热的原因之一。

燃气轮机(6.2)

燃气轮机是一种内燃机。这种内燃机的空气由于燃料燃烧受热膨胀，从而直接驱动一个特殊形状的叶轮(涡轮)，而不像往复式发动机那样推动活塞上下运动。

由于内部运转连续、平稳，燃气轮机跟蒸汽轮机一样几乎完全没有振动，再加上它最基本的特点——结构简单，这就使得它运动更加可靠而且更易于维护。燃气轮机比活塞发动机重量轻、体积小，因此能制成较大的尺寸，从而通过单机可以产生较高的功率。基于上述原因，燃气轮机在海、陆、空各种形式的运输工具中的使用正在日益增加。从上述这些优点来看，人们可能感到奇怪，为什么燃气轮机没有更早地被采用，特别是并不是什么新的概念。的确，利用热燃气的能量来直接转动叶轮的概念也许比活塞发动机中采用的比较复杂的系统更明显易懂。但事实上，要在实践中应用涡轮机的原理则更为困难。

早期的效率比较低的小型燃气轮机是利用活塞发动机的废气来工作的，并用它来驱动增压器。只是到了20世纪30年代才成功地制成了自动旋转的燃气轮机，并用作飞机推进器。差不多在制成航空涡轮机的同时，还研制成用于固定用途以及用作铁路机车发动机的燃气轮机。

燃气轮机主要由空气压缩机、燃烧室、涡轮叶轮组成。

压气机 燃气轮机用的压气机有两种基本类型：即轴流式和离心式压气机。在少数特殊情况下，也使用被称为混流式的压气机，这就是部分离心式部分轴流式的压气机。轴流式压气机用得最广泛，因为它能够高效率地处理大容积的空气。但是对于500马力或500马力以下的小型燃气轮机，则采用离心式压气机而不用轴流式压气机。

燃烧室 燃气轮机的燃烧器有时叫燃烧室。它有各种各样的形状和形式，例如环形、筒形或环筒形。燃气轮机的燃烧室的部件有：燃烧喷嘴、燃烧段以及通向涡轮进口的过渡段。

燃烧室用的空气由压气机压入发动机。燃料同压缩空气混合，然后在燃烧室里燃烧。再由涡轮把释放出来的热能转换成旋转能。由于燃烧产物的初始温度很高，通常采用过量空气来冷却燃烧产物，使之降到涡轮进口的设计温度。

涡轮叶轮 燃气轮机使用的涡叶轮有两种，一种是向心式，另一种是轴流式。小型燃气轮机用径流式涡轮叶轮。对于大容积流量，几乎全采用轴流式涡轮叶轮。虽然某些小型燃气轮机使用的涡轮是纯冲动式，但大多数高性能的涡轮既不是纯冲动式，也不是纯反动式。高性能的涡轮通常是按不同大小的各种冲力的反力相配合设计而成，以便获得最佳性能。

压气机与涡轮叶轮都安装在同一根轴上一起转动，由燃烧室出来的高温燃气，冲击涡轮叶片，使轴转动，从而带动压气机。从大气中来的空气通过压气机的进口吸入，然后向前流经每一级叶片(轴流式压气机)。随着空气压力逐渐增大，其体积则逐渐减小，在末一级压缩到最大限度。然后，高压(同时也是高温)空气被排入通向燃烧室的导管。燃烧室有一个或多个燃料喷嘴，通过喷嘴使燃料雾化，以便和流动的空气混合。起动时，利用电火花塞将燃料喷雾点燃。燃料与空气的混合气一经点燃，便连续不断地燃烧，因此点火装置就可以关掉。

以筒形燃烧室或环管形燃烧室组成的若干分燃烧室常常用来代替单一的燃烧室(即环形燃烧室)。例如在标准的飞机用燃气轮机中，使用 8～10 个筒形燃烧室，每个燃烧室都有自己的燃料喷嘴。

从燃烧室出来的燃烧产物经过导管、固定导叶片或喷嘴进入涡轮。燃气在涡轮里沿轴向流动，由于燃气的大部分能量传给了涡轮叶轮，燃气的温度和压力都逐渐下降。

图 6.3(见原文)为燃气轮发动机的基本原理示意图，从中可以清楚地看出推迟研制成功燃气轮机的种种技术方面的困难。(A)是进气口，空气由此进入压气机(B)，由于被压缩，空气以很高的压力(至少为 50 磅/平方英寸)和比原来高的温度进入燃烧室(C)。在燃烧室里燃料被喷射进压缩空气里，并以高效率燃烧。燃烧使温度升高到 1 850℃，甚至更高，从而使空气膨胀。生成的高温、高压燃气连续不断地喷射到驱动压气机的涡轮(D)上。燃气离开涡轮(D)之后，其压力和温度还相当高并且继续膨胀，因此能够以两种方法来加以利用。在燃气轮机本身以及在涡轮螺桨飞机发动机中，排出的气体用来驱动固定在动力轴上的另一个涡轮(或多级涡轮)(E)。这根轴可以用来驱动螺旋桨(例如在涡轮螺桨发动机中)，还可以用来驱动机车的齿轮箱(例如在燃气轮机机车中)。

反之，在单纯的喷气发动机中，喷出的燃气通过尾喷管直接排入大气，形成一股高速喷气流，根据反作用原理，像火箭一样，把发动机推向前进。在内外涵喷气式飞机发动机中,有一个低压压气机和一个高压压气机。从低压压气机出来的一部分空气绕过高压压气机和燃烧室,在尾喷管里形成一般温度较低、速度较慢、力量较强的空气喷气流,这种喷气流对速度较低的喷气式飞机是比较适用的。

涡轮的材料要连续不断地接触温度非常高的燃气,因此对用来制作燃气轮机叶片的金属的要求是非常之高的——甚至比对汽轮机叶片的要求还要高。另一个问题涉及压气机的效率,如果效率低的话,它本身就会消耗过多的功率,从而大量有用的燃气能量就被涡轮(D)用掉,结果成为推力的能量所剩无几,或第二涡轮(E)几乎产生不出多少有用的动力来。因此,一直到效率很高的压气机以及能耐高温的钢种或其他金属制造出来以前,燃气轮机的试制都没有成功。

对于某些用途来说,活塞式发动机仍然优于燃气轮机。对一定的输出功率来说,活塞式发动机的燃料消耗量一般明显地较低,但燃气轮机的重量则较轻。要制造出符合要求的低输出功率的燃气轮机(例如适用于公路车辆的),也还是不容易的,尽管现在正在努力解决这个问题。

燃气轮机由于重量轻、尺寸小,用作飞机推进器有许多独特的优点,所以首先在飞机制造业中得到重要的应用并大大促进了它的发展。燃气轮机作为航空发动机既可用作单纯的喷气推进装置,也可用来驱动普通的螺旋桨。

在高空飞行和空速很大时,喷气推进发动机的效率最高,因此它特别适用于高性能的军用飞机。现代军用喷气推进发动机能够产生惊人的动力。在紧急情况下,还能够借助一个加力燃烧室使动力进一步增大,因为这种燃烧室使即将进入排气喷管的燃气的温度增高。这样的加力燃烧可提高燃气的排气速度以及提高发动机的前进推力。

燃气轮机在飞机上另一应用是用作涡轮螺桨发动机。在这一应用中,燃气轮机具有两种用途:它驱动一个普通的螺旋桨,以及利用从发动机喷管排出的喷气的反作用力产生附加的推力。这样,就把螺桨式飞机所固有的起飞距离短的优点与普通喷气推进发动机飞机速度快、飞行高度高的能力结合起来。

介于普通喷气推进发动机和涡轮螺桨发动机之间的是后来研制成功的所谓涡轮风扇发动机。它与普通喷气推进发动机的区别在于:在进气口安装一个风扇,从而使进气口进入的空气量要比实际上流过发动机内涵的多得多。风扇把进入的空气稍稍压缩,然后将大部分空气引进环绕发动机的旁路空气导管,空气在导管里加速,并以比通过进气口时更高的速度排出来,从而增加了发动机的推力。余下的空气流过发动机的内涵,并且在那里如同在普通的喷气发动机中一样,通过涡轮和排气喷管被压缩、加热然后膨胀。

被分流流过环绕着发动机内涵旁路管道的空气同流过发动机内涵的空气之比称为双涵空气流量比(或涵道流量比)。双涵空气流量比根据不同的用途其比值大不相同。大型涡轮风扇发动机的双涵空气流量比通常高达8:1。一般说来,高双涵空气流量比和高压缩比能够节省燃料。

涡轮风扇发动机有许多优点。发动机所增加的推力可以使飞机不必携带许多水(这是很重的附加载荷);飞机在暖和的天气起飞时,有时就需喷注这些水以增加普通发动机的推力。当发动机在合适的速度和高度范围内工作时,可节省燃料 20% 左右。这些优点已经使得这类发动机成为在商业上应用于大型喷气式飞机的一种最受欢迎的发动机。

在发电领域中,同柴油机和蒸汽轮机相比,燃气轮机的容量受到限制,这是因为燃气轮机内的压力很低,因而需要空气的容积非常之大,所以必须使用大型涡轮和压气机。正是由于这一原因,在现代的中心电站中就没有做过什么认真的努力去设计一个燃气轮机电厂,来取代单机容量高达 1 200 000 kW 的蒸汽动力厂。

燃气轮机在发电领域中有三种用途值得特别提一提:
(1) 与蒸汽发电站联合运动作为增加总效率的一种手段;
(2) 用作备用机组和服务于峰值负荷;
(3) 用于流动发电站。

另有一种很有前途的发电站是汽轮机-燃气轮机联合机组发电站。它利用从普通的燃气轮机排出的高温废气为蒸汽锅炉供氧,以代替预热的燃用空气。由于从燃气轮机排出的燃气中仍然含有输入压气机进气口的空气所含的大约 80% 的氧,所以这样的联合运行是切实可行的。这样的机组能够大大提高电站的总效率,它还可以缩减所需要的锅炉尺寸和重量,节省建筑体积,加快锅炉起动,并可以不用一般的锅炉所需要的强力鼓风机和抽风机。

利用燃气轮机来改进蒸汽电站效率的另一些办法是:通过利用废气来加热给水,或者用废热锅炉来产生蒸汽。

燃气轮机对于提供一个附加的峰值负荷及备用功率来说,是一种非常引人注意的手段。安装用于这一目的的燃气轮机造价比安装附加的蒸汽轮机或水力发电机机组要低。此外,燃气轮机还具有能够实现有效自动控制、结构简单、所需空间小、维修量最小等等优点。燃气轮机另一个类似的用途是用于线端升压器,为远距离输电线服务。第三是用于流动发电站。在这种情况下,燃气轮机可装在铁路车辆或驳船上供紧急情况之用。

除灰及灰的处理(7.1)

在燃用固体燃料情况下,除灰及其处理问题是很重要的。燃料油中的灰量往往很小,其问题主要是在炉膛内和炉墙上。电气除尘器有时也用于改善烟囱排出的视感。

早期煤的燃烧方法是在自然通风的炉排上燃烧,其大部分煤灰是留在炉排上而后排向灰斗再行处理。采用现代化的机械给煤机后,例如抛煤机炉中,部分燃料是在浮悬状态下完成燃烧的,这就使烟气中含有较大的颗粒物质。

采用煤粉燃烧时,煤的全部燃烧都在悬浮状态下完成。结果是在固态排渣的煤粉炉中大约有 80%~90% 的灰被烟气带走。在液态排渣的煤粉炉中,这个数字大约可减少到 50% 左右。

在旋风炉中燃烧时,烟气中飞灰量可以减少到煤的含灰量的 20%~30%。与干态排渣煤粉炉相比较,旋风炉烟气中所携带的灰粒将降低 2/3 或 3/4。从成本观点出发,这一点可能使在排烟中达到规定的含颗粒量的设备投资来说,是重要的。在有可能对旋风炉燃烧作出改进或发展一种经济的或可靠的烟气清洁系统以前,旋风炉仅用于经过很慎重选择的工程。它是为了达到高稳定的运行而采用的高度紊流和高燃烧率,同样也会使烟气中的成分不能满足现行的美国环境保护处理。

从炉膛中除灰 在机械加煤机炉和干态排渣煤粉炉设计中,灰是沉积在灰斗中然后再排除进行处理。这种炉渣的某些可能利用是填地、道路底层材料、屋顶颗粒填充材料、混凝土块骨料和混凝土预制件、柏油混合料、结冰路面覆盖料、保温和喷砂用的砂子。以干法取自机械加煤机炉和煤粉炉的灰渣也可用于上述大部分用途。

烟气中灰粒的清除 为了达到清洁排烟的目的,当燃料呈悬浮燃烧时,现在普遍需要某些型式的去除灰粒的设备去除掉机组烟气中的飞灰。现有好几种型式的灰粒去除设备,它们可以分为电气除尘器、机械除尘器、面袋式除尘器和湿式除尘等。对用这些型式的设备所除去的飞灰来讲,这些飞灰也可以用于上述的灰渣的大多数用途中。

电气除尘器　电气除尘器能在要收集的颗粒上产生一种电荷,由静电力将这些带电荷的颗粒推到集尘板上。这种除尘器在运行上包括四个基本步骤:

1. 在电晕电极和集尘板之间保持一个强的高电压电场;
2. 带飞灰的烟气被强力电场离子化,这些烟气离子又使携带的颗粒带电荷;
3. 处于静电场内的带负电荷的颗粒被吸引到带正电荷(接地的)的集尘板上;
4. 已收集的灰尘受到敲打后掉落到贮灰斗中。

电气除尘器的收集效率与灰粒暴露在静电场内的时间、电场强度以及灰粒的电阻有关。与其他形式设备比较,一般是在有利的投资条件下获得 99% 以上的效率。因此从 1970 年以来安装于商业用的锅炉房内的灰颗粒清除装置绝大部分是电气除尘器。

机械除尘器　机械除尘器的运行是使带有灰粒的烟气切向流入除尘器的本体,因而在要收集的灰粒上就产生一个离心力。灰粒甩在除尘器的壁上,在那里被排除掉。机械除尘器最有效的运动条件是灰颗粒尺寸在 10 μm 以上,当灰粒在 10 μm 以下时,除尘效率大大下降,可能降到 90% 以下。由于对除尘效率要求日益增高,机械除尘器的采用率已经下降。

布袋除尘器　布袋除尘器的运动是将烟气碰撞在由织物构成的细密过滤器上将灰尘捕获,当将灰尘连续收集时,积累的灰粒粘住在织物的表面上。布袋除尘器获得最大效率是当灰尘积聚到堵塞织物前的这段时期,在固定运动周期以后布袋必须清理。紧接着布袋清理以后过滤效率将有所降低,直到灰尘又开始积聚起来。

布袋除尘器可以应用于任何需要干除尘的工艺流程和对要处理的气体中的温度和湿度并不对其产生限制的场合。在效率等于或低于 99% 时,布袋除尘器一般不能与电气除尘器在锅炉上的应用作竞争。可是,对于除颗粒物质,采用布袋除尘器可以获得 99% 以上的效率,在人口密集区的应用可能增加。

湿式除尘器　湿式除尘器是利用适当的液体来收集灰尘,从而将灰尘由烟气中除去(见原文),一种好的湿式除尘器可以使烟气流和液体之间形成密切的接触,从而达到由烟气中将浮悬颗粒物转移到液体中去的目的。在湿式除尘器运动中,其集尘效率、灰粒大小和压降三者是密切相关的。需要的运行压降是在给定效率下与灰粒大小成反比变化,或者是在给定的颗粒大小下,除尘效率由于运动压降的增加而增加。

和其他的颗粒物质收集设备不同之处是,湿式除尘器是利用一种液体去收集颗粒物质。为了这个缘故,往往除集尘外,常常还执行附加工艺过程的功能,如气体吸收、化学反应和热传导等,在湿式除尘器中采用合适的冲洗液体时可以同时完成除尘和除去气体污染物质。

油灰腐蚀(7.2)

高温腐蚀 当钠和钒的复合物熔化时是具有腐蚀性的,在油灰沉积物中经常有这种复合物。腐蚀的机理可能是由于金属的加速氧化作用,即由于熔融灰中的组成成分将氧传送到金属表面上去而引起的,还由于灰将金属表面正常的氧化保护层除去而引起的。

腐蚀也可能是由于硫酸盐的侵蚀而产生的,特别是当燃料油中也存在着氯化钠或其他氯化物时。这种腐蚀易于在燃用含低钒量但含有万分之几的氯化钠的燃油锅炉中产生。当围绕管子四周的气氛是还原气氛,或者是氧化和还原交替变化的气氛时,即使燃料油中所含有氯化物是少得可以忽略不计,但硫酸盐的腐蚀仍可能是严重的。

一个可以测量得出来的腐蚀率可以在较大的金属温度和烟温范围内观察出来,这取决于油灰沉积物的量及其成分。燃料油中含钒量的高低对腐蚀的影响不是十分明显的,因为燃烧条件或燃料油中氯化物的含量都可能在起主导作用。但是钠的含量对发生显著腐蚀的最低金属温度的影响则是肯定的。

在目前似乎没有任何一种合金不受油灰腐蚀的,一般说来,合金中的含铬量越高,则越能抗腐蚀。这就是在高温过热器管采用 18Cr–8Ni 合金的原因。含铬量大于 30% 的高铬合金可能增加抗腐蚀能力,但这是在牺牲了物理性能的条件下获得的。曾经用过 25Cr–20Ni 合金作为管子的包覆层,但是甚至这种合金也不能起完全保护的作用。在高温合金内加入锡是为了增加强度。高锡合金在氧化气氛条件下有相当抗油灰腐蚀的能力,但是易于受到由于局部还原性气氛或由于灰沉积物中存在氯化物而引起的硫化物侵蚀。要完全避免这种条件是有困难的,因此高锡合金的优点可能是有限的。无论如何,价格昂贵的材料要以长的使用寿命来证明是否合算,但这并不是经常可以预测准确的。

低温腐蚀　在燃油锅炉中的低温腐蚀问题,是由于炉烟中硫酸的形成和凝结而引起的,这与上述的燃煤锅炉的情况相似。

由于以下的两种原因,燃油锅炉比大多数燃煤锅炉易于受低温腐蚀:

(1) 油灰沉积物中的钒是将 SO_2 转换成 SO_3 的一个良好催化剂;

(2) 在烟气中的灰量较少。在烟气中的灰粒会减少烟气中的 SO_3 含量。由于油中的灰比煤中的灰少得多,所以这种显著的不同是在预料之中的。此外,煤灰比油灰的碱性大,这有助于中和任何淀积的酸,而油灰一般就缺少这种性能。

在某些情况下,燃油锅炉可能由烟囱排出酸性的灰粒,这种酸性灰粒会污染或腐蚀厂房附近有色彩物体的表面。酸性的沉积物或烟炱通常是由于金属表面(如空气预热器、烟道和烟囱)在低于烟气露点很多的情况下运动而引起的,或者由于流过锅炉通道中吸收了硫酸气的烟灰所引起的。有下列几种方法用来防止排出酸性的烟炱:

1. 在烟气中将 SO_3 的形成减到最小程度;
2. 将烟气中的 SO_3 中和;
3. 保持所有与烟气接触的金属表面温度高于 $250°F$;
4. 燃料油完全燃烧,以消除烟炱颗粒。

控制方法　曾经采用或建议过控制燃油锅炉的沾污和腐蚀的一些方法,但是在每种情况下,这些方法的适用性都受到经济情况的支配。无疑地,减少进入炉膛的灰量和硫量是最有把握的控制手段,但是只要灰的组成成分已经沉积在管子上,要将其影响减到最小也是不可靠的。由于污染和腐蚀的严重性不仅取决于燃料油的特性,还取决于锅炉设计和运行中的变化,因此,对于这些问题,无法规定出一个笼统的解决办法。

燃料油的供应　虽然在美国,选择用油和用混合油的方式已实行到某种程度,但是这是为了在用户厂中的安全和可靠的运输和贮存而执行的,并不是为了解决污染的困难。由于对钠、硫和钒的极限限度不是为了避免沾污,也不是为了避免腐蚀而准确规定的,因此不能充分利用这些方法来作为控制的手段。

对燃料油的脱硫和除去灰分是两种可用的处理方法。对渣油用水冲洗的方法已经在少数船舶锅炉上应用得很成功。但是这一措施只能除去钠和以铁锈和沙子为主的沉淀物,因此,要广泛采用这种方法是有疑问的。燃用低含硫量,低灰分的原油和采用对燃料进行脱硫的方法预期会增加。

燃料油添加剂 在锅炉停役期间用冲洗的习惯做法以及在有限的范围内在锅炉运行时用水冲洗,这都能克服燃用现在的燃料油时有所遇到的困难。此外,对这种问题进行继续研究的结果,发现了在燃料油灰最令人麻烦的地方可以采用的一种其它方法。简单地说,这种方法是向燃料油中或向炉膛中加入少量能足够改变油灰特性的材料,就可以用蒸汽吹灰器或空气吹灰器或空气枪将灰除去。

添加剂对减轻与过热器沾污、高温灰的腐蚀和低温硫酸腐蚀等有关的困难是有效的。最有效的添加剂是氧化铝、白云石和氧化镁。高岭土也是氧化铝的一种原料。

沾污和高温腐蚀的减轻主要是靠生成了呈粉状或脆性而且易于用吹灰器或吹灰枪吹去的高熔点的灰沉积物。当灰呈干态时,腐蚀会大大地减轻。

形成的耐熔硫酸盐与烟气中的 SO_3 气体发生反应后,可以减少低温度硫酸腐蚀,这样就除去了 SO_3 气体,烟气的露点能降低到足以保护金属表面的温度,这样形成的硫酸盐化合物是比较干燥的,易于用一般标准的清理设备来清除。

一般说来,所用添加剂的量约等于燃料油中的含灰量。在某些情况下,为了能获得最好的效果,需用稍为不同的比例,特别是为了减低高温腐蚀,一般公认的是以油中的含钒量为依据,所用添加剂,按重量的比例与含钒量之比应为 2:1 或 3:1。

曾经成功地用过几种方法将添加剂加入炉膛中去。其中普遍采用的一种方法是将规定剂量的添加剂溶液,有控制地加入燃烧器的供油管道中去。为了添加剂能很好地弥散和对油雾化器的磨损减少到最小的程度,要将添加剂粉碎到能 100% 通过 325 目的筛子,也就是 44 μm 的筛子。

对用高压回流油系统的燃油锅炉,有利的是在所需要的位置,将添加剂粉末吹入炉膛内。为了很好地弥散,添加剂粉末一定要能 100% 通过 325 目的筛子。

第三种方法,也就是最近采用的那一种方法,是将添加剂调成水浆的形式,通过专门的吹灰器或吹灰枪喷入锅炉。这种方法的优点是添加剂能正确地用在所需要的地点,这就有可能减少需用的添加剂量。用这个系统,一定要小心观察,以避免造成对管子的热冲击,也就是冷淬裂纹。在添加剂水浆中有氯化物时,就有可能对奥氏体钢产生应力腐蚀裂纹,这是应该注意的。氯化物或者于水中,或者来自于添加剂。

对各种添加剂的选用,取决于各个厂是否能获得这些添加剂及其价格是否合适,还取决于所选用的方法。例如,在用添加剂浆的方法时,用氧化铝就比用其他材料对喷雾板的磨损要快些。

从清理问题方面来讲,对每一台设备所生成的沉积物的量是要考虑的一个重要问题。采用不同的添加剂时,对其所生成沉积物的量进行比较,表明白云石生成的沉积物量最多,这是由于白云石与硫酸盐化合的能力强;氧化铝和高岭土生成的沉积物量最少;氧化镁所生成的沉积物在这两者之间。但是,在有合适的清理设施时,沉积物是易于清除的,因此所生成的量应该不成为一个问题。

用过剩空气量控制 如上所述,在燃烧渣油时所遇到的高温沉积物(沾污)、高温腐蚀和低温硫酸腐蚀等问题,都是由于有呈最高氧化状态的钒和硫的存在而引起的。如果将过剩空气量由7%减少到1%或2%,就有可能避免完全氧化的钒化合物和硫化合物的形成,因此,也就减轻了锅炉的沾污和腐蚀的问题。

在一台试验锅炉上进行的一系列试验中发现,当过剩空气量由7%的平均值减到1%~2%的水平时,则304型不锈钢过热器合金管在2 100℉温度烟气中维持在1 250℉的温度时,其最大腐蚀率可减低75%以上。此外,与在过剩空气量约为7%时生成的紧紧粘在管子上的硬而且密集的灰沉积物相对照,在过剩空气量为1%~2%时,在过热器管束上所形成的灰沉积物是软的,并且是粉状的,其灰的聚集率也只有硬的密集的灰聚集率的一半那么大。在1%~2%的过剩空气量下运行,并保持所有的金属温度高于烟气中水的露点,实际上清除了碳钢的低温腐蚀。但是,假若在燃烧器处过剩空气量有波动,即使在短时间波动量仅达到5%的水平,则部分在低过剩空气量燃烧所得到的有益的效果也都损失了。低过剩空气量下的碳损失约为0.5%,这个数值一般来说,是能为电力公用事业和工业所接受的。

在美国和欧洲的大型工业锅炉曾有好几年都在低的过剩空气量下运行,

其结果证明这对减轻低温腐蚀是有好处的。但是,它对减轻高温结渣和高温腐蚀是否有好处,还没有得出结论。无论如何,必须对各个燃烧器的燃料和空气的平均分配给以极大的注意,必须连续不断地监视燃烧情况,以保证燃烧气体在进入对流通道的管束以前,燃料已完全燃烧。

压力测量(7.11)

测量压力、温度、流量、蒸汽的干度和蒸汽的纯度所用的仪表和测量的方法,是在蒸汽发生设备的运行中必不可少的。为了确保设备安全、经济、可靠的运行,所用的仪表和测量方法所涉及范围是由最简单的手动装置到用于对锅炉和其有关设备实行完全自动控制的测量设备。

试验监测仪表往往是便携式的。它用于设备的性能试验中,以确定所要求的流量、压力和温度是否已经符合设计和运行的条件,使用户和设备供应者都感到满意。对这些仪表的要求在 ASME 性能试验法规中作了概述。这些仪表需要技术熟练的操作者小心地管理和经常地校验。这种仪表不适宜用于长期连续的商业运行。

商业所用的仪表是那些永久固定安装的仪表,并且预期在持久的时期内会有满意的准确度。要强调仪表的可靠性和复现性。这往往要求对绝对的准确度作些让步。但是,商用仪表的准确度正在逐步改进,现在用于试验目的的商用仪表也正在增加。

压力测量

压力表可能是最早用于锅炉运行的仪表。在第一台"水管安全式"锅炉问世一百多年以后的今天,虽然采用了现代化控制设备和联锁装置使锅炉超压在实际上是不可能的,但是用压力表来测定汽包的压力仍是需要的。图7.9(见原文)示出了已经多年采用作为指示压力的波登管式压力表。虽然这种仪表在结构上和准确度方面已经作了许多改进,但是其基本原理还是没有什么变化。

压力测量仪表根据压力的大小、所需要的准确度和其他条件,有各种不同的型式。

流体压力计是根据压力的大小在表内装有各种不同的流体。这种表在仔细运用时,可以有高的准确度。装用的流体是不同的,由测量低压时采用的比水为轻的流体,到测量比较高的压力时采用的水银,图 7.10(见原文)示出一个用于测量低压力时能读出小压差的倾斜式差压计。磁力作用的膜片式差压计现已用于低压测量。图 7.11(见原文)示出高压水银压力计。这些压力计是用于压力测量或压差测量的准确工具,符合于 ASME 性能试验法规的要求。在测量小压差而精确度又较高的测量中,例如要读出流量孔板的压差的准确读数时,就可以用管压力表(或者叫做微压计)来测量。图 7.12(见原文)所示为一种管压力计。

波登压力表可用于各种不同程度的精确度和准确度的范围大的静压测量。必需的精确度和准确度是由应用的要求来决定的。作为运行指导用的压力表不需要高的精确度,一般表计的分刻度约为表盘的全刻度范围的 1% 就可以了。在某些试验过程中,如承压部件的静水压试验和锅炉效率试验,就需要较高的精确度。分刻度为表盘的全刻度范围的 0.1% 的仪表是合用的,并且是为了这些目的所必须采用的。在要求得到高精确度的温度和压力,以便能准确地确定蒸汽和水的焓的锅炉效率试验中,这时对压力的测量采用自重压力计比采用波登压力计更好些。

膜片式压力表可以作测量压差之用。图 7.13(见原文)所示为一种典型的能读出小压差的挠性膜片压力表,用在总压力不超过 1 psig 的地方,读出的压差单位为英寸水柱。用对称安装的两个波纹管式的压力表(见原文图 7.14),可以读出范围大的压差。这种压力表适合于读出流过锅炉回路的流体压降。在压力高达 6 000 psi 时,可以用来测量从 2 到 1 000 psi 的压差。

目前市场上有许多测量压力和压差用的技术先进的装置。这些装置一般称为变换器,它是根据不同的原理工作的。例如,有装在薄膜上的应变计式的变换器,或者是晶体变换器,当元件变形时,晶体的电阻就发生变化。由于这些元件需要精密的和经常的较验,因此一般不作为运行指导或设备试验用的基本仪表。但是这种仪表的可靠性正在提高,并且它易于应用,因此压力变换器的应用愈来愈广泛。

压力读数

在记录和报告压力读数时,如果表计有连接的水柱的情况,则对表计的读数一定要作对水柱的修正。如果有需要时,将压力表的读数加上大气压,换算成绝对压力值。水柱仅仅是添加在表计的额外压力,而不是实际压力所起的作用,它不过是在表计上面的凝结水柱或水柱的实际压力。图7.15(见原文)说明对压力表读数作水柱修正的应用。在实际使用中,在系统中没有压力时,将仪表水柱充满水,然后将表计重新校正到零,这种作法是完全可以的。

在各种形式测量装置两端的压降可作为测量流量的一种手段,诸如孔板、喷嘴或皮托管等的压差。这将在本章末叙述。

压力测量仪表的连接

确定测量装置连接到压力源的位置的指导原则,不管测量压力的大小、测量设施的形式或被测量的流体的类型是怎样的,一般都是一样的。

在管道、烟道或导管的压力连接管或取压接头一定要放在能避免由于流体冲击或涡流而会引起误差的位置。这样就可以保证所测得的是真正的静压。连接管线要尽可能短和尽可能直接连接,而且没有泄漏。为了得到压差数值时,宁可用一个压差测量装置而不用在两个仪表上取得读数后,再求出其差值。

7.12 洁净煤技术

众所周知,煤是一种"脏"燃料,因此,必须开发洁净煤技术,以满足严格的环境法要求。

第一个方法是开发除污染设备,以减少现有煤粉炉的排放污染物。这一设备处理过程包括炉内燃烧处理(一次过程)和/或炉膛出口烟道气的处理(二次过程)。

第二个方法是在锅炉设计中完全采用流化床燃烧这一新技术,它可以保证炉内煤燃烧的状态,以同时消除 NO_x 和 SO_x。除此之外,煤气化技术也包括在内。

本文所考虑的洁净煤技术包括:

1.对已有锅炉,一次和二次除污染系统;

2. 装有烟气净化设备的煤粉炉；
3. 常压循环流化床燃烧；
4. 增压鼓泡流化床燃烧；
5. 增压循环流化床燃烧；
6. 整体煤气化(蒸汽－燃气)联合循环；
7. 混合循环应用于循环流化床。

对已有电厂的洁净煤技术改造

· 一次过程

脱氮装置。燃烧器的设计越来越注重控制燃烧过程中氮氧化物的生成量。这些燃烧器被称作"低 NO_x 燃烧器"，其方法是空气分段送入并改变燃料分配(以分段燃烧)。其原理是避免过高的火焰温度，以减少炉内的过量氧气，从而降低氮氧化物的生成量。另一种一次过程是将炉膛燃烧用的空气分段，称为"过燃风"。还有一种方法是将燃料分段送入炉膛，称为"再燃料"。

脱硫装置。一次除硫工艺是向炉内喷入细粉状石灰或石灰石，以吸收燃料过程中产生的二氧化硫。如有必要，可向烟气中喷入熟石灰和水，以提高脱硫效率。这一工艺的效率适中，约为40%～70%，但花费较低。

· 二次过程

脱氮装置。可使用有催化或无催化化学过程，以减少 NO_x 排放量。最常用的二次过程(95%的已安装系统)选用选择性催化氧化过程。氨气与烟气在炉膛出口空气预热器之前混合，然后混合气体通过附有催化剂的反应器(反应)生成 N_2 和水。运行时温度控制在 350～430℃。

脱硫装置。新近安装的机组中，一般使用以湿石灰/石膏作原料的烟道气除硫系统，以减少 SO_2 的排放量。SO_2 是以 $CaSO_4$ 的形式从烟气中清除掉的。该工艺必须通过一个湿式过程生成悬浮的钙的碳酸盐、亚硫酸盐、硫酸盐产物。

常压循环流化床燃烧

常压循环流化床燃烧的电厂的工作原理是，煤在流化床炉体内完全燃烧发出热量，(加热水)以产生高温高压的水蒸气。炉内压力大致为常压，流化速度很高。被带出炉膛的固体颗粒被搜集并重新送回炉内。这种固体物质的炉内循环可保证煤在约850℃的炉温下充分燃烧（这一温度有利于二氧化硫与石灰石合并使氮氧化物生成量最少）。蒸汽膨胀冲动汽轮机,汽轮机带动交流发电机发电。

增压鼓泡流化床燃烧

在增压鼓泡流化床燃烧的电厂中,锅炉工作在 $1.0 \times 10^6 \sim 1.6 \times 10^6$ Pa 的压力下,炉床的流化速度很低。这样,流化床上的固体颗粒与上部的气化层完全分开。在这样的流化速度下,气化鼓泡可通过炉床到达其表面,因此被称作"鼓泡床"。电力由两台发电机发出,一台连接蒸汽轮机,它通过蒸汽扩容过程带动发电,另一台连接燃气轮机,它通过燃气的膨胀做功带动发电。增压鼓泡流化床燃烧技术是一个联合循环。

增压循环流化床燃烧

在增压循环流化床燃烧的电厂中,锅炉工作在 $1.0 \times 10^6 \sim 1.6 \times 10^6$ Pa 的压力下,炉床的流化速度很高,近似于常压循环流化床燃烧。增压循环流化床燃烧,其循环流化床上的特点与常压循环流化床燃烧相同。惟一不同的是,增压循环流化床燃烧,其炉膛是在增压的条件下运行。

整体煤气化（蒸汽－燃气）联合循环

在整体煤气化联合循环中,首先将煤气化产生的煤气净化,特别是除尘、除硫化物,再燃烧,(燃气)一般进入燃气轮机以带动发电。余热锅炉利用燃气的部分显热产生蒸汽。这些蒸汽也被用来驱动蒸汽轮机发电。

今天,残煤或残油的气化新技术为高效率的联合循环发电提供可能。整体煤气化联合循环技术分多种类型。它们既可以按气化床的种类（固定床、流化床）划分,也可以按所用的氧化剂（空气或氧气）种类和按燃气净化系统不同来划分。

Words and Expressions

A

a variety of 种种
absorbant [əb'sɔːbənt] n. 吸收剂
absorption [əb'sɔːpʃən] n. 吸收(过程)
acceleration [æk‚selə'reiʃən] n. (物)加速,加速度
accumulation [əkjuːmju'leiʃ(ə)n] n. 积聚,堆积物
accumulator [ə'kjuːmjuleitə] n. 贮液器,收集器
acidic [ə'sidik] a. 酸性的
acmite ['ækmait] n. 锥辉石
additional [ə'diʃənəl] a. 额外的,附加的,补充的
adiabatically [‚ædiəbətikli] ad. 绝热地
adjacent [ə'dʒeisənt] a. 接近的,邻近的,附近的
adjacent [ə'dʒeisənt] a. 接近的,邻近的
adjacent [ə'dʒeisənt] a. 邻近的,因此相连的
aerodynamics ['ɛərəudai'næmiks] n. 空气动力学
aeronautical [‚ɛərəu'nɔːtikl] a. 航空(学)的
aerothermodynamics n. 空气热力学
aero-generator n. 空气发电机
air injection staging 空气分段送入
air-preheater n. 空气预热器
alkaline absorbent 碱性吸收剂
alloy ['æbi] n. 合金
alternator ['ɔːltə(ː)neitə] n. 交流发电机
alternator ['ɔːltəneitə] n. 交流发电机
ambient ['æmbiənt] a. 周围的,大气的

analcite [ə'nælsait] n. 方沸石
analogy [ə'nælədʒi] n. 类比,类推
and the like 等等,诸如此类
angular ['æŋgjulə] a. 角形的,用角度量的
anhydrite [æn'haidrait] n. 酸酶
anhydrous [æn'haidrəs] adj. 无水的
annular ['ænjulə] a. 环形的
anthracite ['ænθrəsait] n. 无烟煤,白煤,硬煤
anthracite ['ænθrəsait] n. 无烟煤
anthracite ['ænθrəsait] n. 无烟煤
appendage [ə'pendidʒ] n. 附属物
appreciable [ə'pri:ʃiəbl] a. 相当大的
approximate [ə'prɔksimit] a. 近似的,大概的
approximately [ə'prɔksimətli] adv. 大概,近乎
aqueous ['eikwiəs] a. 水的,水状的
aragonite [ə'rægənait] n. 散文石
arch [a:tʃ] n. 拱,拱顶
arch [a:tʃ] n. 拱门,弓形结构
ash [æʃ] n. 灰
ASHRAE = American Society of Heating Refrigerating and Air-conditioning Engineers 美国供热制冷和空调工程师协会
associate [ə'souʃiit] vt&vi. (使)发生联系,(使)联合; n. 伙伴,同事
assumed [ə'sju:md] a. 假装的,虚构的,假想的
at a stroke 一下子,一次
atomic [ə'tɔmik] a. 原子的,核子的,核能的
attainment [ə'teimənt] n. 达到
augment [ɔ:g'ment] v. 增加
auxiliary [ɔ:g'ziljəri] a. 辅助的,附加的
auxiliary [ɔ:g'ziljəri] a. 辅助的

auxiliary [ɔːgˈziljəri] n. (复)辅助设备
axial-turbine 轴流式透平,轴流式汽轮机

B

back pressure turbine 背压式汽轮机
balding [ˈbɔːldiŋ] adj. 叶片,叶栅
baseboard n. 踢脚板
be replaced by 被代替
bearing [ˈbɛəriŋ] n. 轴承
beverage [ˈbevəridʒ] n. 饮料
bin [bin] n. 仓,箱
binder [ˈbaində] n. 黏合
bio-fluid [ˈbaiəˈfluːd] n. 生物流体
bituminous [biˈtjuːminəs] a. 烟煤的
bituminous [biˈtjuːminəs] adj. 烟煤
bituminous [biˈtjuːminəs] u. 烟煤的
blade [bleid] n. 叶片,刀片
blading [ˈbleidiŋ] n. 叶片(装置)
bleed off 放出
blower [ˈbləuə] n. 鼓风机,风扇
blower [ˈbləuə] n. 鼓风机
blower [ˈbləuə] n. 鼓风机
bodily [ˈbɔdili] a. 具体的,有形的
boil off 汽化,蒸发
boil off 汽化
boiler [ˈbɔilə] n. 锅炉,煮器
bomb [bɔm] n. 高压弹,炸弹
bonnet [ˈbɔnit] n. 烟囱帽,阀帽
boost [buːst] vt. 升高,增加

bore [bɔː] n. 激浪
bottom ['bɔtəm] n. 底部,炉底
boundary ['baundəri] n. 界线,分界,边界
boundary ['bəundəri] n. 界线,边界
brake [breik] n. 制动器,刹车
break down 分解
breeze [briːz] n. 灰渣,焦炭屑
brewery ['bruəri] n. 酿酒厂
bubble ['bʌbl] n. 气泡,泡沫 v. vi. 起泡,沸腾
Bubbling Fluidized Bed(BFB) 鼓泡流化床
buffet ['bʌfit] v. 打击,与……搏斗
bulk [bʌlk] n. 大部分,堆
bunker ['bʌŋkə] n. 燃料舱,煤箱
bunker ['bʌŋkə] n. 容器,仓
buoyancy ['bɔiənsi] n. 浮力
buoyant ['bɔiənt] a. 浮升的
burner ['bəːnə] n. 燃烧器
burning ['bəːniŋ] a. 燃烧的 n. 燃烧
butterfly ['bʌtəflai] n. 蝴蝶
by imparting to 通过把……给与
bypass governing 旁路调节
by-pass n. 旁路,支流 a. 旁通 v. 分流

C

calcium sulfate 硫酸钙
calcium sulfite 亚硫酸钙
calcium ['kælsiəm] n. 钙
calorimeter [ˌkælə'rimitə] n. 热量计,量热器
capacity [kə'pæsiti] n. 容量,生产力,功率

carbon ['ka:bən] n. 碳
carbonate ['ka:bəneit] vt. 碳酸盐
carborundm [,ka:bə'rʌndəm] n. 金刚砂,碳化硅
caretaker ['kɛəteikə] n. 看管人
casing ['keisiŋ] n. 汽缸,气缸,机匣,机壳
casings ['keisiŋz] n. 壳
catalyst ['kætəlist] n. 催化剂
categorize ['kætigəraiz] v. 把……分类
category ['kætigfəri] n. 种类,部类
category ['kætigəri] n. 种类,类型
centrifugal [sen'trifjugəl] a. 离心的;n. 离心,离心机
centrifugal [sen'trifjugəl] a. 离心的
chain-grate 链条炉排
challenge ['tʃæləndʒ] n. 异议,质问,需要
chamber ['tʃeimbə] n. 室,房间,箱
chamber ['tʃeimbə] n. 室,容器
chaotic [kei'ɔtik] a. 浑沌的,混乱的
charge [tʃa:dʒ] v. 注入,装填
check with 与……联系,与……接洽
chill ['tʃil] n. & vt. 冷冻,使变冷,寒冷
chloride ['klɔ:raid] n. 氯化物,漂白粉
churn [tʃə:n] v. 搅拌
Circulating Fluidized Bed(CFB) 循环流化床
circulation [,sə:kju'leiʃən] n. 循环
civil engineer 土木工程师
classification [,klæsifi'keiʃən] n. 分类,分类法
clatter ['klætə] n. v. (机械转动等)(发出)卡搭声
Clean Coal Technology(CCT) 洁净煤技术
clearance volume 余隙,容积

clearance ['kliərəns] n. 余隙
client ['klaiənt] n. 委托人, 买方, 顾客
cling [kliŋ] vi. 粘住, 依附, 坚持
coal gasification 煤气化
coefficient [ˌkəui'fiʃənt] n. 系数
coefficient [ˌkəui'fiʃənt] n. 系数
cohesive [kəu'hi:siv] a. 内聚的
coil [kɔil] n. 蛇[盘, 旋, 螺]管
collision [kə'liʒən] n. 猛烈相撞, 抵触(意见)冲突
combustion [kəm'bʌstʃən] n. 燃烧
combustion [kəm'bʌsʃən] n. 燃烧, 氧化
combustor [kəm'bʌstə] n. 燃烧室
come out of 有……结果
come to light 被人发现
comissioning [kə'miʃəniŋ] n. 试运转, 使用
commercial turbine 商业透平, 商业汽轮机
commercial [kə'mə:ʃəl] a. 大量生产的, 商业的
compatibility [kəmˌpæti'biliti] n. 兼容性
compensate ['kɔmpenseit] v. 抵消, 弥补, 补偿
complexity [kɔmp'leksiti] n. 复杂性, 复杂的物
comply with 照做
component [kəm'pəunənt] n. (组成)部分, 成分
compressibility [kemˌpresi'biliti] n. 压缩性, 压缩系数
compressible [kəm'presəbl] a. 可压缩的
compression [kəm'preʃən] n. 压缩
compressor [kə:m'presə] n. 压缩机, 压气机
compressor [kəm'presə] n. 压缩机
concentrate ['kɔnsentreit] vt. 浓缩, 冷凝
concentrated [kən'sentreitid] a. 浓缩的

concentration [ˌkɔnsen'treiʃən] n. 浓度,浓缩
condensate [kɔn'denseit] n. 冷凝物
condenser [kən'densə] n. 冷凝器
condensing turbine 凝汽式汽轮机
conductance [kən'dʌktəns] n. 导热率
conductivity [ˌkɔndʌk'tiviti] n. 导热系数
conduit ['kɔndit] n. 管道,管路
configuration [kən'figju'reiʃən] n. 构造,结构
configuration [kənˌfigju'reiʃən] n. 结构,形状,外形
confine [kən'fain] v. 限制
constituent [kən'stitjuənt] a. 组成的
contaminant [kən'tæmineit] n. 污染物,毒害
contaminant [kən'tæminənt] n. 污染物
continuum [kən'tinjuəm] n. 连续体
control stage 调节级
convection [kən'vekʃən] n. 对流
converging nozzle 渐缩喷嘴
convey [kən'vei] v. 传送,输运
convincing [kən'vinsiŋ] a. 有说服力的
coolant ['kuːlənt] n. 冷却剂,载热剂,冷却油
copper oxide 氧化铜
correlation [ˌkɔri'leiʃən] n. 相互关联,交互作用,关联式
correlation [ˌkɔri'leiʃən] n. 关系式
corrosion [kə'rəuʒən] n. 腐蚀,腐蚀作用
cost-effective a. 划算的,经济的
Coulomb friction 库伦系数
coverage ['kʌvəridʒ] n. 有效范围
crankcase ['kræŋkeiz] n. 曲轴箱
crank-shaft n. 曲轴

credit (to)　v. 把……归于,认为……
cross-over　n. 交叉
cross-sectional area　横截面积
crusher　['krʌʃə]　n. 破碎机
cryogenics　[kraiə'dʒeniks]　n. 低温学,低温技术
Curtiss stage　柯蒂斯级,复速级
cyclic　['saiklik]　a. 循环的
cyclone　['saikləun]　a. 旋风的
Cyclone-Furnace firing　旋风炉
cylinder　['silində]　n. 气缸,汽缸
cylinder　['silində]　n. 气缸,圆筒
cylinder　['silində]　n. 气缸,圆筒
cylinder　['silində]　n. 气缸,圆筒
cylinder　['silində]　n. 圆筒,圆柱体,汽缸

D

dairy　['dɛəri]　n. 牛奶房,制酪场,制酪业
damper　['dæmpə]　n. 节气闸
deaerate　[di:'eiəreit]　v. 使除去气体
decelerate　[di:'seləreit]　v. (使)减速
decline　[di'klain]　v. 拒绝,倾斜,跌落
deficiency　[di'fiʃənsi]　n. 缺乏,不够
deformation　[ˌdi:fɔ:'meiʃən]　n. 变形
dehumidify　[di:'hju:midifai]　vt. 除湿
deliver　[di'livə]　vt. 释放,发出
demonstration　['demən'streiʃən]　n. 示范
denitrification device　除氮装置
dense　[dens]　a. 密的,稠密的,浓厚的
density　['densiti]　n. 密度,浓厚

desulfurization [di:ˌsʌlfərai'zeiʃən] n. 脱硫,去硫
desulphurization devices 除硫装置
desuperheated [di:'sju:pə'hi:tid] a. 降温,降低蒸气过热度
deterioration [diˌtiəriə'reiʃən] n. 恶化,磨损,损坏
diaphragm ['daiəfræm] n. 膈,隔膜,光圈
diffraction [di'frækʃən] n. 衍射
diffuse [di'fju:z] v. 扩散,散开
diffuser [di'fju:z] n. 散布者,扩散体
diffusion [di'fju:ʒən] n. 扩散,散布
diffusion [di'fju:ʒən] n. 漫射,(气流的)滞止
diffusivity [ˌdifju:'siviti] n. 扩散性,扩散系数
dilute [dai'lju:t] v. 稀释,冲淡
diluted [dai'lju:tid] a. 稀释的
dilution [dai'lu:ʃən] n. 冲淡,稀释物
dimension [di'menʃən] n. 尺寸
diminish [di'miniʃ] vt. 减小,减少
discern [di'sə:n] v. 辨别,分清,看出
discharge from 从……排出,从……流出
discharge [dis'tʃa:dʒ] n. 发射,卸货,偿还
discharge [dis'tʃa:dʒ] v. 排出,发射 n. 发射,放电量
discharge [dis'tʃa:dʒ] vt. 排出,离开
discipline ['disiplin] n. 学科
disorder [dis'ɔ:də] n. (身心,机能的)失调,轻病
displace [dis'pleis] vt. 排(水)
disposal [dis'pəuzəl] n. 丢掉,处理,布置
dissipation [ˌdisi'peiʃən] n. 消耗,消散
dissociation [disˌsəusi'eiʃən] n. 离解作用,分离
dissolve [di'zɔlv] v. 解散,结束,溶解,消失
distortion [dis'tɔ:ʃən] n. 扭曲,变形

documentation [ˌdɔkjumen'teiʃən] n. 提供的条件;文件(或证书等的)提供;文件(或证书等的)利用
downcomer [daun'kʌm] v. 下降管
dramatically [drə'mætikəli] adv. 明显地,显著地
draught [drɑːft] n. 吹风
drift ['drift] n. 吹积物 v. 吹积,漂流
drifting ['driftiŋ] adj. 漂移,偏差
drill [dril] n. 钻床
droplet ['drɔplit] n. 微滴
droplet ['drɔplit] n. 小滴
drum [drʌm] n. 汽包,汽鼓
dry-bottom furnace 固态排渣炉膛
ducts [dʌkts] n. 风管,管道

E

economizer [i(ː)'kɔnəmaizə] n. 省煤器
economizer [i'kɔnəmaizə] n. 省煤器
eddy ['edi] n. 涡流,漩涡
effect on 操作
elastic [i'læstik] a. 弹性的
electrostatic precipitators 静电除尘器
elevation [ˌeli'veiʃən] n. 高度
eliminate [i'limineit] v. 削减,除去
embrace [im'breis] v. 包含
emission [i'miʃən] n. 发出,排出物
emissive power 辐射力
emissivity [imi'siviti] n. 发射率,发射性,辐射系数
emit [i'mit] v. 放射,发出
empirical [em'pirikl] a. 经验的,实验的

emulsify [i'mʌlsifai] vt. 使乳化
enclosure [in'kləuʒə] n. 围绕,封人
encompass [in'kʌmpəs] vt. 围绕,包围
engine ['endʒin] n. 发动机
enthalpy drop 焓降
enthalpy [en'θælpi] n. 焓
enthalpy [en'θælpi] n. 焓,热量
entrain [in'trein] v. 带走,夹带,卷吸
entrance ['entrəns] n. 入口,进入
entropy ['entrəpi] n. 熵(热力学函数)
enumerate [i'nju:məreit] vt. 数,计点,枚举,计算
envelope ['enviləup] n. 壳层,外壳,包裹物
environmental chamber 环境实验室
equilibrium [i:kwi'libriəm] n. 平衡,均衡
equilibrium [ˌi:kwi'libriəm] n. 平衡(状态),均衡
erection [i'rekʃən] n. 建筑,安装
erosion [i'rəuʒən] n. 腐蚀,磨蚀
erosive [i'rəusiv] v. 腐蚀性的,侵蚀的
erratically [i'rætikəli] ad. 不稳定地,无规律地
evaporate [i'væpəreit] v. 使蒸发,使挥发
evaporator [i'væpəreitə] n. 蒸发器
exhaust [ig'zɔ:st] vt. 取出,弄空
exhaust [ig'zɔ:st] vt. 用尽,耗尽;vi. 排气;adj. 用不完的
expedite ['ekspidait] v. 使加速,迅速完成
extinguish [iks'tiŋgwiʃ] vt. 使熄灭,扑灭,使……不复存在
extract [iks'trækt] vt. 提取
extrapolation [ˌekstrəpəu'leiʃən] n. 外推,推断

F

facilitate [fə'siliteit] vt. 使方便
facility [fə'siliti] n. 设备,装置,机构
failure ['feiljə] n. 失败,忽略
fall within 属于……(之列)
fan [fæn] n. 风机,扇子
far-flung ['fɑː'flʌŋ] a. 辽阔的,漫长的
faucet ['fɔːsit] n. 龙头,旋塞
fault-finding n. a. 检查故障(的)
feeder ['fiːdə] n. 给煤机
feedwater [fiːd'wɔːtə] n. 给水,补水
feed-water n. 给水
filing system 档案制度
filing [failiŋ] n. (文件的)整理汇集
filter ['filtə] n. 滤波器,过滤器,筛选 vt. 过滤,渗透
filtrate ['filtreit] v. 过滤
final condition of steam 蒸汽终参数
fire hose 消防水龙头
fitness ['fitnis] n. 适合,恰当
flap [flæp] n. 风门片
flash [flæʃ] n. 闪光,一瞬间; a. 瞬时的,迅速的
flex [fleks] v. 弯曲
flexibility [ˌfleksə'biliti] n. 弹性,适应性,机动性
flexibility [ˌfleksə'biliti] n. 适应性,易曲性
flexibility [ˌfleksə'biliti] n. 易曲性,适应性
fling [fliŋ] v. 抛,猛冲
fluctuate ['flʌktjueit] vi. 波动 vt. 使波动,变动
flue gas 烟道内烟气

flue gas　*a*. 烟气,废气
flue　[fluː]　*a*. 烟道
flue　[fluː]　*n*. 烟道,风道
fluidized bed combustion　流化床燃烧
flux　[flʌks]　*n*. 流动,流量
foam　[fəum]　*n*. 泡沫; *v*. 起泡沫
foam　[fəum]　*vi*. 起泡沫,充满　*vt*. 使起泡沫
foil　[fɔil]　*n*. 叶形饰,翼,薄片
forced draught　送风机
forced-draft　送风机
forced-on-free convection　加上自然对流影响的受迫对流
Fourier's law　傅里叶定律
frequency　['friːkwənsi]　*n*. 频繁,频率
friction　['frikʃən]　*n*. 摩擦(力),阻力
fuel-ash　*n*. 燃料灰
fuel-burning　*a*. 燃料燃烧的
fundamental　[ˌfʌndə'mentl]　*a*. 基础的
furnace　['fəːnis]　*n*. 火炉,炉膛
furnace　['fəːnis]　*n*. 火炉,炉膛
fusibility　[ˌfjuːzə'biliti]　*n*. (可)熔性,熔度
fusion　['fjuːʒən]　*n*. 熔化

G

gall　[gɔːl]　*v*. 咬住,卡死
gaseous ammonia　氨气
gasifier　['gæsifaiə]　*n*. 气化床
gasket　['gæskit]　*n*. 衬圈,衬垫
gasoline　['gæsəliːn]　*n*. 汽油
gear-box　*n*. 变速箱

give up 释放,放弃,中断
govern ['gʌvən] v. 治理,统治,支配
Grashof number 格拉晓夫数
grate [greit] n. 炉架;壁炉
gravimetric [grəvi'metrik] a. 重量分析的,重量的
grid [grid] n. 格子,格栅
grindability [ˌgraində'biliti] n. 可磨性,磨削性
grindability [ˌgraində'biliti] n. 可磨性
gross [grəus] a. 总体的,总的
guarantee [ˌgærən'ti:] n. 保证,保证书
gypsum ['dʒipsəm] n. 石膏

H

handhole [hændhəul] n. 手孔
handing of ash 灰的处理
hand-over n. 移交,交接
hazard ['hæzəd] n. 危险,机会,偶然
hazardous ['hæzədəs] a. 碰运气的,危险的
header ['hedə] n. 联箱,母管
heat content 热值
heat drop process 热力过程
heat engine 热机
heat loss 热损
helical [helikəl] a. 螺旋的,螺旋形的
helium ['hi:ljəm] n. (化)氦
hemispherical [ˌhemi'sferrikəl] a. 半球状的,半球体的
hence [hens] adv. 从此,今后,因此
homogeneous [hɔ'mɔdʒinəs] a. 均匀的
hood [hud] n. 帽

horizontal [ˌhɔri'zɔnt] n. 水平面,水平的物体
horizontal [ˌhɔri'zɔntl] a. 水平的,卧式的
hotwell n. 温泉
humidity [hju(:)'miditi] n. 湿度
humidity [hju:'miditi] n. 湿度
humidity [hju:'miditi] n. 湿气,潮湿,湿度
humidity [hju:'miditi] n. 湿气,潮湿,湿度
hurricane ['hʌrikən] n. 台风
Hybrid cycle 混合循环
hydrocarbon ['haidrəu'ka:bən] n. 碳氢化合物
hydrodynamics ['haidrəudai'næmiks] n. 流体动力学
hydrogen ['haidrədʒən] n. 氢,氢气
hydrology [hai'drɔlədʒi] n. 水文学
hydrolysis [hai'drɔlisis] n. 水解
hydronic [hai'drɔnik] adj. 液体循环加热(或冷却)的
hydropower ['haidrəˌpauə] n. 水力发出的电力
hydrostatics ['haidrəu'stætiks] n. 流体静力学
hydroxyapatite [haiˌdrɔksi'æpətait] n. 含氧酸磷灰石
hydroxyl [hai'drɔksil] n. 氢氧
hydro-static a. 流体静力(学)的

I

ICI 帝国化学公司
ignition [ig'niʃən] n. 点火,点火装置,燃烧
illustrate ['iləstreit] v. 举例说明,显示,说明
illustrate ['iləstreit] v. 显示,加插图,说明
imaginary [i'mædʒinəri] a. 虚构的,想像的
immiscible [i'misəbl] a. 不溶混的
impeller [im'pelə] n. 推进器,叶轮,叶轮激动器

impulse turbine 冲击式透平,冲击式汽轮机
impulsive force 冲击力
impurity [im'pjuəriti] n. 杂质
in conjunction with 与……相结合
in large quantities 大量
in series 串联地,多级地
in the light of 依据,按照
incineration [insinə'reiʃən] n. 焚烧,煅烧
incline [in'klain] v. 倾斜
incompressibly [ˌinkəm'presəbli] ad. 不可压缩地
index ['indeks] n. 索引,指针,路标 v. 指示
indicate ['indikeit] v. 指示,表示,说明
individual [ˌindi'vidjuəl] a. 个别的,单独的,一个人的
induced draught 引风机
induced-draft 引风机
induction [in'dʌkʃən] n. 感应,诱导
ingredient [in'gri:diənt] n. 成分,组成部分,原料,要素
inherent [in'hiərənt] a. 内在的,固有的,根本的
initial condition of steam 蒸汽初参数
inject [in'dʒekt] n. 引入,注入
inlet ['inlet] n. 入口,插入物,注入
innocuous [i'nɔkjuəs] adj. 无害(毒的)
inroad ['inroud] v. 袭击 n. 损害
insignificant [insig'nifikənt] a. 小的,微不足道的,不重要的
installation ['instə'leiʃən] n. 安装,设备
installation [ˌinstə'leiʃən] n. 安装,设置,装置
instrument ['instrumənt] n. 仪器,器具
insulating ['insjuleitiŋ] a. 绝热的
insurmountable [ˌinsə:'mauntəbl] a. 不可克服的,难以超越的

intake ['inteik] n. 入口,吸入,进风量
Integrated Gasification Combined Cycle(IGCC) 整体煤气化(蒸汽—燃气)联合循环
integration [ˌinti'greiʃən] n. 积分
integrity [in'tegriti] n. 完整,完全,完善
interface ['intə(ː)feis] n. 相互关系,分界面
intermediate stage 中间级
intermediate [ˌintə'miːdjət] a. 中间的; n. 中间物
internals [in'təːnls] n. 内部部件
internal-combustion engine 内燃机
interruption [ˌintə'rʌpʃən] n. 中断,妨碍,障碍物
interstage [intə(ː)'steidʒ] a. 级间的,中间的
intertocks [ˌintə'lɔks] n. 联动装置
intimate ['intimit] a. 亲密的,本质的
intolerable [in'tɔlərəbl] a. 不能容忍的,难堪的 adv. 非常地,无法忍受地
intractable [in'træktəbl] a. 难处理的
intuitive [in'tjuitiv] a. 直觉的,直观的
inversely [in'vəːsli] ad. 相反地
inversion [in'vəːʃən] n. 逆温,逆增
investment [in'vestmənt] n. 投资,投资额
inviscid [in'visid] a. 无黏性的
ionization [ˌaiənai'zeiʃən] n. 电离
ionize ['aiənaiz] v. 使离子化 vi. 电离
ionospheric [ˌaiənə'sferik] a. 电离层的
irreversibly [ˌiri'vəːsəbli] ad. 不可逆(转)地
irritate ['iriteit] v. 激怒,使急躁,使兴奋
irrotational [ˌirəu'teiʃənl] a. 不旋转的
is preferable to 优于

isentropic ['aisen'trɔpik] a. 等(定)熵的
isolate ['aisəleit] v. 使隔离,使独立
isotope ['aisəutəup] n. 同位素,核素
issue from 从……喷出,从……流出
issue ['isju:] n. 排出,流出

J

jet [dʒet] . 汽流,射流,喷气式发动机,喷气式飞机

K

kaolin ['keiəlin] n. 瓷土,高岭土
kerosene ['kerəsi:n] n. 煤油
kilowatt ['kiləwɔt] n. 千瓦(特)
kinetic energy 动能
kinetic [kai'netik] a. 动力(学)的,动力的
kinetic [kai'netik] a. 动力的

L

laminar ['læminə] a. 成薄层的,薄层状的
latent heat 潜热
latent ['leitənt] a. 潜在的
lattice ['lætis] n. 格子,晶格
leakage ['li:kidʒ] n. 漏出,泄漏,漏风
leave behind 遗留,把……丢在后面,超过
life-cyclen 整个使用周期
lignite ['lignait] n. 褐煤
lime/limestone 石灰/石灰石
lime [laim] n. 石灰
limestone ['laimstəun] n. 石灰石

linear ['liniə] a. 线性的,直线的
linearly ['liniəli] ad. 线性地
liquefaction [,likwi'fækʃən] n. 液化(作用),熔解
liquify ['likwifai] vt. 使液化
list [list] n. 目录 v. 列表
local ['ləukəl] a. 地方的,当地的
location [ləu'keiʃən] n. 地点,位置,场地
locomotive ['ləukəməutiv] n. 机车 a. 运动的
locomotive [,ləukə'məutiv] n. 机车
logging [lɔgiŋ] n. 阻塞
logical ['lɔdʒikəl] a. 逻辑的,必然的,合理的
lubricate [lu:bri'keit] v. 润滑
lubricating ['lju:brikeitiŋ] a. 润滑的
lubrication [,lju:bri'keiʃən] n. 润滑(作用)
lubrication [,lju:bri'keiʃən] n. 润滑
lump [lʌmp] n. 堆
lung [lʌŋ] n. 肺

M

magnesium oxide 氧化镁
magnetogasdynamics n. 磁性气体动力学
magnitude ['mægnitjud] n. 大小,量值
malfunction [mæl'fʌnkʃən] n. 机能失常,发生故障
malfunction [mæl'fʌŋkʃən] n. 障碍,故障,疾病
manometer [mə'nɔmitə] n. 压力计
margin ['ma:dʒin] n. 系度,亲裕
marine [mə'ri:n] adj. 船舶的,海的
match [mætʃ] n. 匹配,使协调
measurement ['meʒəmənt] n. 量度,测量

mechanism ['mekənizəm] n. 机理,机构
mechanism ['mekənizəm] n. 机械装置,机械结构
medium ['mi:diəm] n. 媒体
medium ['mi:djəm] n. 介质,方法
medium-pressure a. 中压的
megawatt ['megəwɔt] n. 兆瓦(特)
metallurgical [ˌmetə'lə:dʒikəl] a. 冶金的 n. 冶金学者
meteorology [ˌmi:tjə'rɔlədʒi] n. 气象学
migration [maig'reiʃən] n. 流动
modification [ˌmɔdifi'keiʃən] n. 更改,改装,修改
modification [ˌmɔdifi'keiʃən] n. 修改,减少,变形,缓和
modify ['mɔdifai] vt. 更改,改变
moisture ['mɔistʃə] n. 水分,湿气
molecular [mou'lekjulə] a. 分子的
molecule ['mɔlikju:l] n. 微小颗粒,分子
molten ['məultən] a. 熔化的,熔铸的
molten ['məultən] adj. 熔化的
molybdenum [mɔ'libdinəm] n. 钼
momentum [məu'mentəm] n. 动量,运动量
monatomic [ˌmɔnə'tɔmik] a. 单原子的
monochromatic emissive power 单色辐射力
monoxide [mə'nɔksaid] n. 一氧化物
moving bucket/blade 动叶
multiaxial turbine 多轴汽轮机
multicylinder turbine 多缸汽轮机
multistage ['mʌltisteidʒ] a. 多级(的),分阶段进行的
multistage ['mʌltisteidʒ] a. 多级的
multistage ['mʌltisteidʒ] adj. 多级

N

nacelle ['næ'sel] n. 机舱
narrows ['nærəuz] n. 海峡
NATO 北大西洋公约组织(即北约)
negative ['negətiv] a. 负的
neutralize ['nju:trəlaiz] v. 使中立,中和,取消
neutralizing the acidity 中和酸
neutron ['nju:trɔn] n. 中子
Newtonian [nju'təuniən] a. 牛顿的
nitrogen oxide 氮氧化物
nonhomogeneous ['nɔnhɔmə'dʒi:niəs] a. 非均匀的
nonviscous ['nɔn'viskəs] a. 非黏性的
non-linear a. 非线性的
non-uniformity 不均匀性
note down 记录下,摘下
nozzle box 喷嘴室
nozzle governing 喷嘴调节
nozzle ['nɔzl] n. 喷管,喷嘴
nozzle ['nɔzl] n. 喷嘴,喷管,燃烧器
nozzle ['nɔzl] n. 喷嘴
numerically [nju(:)'merikəli] ad. 在数字上,数值上的
Nusselt number 努谢尔特数

O

oceanography [,əuʃjə'nɔgrəfi] n. 海洋学
odo(u)rless ['əudəlis] a. 没有香气(气味)的
of the order of 大约,约为
on-line n. (与主机)联机,在线,机内

optimism ['ɔptimizəm] n. 乐观(主义)
optimum ['ɔptiməm] n. 最佳值 a. 最佳的
ordinate ['ɔ:dinit] n. 纵坐标
orifice ['ɔrifis] n. (管子等的)孔
orifice ['ɔrifis] n. 孔,口,喷管
orifice ['ɔrifis] n. 口,洞,孔
orthophosphate [ˌɔ:θəu'fɔsfeit] n. 亚磷酸盐
oscillat ['ɔsileit] v. 摆动,振动
out of the centre 偏心地
Over Fire Air(OFA) 过燃风
overhand [əuvəhænd] n. vt. 大修,仔细检查
overlap ['əuvəlæp] n. 重叠(部分)
oxidizer ['ɔksidaizə(r)] n. 氧化剂
oxygen ['ɔksidʒən] n. 氧,氧气

P

paradigm ['pærədaim] n. 范例
parallel to 平行于
parallel to 与……平行
parallel ['pærəlel] a. 相似的,相同的; n. 相似处
parameter [pə'ræmitə] n. 参数 thermodynamics ['θəmɔudai'næmiks] n. 热力学
paramount ['pærəmɔunt] a. 最重要的,首位的
peakload ['pi:k'ləud] n. 峰值负荷
peat [pi:t] n. 泥煤块
pellet ['pelit] n. 小球,弹丸,锭片
penalty ['penlti] n. 惩罚,罚款,困难,障碍
peripheral [pə'rifərəl] a. 周界的,边缘的
peripheral [pə'rifərəl] a. 周界的,边缘的

permit [pə'mit] v. 许可,容许 n. 许可证
perpendicular to 垂直于
pertinent ['pə:tinənt] a. 恰当的,相关的
pertinent ['pə:tinənt] a. 相关的,有关系的
petroleum [pi'trəuliəm] n. 石油
pharmaceutical [ˌfa:mə'sju:tikl] n. 制药厂
photochemical [ˌfəutəu'kemikəl] a. 光化学的
pick up 吸收
piping ['paipiŋ] n. 笛声,尖叫声
piston ['pistən] n. 活塞,柱塞
piston ['pistən] n. 活塞
piston ['pistən] n. 活塞
pit [pit] n. 沟,槽
plasma ['plæzmə] n. 等离子体
plaster ['pla:stə] n. 熟石膏,烧石膏
plateau ['plætəu] n. 平稳段,平稳状态
platen ['plætən] n. 屏
plenum ['pli:nən] n. 充满,充实
plot [plɔt] v. 测绘
plot [plɔt] v. 作图(表示)
plutonium [plu:təuniəm] n. 钚
pneumatic [nju:'mætik] a. 空气的,气体的,气动的
pneumatic [nju:'mætik] a. 空气的,气体的,气动的
pneumatic [nju:'mætik] a. 空气的,气体的,气动的
poison ['pɔizn] n. 毒,毒物 v. 毒害,毒死
polarize ['pəuləraiz] v. 偏振,极化
polyatomic [ˌpɔliə'tɔmik] a. 多原子的
powder ['paudə] n. 煤粉
power capacity 容量,功率

power hammer　汽锤
Prandtl number　普朗特数
precaution　[priˈkɔːʃən]　n. 预防, 防备
precipitator　[priˈsipiteitə]　n. 除尘器, 聚尘器
precision　[priˈsiʒən]　n. 精确度, 准确(性)
preclude　[priˈkluːd]　v. 预防, 排除
predominate　[priˈdɔmineit]　vi. 支配, 统治
prescribe　[priˈkraib]　v. 限定, 限制
presentation　[prezənˈteiʃən]　n. 表达
pressure drop　压降
procedure　[prəˈsiːdʒə]　n. 程序, 工序
progressive　[prəˈgresiv]　a. 进行的
projected area　投影面积
promote　[prəˈməut]　v. 升级, 促进, 发起
propeller　[prəˈpelə]　n. 螺旋浆, 推进器
proportionality factor　比例系数
proportionality　[prəˌpɔːʃəˈnæliti]　n. 比例
proposal　[prəˈpəuzəl]　n. 建议, 计划
propulsion　[prəˈpʌlʃən]　n. 推进(装置), 推动
propulsion　[prəˈpʌlʃən]　n. 推进(装置), 推力
proton　[ˈprəutɔn]　n. 质子
pulverize　[ˈpʌlvəraiz]　v. 将……粉碎
pulverize　[ˈpʌlvəraiz]　v. 将……弄碎, 磨碎
pulverize　[ˈpʌlvəraiz]　v. 研磨, 使成粉末
Pulverized Coal(PC)　煤粉
pulverizedcoal　煤粉
purge　[pəːdʒ]　n. 清洗, 净化
purity　[ˈpjuəriti]　n. 纯度
pyramidal　[ˌpirəˈmikəl]　a. 金字塔形的, 角锥状的

Q

qualification [ˌkwɔlifiˈkeiʃən] n. 限定,条件
quantitatively [ˈkwɔntitətivli] ad. 定量地
quantum [ˈkwɔntəm] n. 量子

R

radial-turbine 辐流式透平,辐流式汽轮机
radiant asymmetry 辐射不对称
radioactive [ˌreidiəuˈæktiv] a. 放射性的,放射引起的
radioactive [ˌreidiəuˈæktiv] a. 放射性的
railway locomotive 火车机车
range effect 量级分布效果
rank [ræŋk] n. 等级
rap [ræp] v. 叩击,敲击
rapid [ˈræpid] n. 急流
Rateau stages 托拉级,压力级
raw-coal 原煤,未加工的煤
reaction turbine 反击式透平,反击式汽轮机
reactionary force 反击力
recede [riˈsiːd] v. 失去重要性
reciprocate [riˈsiprəkeit] v. 互换(位置),往复移动
reciprocate [riˈsiprəkeit] v. 回报,回信,互换
reciprocate [riˈsiprəkeit] v. 往复移动
reclaim [riˈkleim] v. 收回,要求,归还
recover [riˈkʌvə] vt. 回收
reduction gearing 减速齿轮
reed [riːd] n. 簧片
reestablish [ˈriːisˈtæbliʃ] vt. 重建,恢复,另行安装,使复原

reexpand ['ri:iks'pænd] v. 再膨胀
reflectivity [riflek'tiviti] n. 反射率
refractory [ri'fræktəri] adj. 耐火材料;耐火的,耐热的
refrigerant [ri'fridʒərənt] n. 冷冻剂
refrigerant [ri'fridʒərənt] n. 制冷剂,冷冻剂,冷媒
refrigerated warehouse 冷藏库
refrigeration [ri‚fridʒə'reiʃən] n. 制冷
refrigerator [ri'fridʒəreitə] n. 冷藏器,冷藏间
REGENERATIVE [ri'dʒenərətiv] adj. 再生式,回热式,蓄热式
regime [rei'ʒi:m] n. 区域,状态
regulate ['regjuleit] vt. 管制,调节,校准
reheater ['ri:'hi:tə] n. 再热器
relative to 相对于,关于
relativistic [‚relǝti'vistik] a. 相对论性的
reliability [rilaiə'biliti] n. 可靠性
render ['rendə] v. 反映,执行
replete [ri'pli:t] a. 充满的
requisite ['rekwizit] a. 需要的,必不可少的 n. 必需品
reservoir ['rezəvwa:] n. 蓄水池
residual [ri'zidjuəl] a. 残留,剩余的
restrain [ris'trein] v. 限制,约束
resultant [ri'zʌltənt] a. 总的,生成的 n. 合力,组合
retail ['ri:teil] n. 零售,零卖
retarder [ri'ta:də] n. 抑制剂,控制剂,阻滞剂
reversible [ri'və:səbl] a. 可逆的
reversibly [ri'və:səbli] ad. 可逆(倒)地
reversing blade 转向导叶片
rheological [‚riə'lɔdʒikl] a. 流变的
rim of disk/wheel 轮缘

rink ［riŋk］ n.（室内）滑冰场,冰球场
roof-mounted　屋顶安装的
rotary ［'rəutəri］ a.旋转的,转动的
rotary ［'rəutəri］ a.旋转的,转动的
rotating shaft　转轴
rotor ［'rəutə］ n.转子,旋转部
rotor ［'rəutə］ n.转子,旋转部
routine ［ruː'tiːn］ a.日常的,例行的
rudimentary ［ˌruːdi'mentəri］ a.基本的,初步的

S

saturate ［'sætʃəreit］ v.使饱和
saturated vapor　饱和蒸汽
saturated ［'sætʃəreitid］ a.饱和的
saturation ［ˌsætʃə'reiʃən］ n.饱和(状态)
schedule ［'skedʒul］ n.时刻表,进度
scraper ［'skreipə］ n.刮刀
scrub ［skrʌb］ vt.擦洗,洗涤
scrubber ［'skrʌbə］ n.刷子,刷洗工具,擦洗者
Selective Catalytic Reduction(SCR)　选择性催化剂脱氮装置
sensible heat　显热
sequence ［'siːkwəns］ n.连续,次序
series-connected　a.串联的
serpentine ［'səːpəntain］ adj.蛇纹石
setting ［setiŋ］ n.定位,调整
settling ［'setliŋ］ n.沉淀,沉降
shaft ［ʃaːft］ n.轴
shear stress　剪切力,切应力
shock wave　冲击波

shrink [ʃriŋk] vt. 收缩,减小,热套
shuffle [ˈʃʌfl] vt. 搅乱,弄混
side by side 并排地
silica [ˈsilikə] n. 硅土,氧化硅
singe shaft turbine 单轴汽轮机
single-cylinder turbine 单缸汽轮机
single-stage 单级
skim [skim] v. 掠去,掠过,浏览
slab [slæb] n. 厚片,平板
slag [slæg] n. 熔渣,渣滓
slaked lime 熟石灰
sliding pressure governing 滑压调节
slip [slip] n. 滑动,滑动量
slugging [ˈslʌgiŋ] n. 缓动
slurry [ˈslə:ri] n. 泥浆,水泥浆
smog [smɔg] n. 烟雾
sodalite [ˈsəudəlait] n. 方钠石
sodium-vanadium 钠－钒
solely [ˈsəulli] adv. 单独地,完全
solid sludge 污泥,泥渣
solidification [ˌsɔlidifiˈkeiʃən] n. 凝固,浓缩
solution [səˈlju:ʃən] n. 溶液,溶体
sophisticated [səˈfistikeitid] adj. 精密的,尖端的
SO_2 removal efficiency 脱硫效率
space [speis] v. 把……分隔开,留间隔
specialization [ˌspeʃəlaiˈzeiʃən] n. 专门化,学科
specific volume 比容
specification [ˌspesifiˈkeiʃən] n. 说明书
spherical [ˈsferikəl] a. 球的,球形的

split [split] v. 劈开,分裂
spray [sprei] n. 喷雾,喷嘴,喷射
spray [sprei] v. 喷射
squeeze ['skwi:z] v. 挤,压,使缩减
stack-gas n. 排放的烟气
staff [stə:f] n. 全体职员
stagnant ['stægnənt] adj. 停滞的,不流动的
standby ['stændbai] n. 备用设备;a. 备用的
stationary ['steiʃənəri] a. 固定的,稳定的
statutory ['stætjutri] a. 法定的,规定的
stay constant 不变的
steam engine 蒸汽机
steam extraction 抽汽
stellar ['stelə] a. 星球的,恒星的
stoker ['stəukə] n. 层燃炉,司炉,加煤机
stoker ['stəukə] n. 层燃炉
stoker ['stəukə] n. 加煤机,抛煤机
straight out 直接地
strainer ['streinə] n. 过滤器,滤网
stratify ['strætifaⁱ] v. 分层
stringent ['strindʒənt] a. 严格的
subcritical ['sʌb'kritikəl] a. 亚临界的,低于临界的
subdivide ['sʌbdi'vaid] v. 把……再分
subject ['sʌbdʒikt] v. 受验者
subsonic ['sʌb'sʌnik] a. 亚音速的
suction piping 吸液管路
suction ['sʌkʃən] n. 吸入,抽吸
sulfite ['sʌlfait] n. 亚硫酸
sulfur contents 含硫量

sulfur dioxide　二氧化硫
sulfur　['sʌlfə]　n. 硫磺,含硫磺的
sulphate　['sʌlfeit]　n. 硫酸盐
sulphite　['sʌlfait]　n. 亚硫酸盐
sulphur dioxide　二氧化硫
supercharge　['sju:pətʃa:dʒə]　n. 增压器
superheat　n. v. 过热
superheated　[sju:pəhi:tid]　a. 过热的
superheater　['sju:pəhi:tə]　n. 过热器
superheater　n. 过热器
superimpose　['sju:pərim'pəuz]　vt. 加上,附加,叠加
super-charge　v. 对……增压
surge-tank　n. 备用箱
suspension　[səs'penʃən]　n. 熟悉,通晓
suspension　[səs'penʃən]　n. 悬浮,暂停
suspension　[səs'penʃən]　n. 悬浮,暂停
suspension　[səs'penʃən]　n. 悬浮
sustain　[səs'tein]　v. 支持,维持,证明
swirl　[swə:l]　n. 旋涡,涡动
symmetrical　[si'metrikəl]　adj. 对称的
symmetricical　[si'metrikəl]　v. a. 对称的,整齐的
synchronous　['siŋkrənəs]　a. 同步的

T

take a set　凝固,硬化
take up　占据
tangent　['tændʒənt]　a. 正切的,相切的
tangential　[tæn'dʒenʃəl]　a. 切向的
tangential　[tæn'dʒenʃəl]　a. 正切的,切线方向的

tangible ['tændʒəbl] a. 确实的, 实质的
temperature-entropy diagram 温熵图
tendency ['tendənsi] n. 趋势, 倾向
terrestrial [ti'restriəl] a. 地球(上)的, 陆地的
terrestrial [ti'restriəl] a. 地球上的, 陆地的
thereof ['ðɛər'ɔf] ad. 关于它的
thermal ['θə:məl] a. 热的
thermal [θə:məl] a. 热的
thermally neutral 热中性状态
thermoelectric [ˌθə:məui'lektrik] a. 热电的
thermostatic(al) [θə:mou'stætik(əl)] a. 恒温(器)的
thermo-dynamics n. 热力学
thixotropic [ˌθiksə'trɔpik] a. 触变性的
thorium ['θə:riəm] n. [化]钍
throttle governing 节流调节
throttle ['θrɔtl] n. 节流阀 v. 节流
throttle ['θrɔtl] vt. 节流
tidal ['taidl] a. 潮汐的
tip [tip] vt. 端点, 端头
tolerance ['tɔlərəns] n. 容忍, 抗拒药物的能力
topping turbine 前置式汽轮机
tornado [tɔ:'neidəu] n. 龙卷风, 旋风
tortuous ['tɔ:tjuəs] a. 弯曲的
toxic ['tɔksik] a. 有毒的, 有害的
trade off 交替使用
transient ['trænziənt] a. (物)瞬变的
transmissivity [træczmi'siviti] n. 透射系数, 透射率
transparency [træns'pɛərənsi] n. 透明, 透明物, 透明性, 透明度
trap [træp] n. 捕捉, 搜集

trap [træp] v. 用陷阱捕捉,诱捕
tremendous [tri'mendəs] a. 巨大的,惊人的
tremendous [tri'mendəs] a. 巨大的,可怕的
trip [trip] vi. 解扣,跳闸
trunk [trʌŋk] n. 树干,主要部分
tube bundle 管束
tubular ['tju:bjulə] a. 管的,管状的,由管构成的
turbofan n. 涡轮风扇(发动机)
turbulence ['tə:bjuləns] n. 紊流,扰动
turbulence ['tə:bjuləns] n. 紊流,湍流
turbulization [tə:bjulai'zeiʃən] n. 湍流,紊流,涡流
two-phase flow 两相流

U

ultimate ['ʌltimit] a. 最后的,最终的
ultralow ['ʌltrələu] a. 超低的
under construction 正在建设中
underway 在进行中
undesirable ['ʌndi'zaiərəbl] a. 令人不快的,讨厌的,不需要的
unicellular ['ju:ni'seljulə] a. 单细胞的,单孔的
unidirectional ['ju:nidi'rekʃənl] a. 单向的
uniformly ['ju:nifɔ:mli] adv. 一律地,一样地
uninspiring [ʌnin'spaiəriŋ] a. 平凡的
uninterrupted ['ʌnˌintə'rʌptid] a. 不间断的
unitary ['ju:nitəri] a. 具有单一特征的,整体式的,一体的
Univer-Pressure boiler 常压锅炉
unorthodox ['ʌn'ɔ:θədɔks] a. 非正统的,异端的
upkeep ['ʌpki:p] n. 保养,维修,维持
uranium [ju'reiniəm] n. 铀

utility ['juːtiliti] n. 实用,公用事业
utilizer ['juːtilaizə] n. 利用装置

V

vacuum ['vækjuəm] n. 真空(度)
vacuum ['vækjuəm] n. 真空
valency ['veilənsi] n. (化合)价,(原子)价
valve [vælv] n. 阀门
vane [vein] n. 叶片,轮叶,刀片,节气阀
vane [vein] n. 叶片,翼
vegetal ['vedʒitl] a. 植物的,蔬菜的
velocity-compounded stage 复速级
vent [vent] v. 排放出 n. 出口
ventilate ['ventileit] v. 使通风,安装通风设备
ventilate ['ventileit] v. 使通风,使换气
ventilation [venti'leiʃən] n. 通风,流通空气
vestibule ['vestibjuːl] n. 前厅,通廊
via [vai] prep. 经过,通过
vibrate [vai'breit] v. 使振动,使摇摆
vibrating-grate 振动炉排
vibrating-grate 振动炉排
vibration [vai'breiʃən] n. 振动,动摇,共鸣,感应
vice versa 反过来(也是这样)
viscosity ['vis'kɔsiti] n. 黏性,黏滞度
viscosity [vis'kɔsiti] n. 黏性,黏度
viscosity [vis'kɔsəti] n. 黏稠,黏性
viscous ['viskəs] a. 黏性的,黏滞的
volatile ['vɔlətail] a. 挥发性的,易变的
volatile ['vɔlətail] a. 挥发性的

volumetric [ˌvɔljuˈmetrik] a. 容积的
vortex [ˈvɔːteks] n. 涡流,漩涡
vulnerable [ˈvʌlnərəbl] a. 难防守的,易受伤的,脆弱的

W

warehouse [ˈwɛəhəus] n. 仓库,货栈; vt. 把……入库
waterfall [ˈwɔtəfɔːl] n. 瀑布
water-cooled wall 水冷壁
water-wall tube 水冷壁管
wet-bottom furnace 液态排渣炉膛
whence [hwens] ad. 从何处
whereby [hwɛəˈbai] ad. 由此,从而
whirlpool [ˈhwəːlpuːl] n. 漩涡
with a view of 为了……的目的
worked-out 用过的,废弃的
wrist pin n. [活赛,曲柄]销

X

xonotlite [ˈzəunətˌlait] n. 硬硅钙石

Y

yield [jiːld] n. 屈服(点),极限

Z

zeolite [ˈziːəlait] n. 沸石

附 录 I

常用缩写词

a　absolute 绝对的
　　ampere 安培
A　angstrom 埃(10^{-8}厘米)
AAEC　Australian Atomic Energy Commission 澳大利亚原子能委员会
ABAI　American Boiler & Affiliated Industries 美国锅炉及附属设备制造商协会
abbr　abbreviation 缩写
ABC　automatic boiler control 锅炉自动控制
ABMA　American Boiler Manufactures Association 美国锅炉制造商协会
abr　abridged 节略
　　abridgement 节略
abs　absolute 绝对的
ABS　American Bureau of Standards 美国标准局
Abs E　absolute error 绝对误差
abstr　abstract 提要,简解
abs visc　absolute viscosity 绝对粘度
abt　about 大约
AC　air-coal 风-煤,空气-煤[粉]
　　alternating current 交流电
acc　acceleration 加速度
　　according to 按照

ACC　automatic combustion control 自动燃烧调节
ACE　automatic computing equipment 自动计算设备
ACM　Association for computing machine 计算机协会(美)
　　　automatic computing machine 自动计算机
ACRS　Advisory Committee on Reactor Safeguards 反应堆安全监察咨询委员会
ACS　American Ceramic Society 美国陶瓷学会
　　　American Chemical Society 美国化学学会
ADC　analog digital converter 模拟数字变换器
add　addenda 补遗
ADI　American Documentation Institute 美国文献资料工作研究学会
adj　adjustment 调节,调整
ADP　automatic data processing 自动数据处理
AE　acoustic emission 声发射
AEA　Atomic Energy Authority 原子能局(英)
AEC　Atomic Energy Commission 原子能委员会(美)
AEEW　Atomic Energy Establishment Winfirth 原子能中心(英)
AEI　Associated Electric Industries Ltd. 联合电气制造公司(英)
AERE　Atomic Energy Research Establishment 原子能研究所(英)
AESC　American Engineering Standards Committee 美国工业标准委员会
AF　audio frequency 声频
　　　automatic following 自动跟踪
AFC　automatic frequency control 自动频率调整
AFWC　automatic feed water control 给水自动调节
AGA　American Gas Association 美国煤气协会
AGC　automatic gain control 自动增益控制
agg　aggregate 总计,总数
AICE, AIChE　American Institute of Chemical Engineers 美国化学工程师学会

AIEE American Institute of Electrical Engineers 美国电气工程师学会
AIME American Institute of Mining, Metallurgical & Petroleum Engineers 美国采矿、冶金与石油工程师学会
AIMME American Institute of Mining & Metallurgical Engineers 美国采矿及冶金工程师学会
AISC American Institute of Steel Construction 美国钢结构研究所
AISE American of Iron & Steel Engineers 钢铁工程师学会
AISI American Iron and Steel Institute 美国钢铁学会
ALGOL algorithmic language 算法语言（电子计算机用的一种自动化语言）
alk alkali 石
  alkaline 碱性
alt alternating 交变,交替
  alteration 改变,变化
  altitude 高度
AM amplitude modulation 调幅
amb ambient 周围的
amp ampere 安培
amt amount 数量,合计
amu atomic mass unit 原子质量单位
ANACOM analog computer 模拟计算机
ANGA American natural Gas Association 美国天然气协会
ANL Argonne National Laboratory 阿贡国家实验所(美)
ANSI American National Standards Institute 美国全国标准学会
Anth anthracite 无烟煤
AOV automatically operated valve 自动阀
APC American Power Conference 美国动力会议
APCA Air Pollution Control Association 空气污染控制协会
API American Petroleum Institute 美国石油学会

app　　apparatus 仪表,工具,装置,设备
appl　　applied 应用的,实用的,外加的
appr, approx　　approximate 近似的
appx　　appendix 附录
ap　　aqueous 水的
ARC　　automatic remote control 自动遥控
ASA　　American Society of Acoustics 美国声学学会
　　　　American Standards Association 美国标准协会
asb　　asbestos 石棉
ASC　　automatic sequence control 自动顺序控制
ASCE　　American Society of Civil Engineers 美国土木工程师学会
ASHAE　　American Society of Heating & Air-condition Engineers 美国采暖与空气调节工程师学会
ASHRAE　　American Society of Heating Refrigerating & Air Conditioning Engineers 美国采暖、制冷及空气调节工程师学会
ASHVE　　American Society of Heating & Ventilating Engineers 美国采暖及通风工程师学会
ASM　　American Society for Metals 美国金属学会
ASME　　American Society of Mechanical Engineers 美国机械工程师学会
ASME PTC　　ASME Power Test Codes 美国机械工程师学会动力试验规程
ASNT　　American Society for Nondestructive Testing 美国无损检验学会
ASQC　　American Society for Quality Control 美国质量检验学会
Assn　　Association 协会,学会
assoc　　association 协会,学会
ASST　　American Society for Steel Treating 美国钢材处理学会
ASTC　　automatic steam temperature control 蒸汽温度自动控制
ASTM　　American Society for Testing Materials 美国试验与材料学会

at atmosphere 大气压

at atomic heat 原子热容量

atm atmosphere 大气压

att attached 附件

at wt atomic weight 原子量

aut automatic 自动的

aux auxiliary 辅助的

av , avg average 平均的

AWS American Welding Society 美国焊接学会

BAEA British Atomic Energy Authority 英国原子能管理局

BAERE British Atomic Energy Research Establishment 英国原子能研究中心

BBC Brown Boveri & Company Ltd 勃朗·鲍维利公司(瑞士)

bbl barrel 桶(美制＝159公升,英制＝163.7公升)

BBS British Standard Sieve 英国标准筛

BCS British Computer Society 英国计算机协会

BCURA British Coal Utilization Research Association 英国煤炭利用研究协会

BE boiler extration valve 炉膛排水阀

BEAMA British Electrical & Allied Manufacturers Association 英国电气制造商协会

BES burner executive system 喷燃器执行系统

BESA British Engineering Standard Association 英国工程标准协会

BEV billion electron volts 十亿电子伏

BFP boiler feed pump 锅炉给水泵

BFPT boiler feed pump turbine 带动锅炉给水泵的汽轮机

BH Brinell hardness 布氏硬度

BHP boiler horsepower 锅炉马力

　　　brake horsepower 制动[有效]马力(轴功率)

BHRA British Hydromechanics Research Association 英国流体力学研究学会
BISRA British Iron & Steel Research Association 英国钢铁研究协会
Bit bituminous 烟煤
BIW British Institute of Welding 英国焊接研究所
BM Bailey Meter Co. 倍莱仪表公司
  bill of material 材料清单
BMN Beckman Instruments Inc. 贝克曼仪器公司
BNES British Nuclear Energy Society 英国核能学会
BNL Brookhaven National Laboratory 布鲁克海文国家实验所(美)
bp boiler pressure 锅炉压力
  boiling point 沸点
BP, Br Pat British Patent 英国专利
BR breeding ratio 再生系数
Brit British 英国的
BRRA Basic Refractory Raw-materials Association 碱性耐火材料原料协会
BS British Standard 英国标准
  Bureau of Standards 标准局(美)
bsh bushel 蒲式耳(等于8加仑)
BSI British Standards Institution 英国标准协会
BSS British Standard Sieve 英国标准筛
  British Standard Specification 英国标准规范
BSWG British Standard Wire Gauge 英国标准线规
BT boiler throttle valve 锅炉节流阀
BTB boiler throttle by-pass valve 锅炉节流旁路阀
BTU British thermal unit 英热单位(等于252卡)
Bull Bulletin 会报,公报
B & W Babcock & Wilcox Co. 拔柏葛[－威尔考克斯]公司

BWC　boiler water concentration 炉水浓度
BWR　boiling water reactor 沸水[反应]堆
BWRA　British Welding Research Association 英国焊接研究学会
c　centi 百分之一
　　constant 常数,恒定的
　　cubic 立方的
　　cycle 周,循环
C　carbon 碳
　　centigrade 摄氏温标,百分度,摄氏
　　current 电流
CAD　computer aided design 用计算机设计
cal　calorie 卡
CBL　Common Business Oriented Language 通用商业性语言(电子计算机用的一种自动化语言)
CC　cubic centimeter 立方厘米
CCT　continuous cooling transformation 连续冷却相变
CE　Combustion Engineering Co. 燃烧工程公司(英)
　　Consolidated Edison Company 联合爱迪生公司
CEA　Central Electricity Authority 电力总局(英)
　　Combustion Engineering Association 燃烧工程协会
CEGB　Central Electricity Generating Board 中央电力局(英)
CERL　Central Electricity Research Laboratories 中央电力研究试验所
cf　compare 比较
　　confer 参看
CFM　cubic feet per minute 英尺^3/分
CFS　cubic feet per second 英尺^3/秒
cg　center of gravity 重心
CG　chain grate 链条炉排
CGE　Canadian General Electric Co Ltd. 加拿大通用电气公司

CGS   centimeter-gram-second 厘米－克－秒制
chap, ch   chapter 章
chem   chemical 化学的
CHU   caloric heat unit 测热单位
       centigrade heat unit 百度热量单位
cit   cited 引用
CM   centimeter 厘米
CMER   continuous maximum and most economical rating 连续最大和最经济的功率
CMIA   Coal Mining Institute of America 美国采煤研究所
CMR   continuous maximum rating 最大连续功率
CNC   Computer Numerical Control 群控,计算机数值控制
Co   company 公司
COD   crack opening displacement 裂纹张开位移
coef, coeff   coefficient 系数
const   constant 常数
Corp   corporation 公司
cp   centipoise 厘泊
       chemically pure 化学纯
CPC   card programmed electronic calculator 卡片程序电子计算机
cpm   counts per minute 每分钟次数
       cycles per minute 次/分
cps   cycles per second 周/秒·赫兹,每秒循环次数
crit   critical 临界的
CRT   cathode ray tube 阴极射线显像管
CRV   convection recirculating valve 对流段再循环阀
CS   centistoke 厘池(运动粘度单位)
CSIR   Council for Scientific & Industrial Research 科学与工业研究委员会

CT current transformer 电流互感器
ct cent 百分之一
CTU centigrade thermal unit 百分度热单位,磅-卡(454卡)
cu cubic 立方的
CUC Coal Utilization Council 煤炭利用委员会(英)
cu ft cubic foot 立方英尺
cu in cubic inch 立方英寸
cu m cubic metre 立方米
cu mm cubic millimeter 立方毫米
CWT hundred weight 英担(英制=112磅,美制=100磅)
d depth 深度
D diameter 直径
DAC digital analog converter 数[字]模[拟]转换器
　　　digital-to-analog convertion 数[字]模[拟]转换
db decibel 分贝
　　　dry bulb 干球
DC digital computer 数字计算机
　　　direct current 直流电
DDC direct digital control 直接数字控制
def definition 定义
deg degree 度,级
Dept department 局,科,部门,车间,处,系
dev deviation 偏差
dia diameter 直径
diag diagram 图,图解
diff difference 差,不同
dil dilute 稀释,冲淡
dim dimension 尺寸,量纲
dist distance 距离

dm decimeter 分米
DNB departure from nucleate boiling 偏离核态沸腾
DNC Direct Numerical Control 群控,直接数值控制
do ditto 同前,同上,如前所述
doz dozen 一打,十二个
dp differential pressure 压差,压力降
DP data processing 数据处理
DSH desuperheater 减温器
DSIR Department of Scientific & Industrial Research 科学与工业研究总署
DVM digital voltmeter 数字电压表
Dwg drawing 图,图纸
EBR Experimental Breeder Reactor 实验性增殖反应堆
ECMB European Committee of Manufacturers of Burners 欧洲燃烧器制造商协会
Eco economizer 省煤器
ed edition 版,版次
EDP electronic data processing 电子数据处理
EEC English Electric Co Ltd 英国电气公司
　　　European Economic Community 欧洲经济共同体
EEI Edison Electric Institute 爱迪生电气研究所
eff efficiency 效率
eg exempli gratia 例如
EGD Electrogasdynamics 电气体动力学
EI Engineering Index 工程[技术文献]索引
elec electrical 电的
el, elev elevation 高度
EMF electromotive force 电动势
enc, encl enclosure 附件

encyc　encyclop(a)edia 百科全书
Engng, Engg　engineering 工程
eq　equation 方程[式]
equip　equipment 设备,装置
equiv　equivalent 相等的,相当的,等效的,当量
ERE　Esso Research & Engineering Co 埃索工程研究公司
ERW　electric resistance welding 电阻焊
esp　especially 特别,尤其
ESSA　Environmental Science Services Administration 环境科学服务管理局(美)
est　estimated 估计的
et al　et alibi 等等
etc　et cetera 等等
et seq　et sequentia 及以下等等,参看以下等句或等项
Eu　Euler number 欧拉数
EURATOM　European Atomic Energy Community 欧洲原子能联营
EV　electron volt 电子伏特
EX　example 例,实例
excl　excluding 除去,不包括
exp　experiment 实验,试验
　　exponent 指数
ext　external 外部的
f　foot 英尺
　　force 力
　　frequency 频率
F　Fahrenheit 华氏[温标]
　　force 力
　　function 函数
FBB　fluidized bed boiler 沸腾床锅炉

附 录 Ⅰ　375

FBI　Federation of British Industries 英国工业联合会
FBR　Fast-Breeder Reactor 快中子增殖反应堆
FC　fixed carbon 固定碳,结合碳
FCB　fast cut back 快速切断
FD　forced-draft-fan 送风机
fig　figure 图
fl　fluid 流体,液体
fl pt　flash point 闪点,闪火点
FM　frequency modulation 调频
Fortran　formula translation 程序设计语言(电子计算机用的一种自动化语言)
FP　feed pump 给水泵
　　flash point 闪点
FPC　Federal Power Commission 联邦电力委员会(美)
fph　feet per hour 英尺／时
fpm　feet per minute 英尺／分
fps　feet per second 英尺／秒
FPS unit　foot-pound-seconds unit 英尺－磅－秒单位,英制单位
Fr　Froude number 弗鲁德数
FrP　French Patent 法国专利
FPV　furnace recirculating valve 炉膛再循环阀
FSH　final superheater 末级过热器
FSS　fuel safety system 燃料保护系统
ft　foot 英尺
ft hd　feet head 以英尺表示的压头
FW　Foster Wheeler Corporation 福斯特·惠勒公司
FWB　feedwater by-pass valve 给水旁路阀
FW-JB　Foster Wheeler Ltd-John Brown Land Boilers Ltd 福斯特·惠勒－约翰·布朗陆用锅炉公司

FWPCA Federal Water Pollution Control Administration 联邦水质污染管制局(美)
g gauge 表计
  gram(me) 克
gad general assembly drawing 总装配图,总图
G generator 发电机,发生器
  giga 千兆,十亿(10^9)
gal gallon 加仑
GB Great Britain 英国
GCFBR gas-cooled fast breeder reactor 气体冷却快中子增殖反应堆
GCR Gas-Cooled Reactor 气冷反应堆
GEC General Electric Co Ltd 通用电气公司(英)
  General Electric Company 通用电气公司(美)
GGA Gulf General Atomic, Inc 海湾通用原子能公司
GL ground level 地平面
gm gram(me) 克
g-mol gram-molecule 克分子
GMR Graphite-Moderated Reactor 石墨减速反应堆
gph gallons per hour 加仑/时
gpm gallons per minute 加仑/分
gps gallons per second 加仑/秒
gr grain 格令(等于0.064克)
Gr Grashof number 格拉晓夫数
grad gradient 梯度
GrBrit Great Britain 英国
gr w gross weight 毛重
h hecto 百(10^2)
  height 高度
  hour 时,小时

HAZ　heat affected zone 热影响区
HCV　high calorific value 高热值
Hd　head 扬程,压头
HEI　Heat Exchange Institute 热交换学会
HF　high frequency 高频
Hg abs　inches mercury absolute 真空度,绝对英寸水银柱
HHV　high(er)heat(ing) value 高热值
hon　horizontal 水平的,水平线
HP　high pressure 高压
　　horse power 马力
hp-hr　horsepower-hour 马力-小时
hr　hour 小时
HRT　horizontal return tubular boiler 卧式回火管锅炉
hs　heating surface 受热面
ht　height 高度
HTC　heat transfer coefficient 传热系数
HTGR　High Temperature Gas (Cooled) Reactor 高温气冷堆
HTR　heater 加热器
HWR　heavy water reactor 重水反应堆
Hz　hertz 赫[兹]
IAE　integral of absolute error 偏差绝对值积分[准则]
LATM　International Association for Testing Materisl 国际材料试验协会
ib, ibid　ibidem 在同书,在同章,在同处
IBM　International Business Machines Corporation 国际商业计算机公司
IBWM　The International Bureau of Weight & Measures 国家度量衡局
IBR　Institute of Boiler and Radiator Manufacturers 锅炉及散热器制造商协会
IC　integrated circuit 集成电路

International Combustion Engineering Co 国际燃烧工程公司(英)
ICE　Institute of Chemical Engineers 化学工程师学会
　　　internal combustion engine 内燃机
ICL　International Combustion Engineering Ltd 国际燃烧工程公司(英)
id　　idem 同样,同前,同上
ID　　induced draft 引风
　　　inside diameter 内径
IDF　induced-draft-fan 引风机
IDP　integrated date processing 综合数据处理
i e　 id est 换言之,就是,即
IEC　International Electrotechnical Commission 国际电工委员会
IEE　Institute of Electrical Engineers 电气工程师学会(英)
IFAC　International Federation of Automatic Control 国际自[动]控[制]联合会
IFRF　International Flame Research Foundation 国际火焰研究中心(荷)
IG　　Imperial Gallon 英加仑
ihp　 indicated horse-power 指示马力
IIW　 International Institute of Welding 国际焊接学会
illus　illustrated 附插图[的],插图[的]
　　　illustration 附插图,插图
IME,I Mech E　Institution of Mechanical Engineers 机械工程师学会(英)
in　　inch 英寸
IN　　inlet 入口,进口
Inc　 incorporated 股份[公司]
incl　included 包括
　　　inclusive 包括
　　　index 指数,索引
ind　 index 指数,索引

inf infinity 无穷大
inHg inches of mercury 吋汞柱
inH$_2$O inches of water 吋水柱
inst institute 学会,协会,研究所,学院
institution 学会,协会
IP intermediate pressure 中压
iq idem quod 如同
IR infrared 红外线,红外[线]的
reheater injection valve 再热减温器进水控制阀
IS superheater injection valve 过热减温器进水控制阀
ISA Instrument Society of America 美国测量仪表学会
International Standardization Association 国际标准化协会
ISE integral of squared error 偏差平方积分[准则]
ISO International Standardization Organization 国际标准化组织
isoth isothermal 等温的
ISPR superheater injection pressure reducing valve 过热减温器进水压控制阀
ISU International Standard Unit 国际[标准]单位
ITV industrial television 工业电视
IU International Unit 国际单位
IV intercepter valve 遮断阀
j joule 焦耳
JAERI Japan Atomic Energy Research Institute 日本原子能研究所
JICRT Japan Information Center of Science & Technology 日本科技情报中心
JIS Japanese Industrial Standard 日本工业标准
jour journal 杂志期刊
JT John Thompson Group 约翰-汤姆逊公司,约翰-汤姆逊集团
K kelvin 开氏(绝对温标)

kilo 千
Kcal kilocalorie 大卡
KE kinetic energy 动能
kev kilo electron-volt 千电子伏
Kg kilogram 公斤,千克
Km kilometre 公里
kv kilovolt 千伏
KVA kilovolt-ampere 千伏安
KW kilowatt
kw-hr kilowatt-hr 千瓦小时,度
l left 左
length 长度
liter 升
lab laboratory 实验室,试验所,实验所
LASL Los Alamos Scientific Laboratory 洛斯·阿拉摩斯科学实验所(美)
lat ht latent heat 潜热
lb libra(pound) 磅(等于0.454千克)
lb per sq in pound per square inch 磅/平方英寸
LCV low calorific value 低热值
LEFM linear elastic fracture mechanics 线弹性断裂力学
LF low frequency 低频
LH left hand 左的
LHV low(er) heat(ing) value 低热值
lg logarithm 对数
lib library 图书馆
lim, lm limit 限度,极限
liq liquid 液体,液体的
LMBR liquid-metal breeder reactor 液态金属增殖反应堆
LMFBR Liquid-Metal Fast-Breeder Reactor 液态金属快中子增殖反应堆

LMFR   liquid-metal fuel reactor 液态金属燃料反应堆
LMTD   logarithmic mean temperature difference 对数平均温差
L &N   Leeds & Northrup Company 李兹、诺思拉普公司
LNG   liquefied natural gas 液化天然气
LO Lox   liquid oxygen 液态氧
log   logarithm ［常用］对数
long   longitude 经度，经线
LP   low pressure 低压
LPG   liquefied petroleum gas 液化石油气
Ltd   Limited 有限［公司］
l tn   long ton 长吨
lu   lumen 流明(光通量单位)
lub   lubricant 润滑剂
LWBR   Light-Water Breeder Reactor 轻水增殖反应堆
LWR   light-water reactor 轻水［反应］堆
m   mass 质量
    mean 平均，平均值
    metre 米
    millki 毫(10^{-3})
    minute 分
M   Mach 马赫［数］
    Mega 兆(10^6)
    moment 力矩
ma   milliampere 毫安
Ma   Mach number 马赫数
mae   mean absolute error 平均绝对误差
math   mathematics 数学
matl   material 材料
max   maximum 最大的，最大值

mb	millibar 毫巴
mc	machine 机器,机械
	megacycle 兆周,兆赫
	millicurie 毫居里
MC	manual control 手控
	master controller 主控制器
MCP	master control program 主控程序
MCR	maximum continuous rating 最大连续出力
ME	Mechanical Engineering 机械工程
mech	mechanical 机械的
mehp	mean effective horse power 平均有效马力
meq	milli-equivalent 毫克当量
MEV	million electron-volts 百万电子伏特,兆电子伏特
MF	medium frequency 中频
mfg	manufacturing 制造,生产
mg	milligram 毫克
MHD	magnetohydrodynamics 磁流体力学
MHF	medium-high frequency 中高频
MIG	metal inert gas welding 金属惰性气体保护焊
min	minimum 最小的,最小值
	minute 分
mip	mean indicated pressure 平均指示压力
MISC	miscellaneous 混杂的,各种各样的,多方面的
mixt	mixture 混合物
mk	mark 标记,符号
MKS	meter-kilogram-second 米－公斤－秒制
ml	milliliter 毫升
mm	millimeter 毫米
mm Hg	millimeters of mercury 毫米汞柱

MMSA mining and Metallurgical Society of America 美国采矿冶金学会
mo manually operated 用手操作的,手控的,手动的
mol molecular 分子的
　　　molecule 分子
mol wt molecular weight 分子量
MP medium pressure 中压
　　　melting point 熔点
MPD magnetoplasmodynamic 磁等离子体
mph miles per hour 哩/英寸
mps meters per second 米/秒
MS, ms main steam 主蒸汽
　　　manuscript 原稿
　　　mild steel 低碳钢
MSBR Molten Salt Breeder Reactor 熔盐增殖反应堆
MSR Molten Salt Reactor 熔盐反应堆
MT metric ton 公吨
MTD mean temperature difference 平均温差
mtl material 材料
mv millivolt 毫伏
MW megawatt 兆瓦,千
MWh megawatt-hour 兆瓦小时
na non available 没有
NACA National Advisory Committee for Aeronautics 国家航空咨询委员会(美)
NAM National Association of Manufacturers 全国制造商协会(美)
NAPCA National Air Pollution Control Administration 国家大气污染管制局
NAS National Academy of Science 国家科学院(美)
NASA National Aeronautics and Space Administration 国家航空和宇宙

航行局(美)
NB nota bene 注意
NBBPVI National Board of Boiler and Pressure Vessel Inspectors 国家锅炉及压力容器监察局
NBS National Bureau of Standards 国家标准局(美)
New British Standard 新英国标准
NC numerical control 数[字]控[制]
NCB National Coal Board 国家煤炭委员会(英)
NCR normal continuous rating 额定连续出力
NDI non-destructive inspection 无损探伤,无损检验
NDT non-destructive test 无损探伤,无损试验
neg negative 负的,负极,底片
NEMA National Electrical Manufactures Association 全国电气制造商协会(美)
National Electronic Manufacturing Association 全国电子制造协会
NERC National Electric Reliability council 全国电力安全委员会(美)
Nuclear Engineering Society 核工程学会(英)
nom nominal 额定的,名义的,铭牌的
NPA National Petroleum Association 国家石油协会(美)
NPI National Petroleum Institute 国家石油研究所(美)
NPSH net positive suction head 净吸入压头(泵)
npt normal pressure and temperature 标准压力及温度
NRC National Research Council 全国研究委员会(属美国科学院)
NRCC National Research Council (of Canada) 国家研究院(加拿大)
NRL Naval Research Laboratory 海军研究实验所(美)
NRV Non Return Valve 止回阀
NSA Nuclear Science Abstracts 核子科学文摘
NSS Nuclear Steam System 核蒸汽系统

NSSS Nuclear Steam Supply System 核蒸汽供应系统
ntp normal temperature and pressure 标准温度及压力
Nu Nusselt number 努赛尔特数
n(t)wt net weight 净重
o ohm 欧[姆]
OD outside diameter 外径
OF oil fuel 石油燃料
OFA over fire air 二次风(炉排上的),上部引入的助燃空气
OPEC Organization of Petroleum Exporting Countries 石油输出国组织
oper operation 运用,工作,运算
    operator 操纵员,运行人员
opp opposed 对面,相反的
opt optimum 最佳值
ORNL Oak Ridge National Laboratory 橡树岭国家试验所(属美国原子能委员会)
OSRD Office of Scientific Research and Development 科学研究与发展部(美)
O T Boiler once through boiler 直流锅炉
oz ounce 盎司,(等于1/16磅)
p pitch 节距,齿距,螺距,间隔,行距
    power 功率
P page 页
    pico 微微(10^{-12})
    poise 泊(粘度单位)
    positive 正的,阳的
    pressure 压力
par paragraph 段
pat patent 专利
PAW plasma arc welding 等离子弧焊

PB Publication Board (Report)(U.S. Dept. of Commerce) PB 报告书（美商务部技术服务处发行的政府研究报的总称）
PCC programme controlled computer 程序控制计算机
PCRV Prestressed-Concrete Reactor Vessel 预应力混凝土反应堆壳体
pcs pieces 个,件,片
pct percent 百分数
PCV pressure controlling valve 压力控制阀
PD pitch diameter 节径
pdl poundal 磅达(力的单位)
Pe Peclet number 贝古列数
PE potential energy 位能,势能
PF power factor 功率因数
pulverized fuel 煤粉,粉状燃料
pkg package 包装,整装
PL program language 程序语言
pos positive 正的,阳的,阳极
pp pages 页(复数)
ppb parts per billion 十亿分之一(10^{-12})
ppm parts per million 百万分之一(10^{-6})
PPS purge and prelight system [炉膛]吹扫及点火准备系统
Pr Prandtl number 普朗特数
pri primary 初级,第一的
proc proceedings 论文集,学报,会议录
PS post scriptum 后记,附言,附录
psf pounds per square foot 磅/英尺^2
psi pounds per square inch 磅/英寸^2
psia pounds per square inch, absolute 磅/英寸^2,绝对
psig pounds per square inch, gauge 磅/英寸^2,表计
pt pint 品脱

point 点
PT　potential transformer ［测量用］变压器
pub　publisher 出版者
PVC　polyvinylchloride 聚氯乙烯
PVRC　Pressure Vessel Research Committee 压力容器研究委员会
PWR, pwr　power 功率,动力
　　　　　pressurized water preactor 压水［反应］堆
Q, qt　quart 夸脱(1/4 加仑)
ques　question 问题
quot　quotation 引语
R　radius 半径
　　resistance 电阻,阻力
　　right 右,右方
rad　radian 弧度
RAND　Research and Development Corporation 兰德［研究与发展］公司
R C　reinforced concrete 钢筋混凝土
rd　round 圆的
R &D　Research &Development 研究与发展
Re　Reynolds number 雷诺数
ref　reference 参考,引证,参照
reg　register 记录,指示;记录器,寄存器,调风器
rem　remark 备注
rep, rept　report 报告
req　required 所需要的
res　research 研究
resp　respectively 分别地,各自地
rev　review 评论
　　　revolution 旋转
RH　reheat 再热

  reheater 再热器
  relative humidity 相对湿度
  right hand 右侧,右的
RHN Rockwell hardness number 洛氏硬度值
R & M reports and memorandum 报告及备忘录
RMS root mean square 均方根
rpm revolutions per minute 转/分
rps revolutions per second 转/秒
RR research report 研究报告(特种文献)
RS Riley Stoker Corp 莱雷层燃炉公司
rs rolled steel 轧制钢
RSV reheat stop valve 再热截止阀
SA steam admission valve 进汽阀
sat, satd saturated 饱和的
satn saturation 饱和
sc scale 标度
SC standard conditions 标准状态
SCF standard cubic foot 标准立方英尺
SCFBR Steam-Cooled Fast-Breeder Reactor 蒸汽冷却快速中子增殖反应堆
scfm standard cubic feet per minute 标英尺^3/分
SCR silicon controlled rectifier 硅可控整流器,可控硅
SD standard deviation 标准偏差
  steam lead drain valve 主蒸汽疏水阀
sec second 秒
  secondary 二次的,第二的
sect section 截面,区域,部分
ser serial 连续的,顺次的
  series 级数,系列

SESA　Society for Experimental Stress Analysis 试验应力分析学会
sfc　specific fuel consumption 单位燃料耗量
Sh　Strouhal number 斯特劳哈尔数
SH　superheater 过热器
sh tn　short ton 短吨(=907公斤)
SGR　sodium graphite reactor 钠石墨反应堆
SIC　semiconductor intergrated circuit 半导体集成电路
sig　signal 信号,信号的
SIGMA　shielded inert-gas metal arc welding 惰性气体保护金属电弧焊
SMA　Stoker Manufacturers Association 层燃炉制造商协会(美)
SM -steel　Siemens-Martion steel 平炉钢
soc　society 学会,社团
sol　solution 溶液
SP　specific 比[的],单位的
　　spillover valve 启动蒸汽溢放阀
　　standard pressure 标准气压
spec　special 特殊的
　　specification 规格,说明书
sp ht　specific heat 比热
sq vol　specific volume 比容
sq　square 平方
sq ft　square foot 平方英尺
sq in　square inch 平方英寸
sq yd　square yard 平方码
ss　superheated steam 过热蒸汽
SSFF　Solid Smokeless Fuels Federation 固体无烟燃料联合会(英)
s t(n)　short ton 短吨(等于907公斤)
St　Stanton number 史坦顿数
ST　standard temperature 标准温度

std standard 标准,标准的
STP standard temperature and pressure 标准温度与压力
suppl supplement 补遗
supr superheater 过热器
sym symbol 符号,标志
      symmetric(al) 对称的
sys system 系统
T tee 三通
    temperature 温度
    time 时间
    ton 吨
tab table 表[格]
TC thermocouple 热电偶
TDS total dissolved solids 总固形物
tech technical 技术的
temp temperature 温度
term terminology 术语,专门词汇
th thermal 热的
TIG tungsten inert-gas arc welding 钨极惰性气体保护[电弧]焊
TM technical manual 技术手册
     technical memorandum 技术备忘录
tn ton 吨
Torr Torricellian unit 压力单位(=毫米汞柱)
TR technical report 技术报告
trans transactions 会报,学报
TS tensile strength 抗拉强度
    tool steel 工具钢
TS diagram temperature-entropy diagram 温-熵图
TU thermal unit 热单位

TV television 电视
　　 throttle valve 节流阀
U uranium 铀
UHV ultrahigh vacuum 超高真空
UKAEA United Kingdom Atomic Energy Authority 英国原子能委员会
ULF ultralow frequency 超低频
ult ultimate 极限的,最后的
UP universal pressure 通用压力
USG United States gallon 美制加仑
USP United States Patent 美国专利
USPO United States Patent Office 美国专利局
USS United Stantes Standard 美国标准
UTS ultimate tensile strength 抗拉强度极限
UV ultraviolet 紫外线
v valve 阀
　　 variable 变数
V velocity 速度
　　 volt 伏[特]
　　 volume 容积,卷
VA volt-ampere 伏安
Vac vacuum 真空,负压
val value 数值
vap vapo(u)r 蒸汽
var variables 变数,变量
　　 variety 变化,变种,多种多样
vel velocity 速度
vers, vs versus 对,与……比较
VHN Vickers hardness number 维氏硬度值
VI viscosity index 粘度指数

viscosity indicator 粘度指示器
visc viscosity 粘性
viscous 粘性的
VM volatile matter 挥发物,挥发分
vol volume 体积,卷
VTR video tape recorder 磁带录像机
vv vice versa 反之亦然
W watt 瓦特
weight 重量
width 宽度
work 功
WB wet bulb 湿球
WD water drain valve 分离器疏水阀
We Weber number 韦伯数
WE Westinghouse Electric Co 威斯汀毫斯电气公司
WG water gauge 水位表
wire gauge 线规
WH Watt-hour 瓦特小时
WI wrought iron 锻钢,熟铁
WP working pressure 工作压力
WPC World Power Conference 世界动力会议
WPC Welding Research Council 焊接研究委员会(英)
WT weight 重量
yd yard 码

# 附 录 Ⅱ

常用计量单位换算

(凡有 * 者为国际单位制规定的基本单位及导出单位)

1. 长 度

*米 (m)	英尺 (ft)(′)	英寸 (in)(′)	码 (yd)
1	3.281	39.37	1.094
0.304 8	1	12	0.333 3
0.025 4	0.083 3	1	0.027 8
0.914 4	3	36	1

1 米 = 100 厘米(cm) = 1 000 毫米(mm)

2. 面 积

*米^2 (m^2)	英尺^2 (ft^2)(′)	英寸^2 (in^2)(′)
1	10.76	1 550
0.092 9	1	144
0.064 52	0.694 4	100

1 米^2 = 10^4 厘米^2 = 10^6 毫米^2

3. 体积、容积

*米^3 (m^3)	英尺^3 (ft^3)(′)	英寸^3 (in^3)(′)
1	35.31	61 024
0.028 32	1	1 728
1.639 × 10^{-5}	5.787 × 10^{-4}	1

升 (l)	美加仑 (U.S.gal)	英加仑 (Imp.gal)
1	0.264 2	0.220
3.785	1	0.832 7
4.546	1.201	1

1 米^3 = 1 000 升

1 桶 = 315 加仑(美) = 36 加仑(英)

4. 质 量

*公斤 (kg)	磅 (lb)	公斤力·秒²/米 (kgf·s²/m)
1	2.205	0.102 0
0.453 6	1	0.046 23
9.807	21.62	1

1 吨(t) = 1 000 公斤

1 公斤 = 1 000 克

1 磅 = 16 盎司(OZ)

1 长吨(英) = 1 016.6 公斤

1 短吨(美) = 907.2 公斤

5. 重量、力

*牛顿 (N)	公斤力 (kgf)	吨力 (tf)	磅力 (lbf)
1	0.102 0	1.020×10^{-4}	0.224 8
9.807	1	0.001	2.205
4.448	0.453 6	4.536×10^{-4}	1
9.807×10^3	1 000	1	2 205

1 牛顿 = 10^5 达因

6. 密 度

*公斤/米³ (kg/m³)	公斤力·秒²/米⁴ (kgf·s²/m⁴)	磅/英尺³ (lb/ft³)
1	0.102 0	0.062 43
9.807	1	0.612 2
16.018	1.633	1

1 公斤/米³ = 1 克/升

7. 重度(比重)

*牛顿/米³ (N/m³)	公斤力/米³ (kgf/m³)	磅力/项尺³ (lbf/ft³)
1	0.102 0	0.062 43
9.807	1	0.612 2
16.018	1.633	1

1 公斤力/米³ = 1 克力/升

附录 Ⅱ

8. 压　力

*牛顿/米² (N/m²)	公斤力/厘米² (kgf/cm²)	磅力/英寸² (lbf/in²)
1	1.020×10^{-4}	1.449×10^{-4}
9.807×10^4	1	14.22
6.894×10^3	0.070 3	1

公斤力/厘米² (kgf/cm²)	巴 (bar)	标准大气压 (atm)	公斤力/米² (kgf/m²)	毫米汞柱 (mmHg)	毫米水柱 (mmH₂O)
1	0.980 7	0.968 1	1	0.073 53	1
1.020	1	0.987 2	13.6	1	13.6
1.033	1.013	1			

1 工程大气压(at) = 1 公斤力/厘米²　　1 公斤力/米² = 10^{-4} 公斤力/厘米²

9. 动力黏度

*牛顿·秒/米² (N·s/m²)	公斤力·秒/米² (kgf·s/m²)	磅力·秒/英尺² (lbf·s/ft²)	泊 (p)
1	0.102 0	2.089×10^{-2}	10
9.807	1	0.204 8	98.07
47.88	4.888	1	478.8
0.1	1.020×10^{-2}	2.088×10^{-3}	1

1 泊 = 100 厘泊

10. 运动黏度

*米²/秒 (m²/s)	英尺²/秒 (ft²/s)	沲 (St)
1	10.76	10^4
0.092 9	1	929.3
10^{-4}	1.076×10^{-3}	1

1 沲 = 100 厘沲

11. 温度

*开氏温度 (K)	摄氏温度 (℃)	华氏温度 (℉)	列氏温度 (°R)

$$K = ℃ + 273.15$$

$$℃ = \frac{5}{9}(℉ - 32)$$

$$°R = 460 + ℉$$

12. 功、能

*焦耳 (J)	公斤力·米 (kgf·m)	磅力·英尺 (lbf·ft)	*焦耳 (J)	千卡 (kcal)	英热单位 (Btu)
1	0.102	0.735 9	1	2.388×10^{-4}	9.48×10^{-4}
9.807	1	7.215	4 187	1	3.968
1.356	0.138 6	1	1 055	0.252	1

1 千瓦·时(kW·h) = 367.1×10^3 公斤力·米 = 860 kcal
1 焦耳 = 1 牛顿·米

13. 功率

*瓦 (W)	公斤力·米/秒 (kgf·m/s)	公制马力 (ps)	英制马力 (Hp)
1	0.102 0	1.36×10^{-3}	1.341×10^{-3}
9.807	1	1.333×10^{-2}	1.315×10^{-2}
735.5	75	1	0.986 5
745.1	76	1.013	1

1 千卡/时 = 0.118 6 公斤力·米/秒 = 1.163 瓦
1 英热单位/时 = 0.252 千卡/时 = 0.293 瓦

14. 热值、发热量

*焦耳/公斤 (J/kg)	千卡/公斤 (kcal/kg)	英热单位/磅 (Btu/lb)
1	2.388×10^{-4}	4.298×10^{-4}
4.187×10^3	1	1.80
2.326×10^3	0.555 6	1

| *焦耳/米³ | 千卡/米³ | 英热单位/英尺³ |
(J/m³)	(kcal/m³)	(Btu/ft³)
1	2.388×10^{-4}	2.682×10^{-5}
4.187×10^3	1	0.112 4
3.725×10^4	8.896	1

15. 导热系数

| *瓦/米·度 | 千卡/米·时·度 | 英热单位/英尺·时·℉ |
(W/m·℃)	(kcal/m·h·℃)	(Btu/ft·h·℉)
1	0.859 8	0.577 8
1.163	1	0.672 0
1.731	1.488	1

16. 传热系数

| *瓦/米²·度 | 千卡/米²·时·度 | 英热单位/英尺²·时·℉ |
(W/m²·℃)	(kcal/m²·h·℃)	(Btu/ft²·h·℉)
1	0.859 8	0.176 2
1.163	1	0.204 9
5.678	4.882	1

17. 面积热强度

| *瓦/米² | 千卡/米²·时 | 英热单位/英尺²·时 |
(W/m²)	(kcal/m²·h)	(Btu/ft²·h)
1	0.859 8	0.317 0
1.163	1	0.368 8
3.154	2.712	1

18. 容积热强度

*瓦/米³ (W/m³)	千卡/米³·时 (kcal/m³·h)	英热单位/英尺³·时 (Btu/ft³·h)
1	0.859 8	9.664×10^{-2}
1.163	1	0.1124
10.35	8.898	1

19. 原子能

原子能量单位 (amu)	兆电伏特 (MeV)	尔格 (erg)	卡 (cal)
1	9.31×10^2	1.492×10^{-3}	3.564×10^{-11}
1.074×10^2	1	1.602×10^{-6}	3.827×10^{-14}
6.705×10^2	6.242×10^3	1	2.389×10^{-8}
2.807×10^{10}	2.613×10^{13}	4.187×10^7	

1 焦耳 = 10^7 尔格

1 兆电子伏特 = 4.450×10^{-20} 千瓦·时 = 1.519×10^{-16} 英热单位

English in Thermal Energy and Power Engineering

责任编辑　　徐　雁
封面设计　　卞秉利

ISBN 978-7-5603-1451-8

定价 28.00元